Break When I'm Dead
by Christian Lawrence
with Douglas Esper

Editor: Brian Paone
Cover Cover Photo: Michael Alago
Front Cover Art Design: Melody Myers
Chapter designs: Amy Hunter
Formatter: Kari Holloway

Published by Scout Media
Copyright 2022
ISBNS: Paperback: 978-1-7368867-8-6
eBook: 978-1-7368867-9-3

www.ScoutMediaBooksMusic.com

everyone who picked up this book and all who
their stories, time, and input. Big shout out to
riends, and all the people who support my
ve continued doing so throughout the years.
ou, there is no me. I would be nothing.

Brain Fair (Shadow's Fall): He has that front-man chromosome, but maybe only like half of it. You can tell he is a showman, but he doesn't suffer from the full-blown lead singer disease. There's no doubt he has a little of the mutation in his genes. He is a natural drummer. He is a sick drummer. He's got the rhythm, he's got the groove, and he's always in the pocket. He manages to get out in front of the audience, which isn't easy from behind the kit. He finds a way to make his presence known. He loves playing drums, but he loves the spotlight as well.

Eric AK (Flotsam & Jetsam): He is one of those players who wants to be a better player every time he plays. And so, he gives his all every performance. Because of this, there is a big, noticeable difference in his drumming ability, from the first time I heard him play to the last time I heard him play. The first time I heard him, I remember thinking, *It's too bad he kinda sucks, 'cause he's a super nice dude.* The last time I heard him play, I thought, *Holy shit, Opus is dopest.*

Brian Fair: Christian is intense. He won't take no for an answer but not in an obnoxious way. He just lets you know he's going to work and grind until you give up or give in and say yes. I appreciate that persistence. He has that punk-rock ethos. He has found a way through a million setbacks and a million other challenges to stay in the game and do exactly what he's wanted to do.

Kai Blackwood (Tokyo Deathsquad): Christian is like the honorary mayor for the night wherever he goes.

Ron 'Bumblefoot' Thal (Sons of Apollo, Asia the Band, Ex-Guns N' Roses): Christian is his own dude, from the hair to the way he talks. I can relate to his strong East Coast accent and vibe. He's focused and organized. He can beat the shit out of a drumkit with Dead By Wednesday, and then shift into a fucking solo acoustic song, where he's singing and playing guitar and hitting his cajon box. He's very versatile.

Christian is more of a musician. Some people are just drummers, which is great too. They sit behind the kit, and they play, but Christian can do a lot of other things as well.

Ricky Bonazza (Butcher Babies): After I put all my eggs in one basket and came to America from Italy on a work visa to play music, I got introduced to my now buddy, Opus, and the DBW crew from a friend, Corey Nash, whom I met at NAMM. I filled in for their bassist, Mike, because he was having a baby at the time. We went out for six weeks to support Flotsam & Jetsam. Crazy things was, I never even met these guys before, though me and Opus hit it off immediately over the phone, both being Pasians. It was my first US tour with people I never met or played with before. Big leap of faith This was one of the best tours ever. It was hard because we had no crew, no bus, and barely any money or equipment. We were fucking road dogs, man, and I appreciated the brotherhood. Me and Opus and the guys remained friends ever since. I really love to think back to that tour. I had a blast.

FORWARD
by Kai Blackwood

I remember hearing Christian play drums in the school band room. He sounded good, even at such an early age. I was a drummer back then as well. I encouraged him and told him to keep at it. Being older, I took him under my wing, and we started to hang out. Not long after, we were in a band together. He was the drummer, and I was the singer. The band had a terrible name, so we were working to change it. One of the names thrown in the pile was Opus. We had gotten it from the penguin character in the Bloom County comic strip. Christian fought for us to change our name to Opus. We knew what it meant, but in 1988, it just wasn't a great fit for the times or for what our band was about.

It got to the point that every time I talked to him, he would ask, "How about Opus?" The way he said it made the idea even goofier. I didn't hate it, but eventually, I told him, "Opus is a terrible name." He kept at it. I said, "It's a horrible idea." He was undeterred.

The other guys in the band said, "We'll call you Opus," but it wasn't chummy; it wasn't kind. They sort of gave him that nickname to make fun of him and his persistence/insistence. He took shit for a while and almost crumbled under that pressure, but he faced it head on and owned it.

He became Opus. The moniker wasn't supposed to sound cool or be a compliment, but he took it and made it his entire brand and identity. He ran with it. That's what he does. He'll take any bulletin board material and instead of letting the negativity get the best of him, he turns it around and makes it a positive.

I think he should stick with signing his name Christian, but then again, I know seven Christians. When someone asks, "Did you see what Christian is doing?" I have to ask, "Which one?" If that same person asks, "Did you see what Opus is doing?" I'll know exactly who they are talking about—as does everyone else in the industry. There is only one Opus.

We're all from that East Coast area, where guys are naturally dicks to each other, and this was no exception. They were trying to be shitty toward him, and yet, he turned it into one of his biggest assets. Oh, you want to hurt this kid's feelings? Your words became his calling card. He has thick skin and determination unlike any other. He has a conviction and a drive and an unwavering will. His belief that he belongs on stage behind that kit can't be cracked by any of your best attempts. Imagine the balls it takes to stand up to your peers like that. Many have tried to knock him off his feet, but Opus rarely breaks his stride or even loses his balance.

Ask people around the world about a drummer named Opus and they probably have a story to share about something he did or said or a song he recorded. They'll talk about his outgoing personality; Jesus Christ, sometimes it's too much. I wish I had a bit of it myself. Some people want him to dial it back a bit, but not me. He is who he is. He is the genuine article. What you see is what you get. Typically, those who don't like it are jealous of what he has done, is doing, and what he is getting ready to do.

Fuck them, Opus. Keep on going.

CHAPTER ONE
A Brush With Death

School was never really quite my thing, although I did manage to go on and get my college degree, in fine arts of all things. And really just to say I did it! At a young age, I was labeled as a bit of a troublemaker, or more so a class clown. I was kicked out of four schools, two being Catholic schools. In one elementary school, St. Michael's in New Haven, I thought it would be funny to write "ass" on the chalkboard while our teacher, a nun, stepped out of classroom. When she came back and saw it, everyone immediately ratted me out. She made me get up in front of the whole class to admit my wrong doings, but instead I proceeded to explain to the nun how Jesus rode on a donkey, and another name for donkey was "ass." She turned red with anger and, well, let's just say I was on to my next school. But the one thing I knew early on was that I was drawn to music and performance. I can hold my own playing guitar, I've been told I have a decent singing voice, and I can play bass if called upon, but I've always loved the drums.

My parents didn't want me to play the drums. That hurt. I could've obeyed their wishes and picked something else. I could've quit music and tried something else, but I also have a natural talent for following my own lead. I signed up to learn percussion at my junior high.

My junior high didn't want me to play drums.

You know how school bands are; they handpick who they want for what instruments they want. I was a troublemaker, a metalhead, and I think they passed me over to avoid any possible disruptions to the process of creating a band. There are a lot of pieces that need to work together. No matter what the actual reason was, the fact that they didn't want me, stung. I felt left out.

My mom suggested I try the cello. I begrudgingly agreed. Every week, I lugged that thing around, and it seemed to break every time I played it. Full disclosure, I didn't treat the cello all that well. I recall dragging it behind me while walking.

I could've picked something else. I could've quit music altogether. Life certainly seemed to be telling me drums weren't for me. With my parents and my school both saying don't do it, it emboldened me. It made me want to try it all that much more. You think I can't succeed as a drummer? Watch me.

Then I found a drum kit for sale on the curb of someone's house down the street. It had a sparkling orange finish on the shells of the three-piece pile of garbage. I'm telling you this was the worst kit money could buy. I spent $35, and I got ripped off. If I recall correctly, drums were by a Japanese company called Max Tone or something equally as generic.

I had a paper route at the time, but I had only saved $25. I had to borrow the last ten bucks from my older brother. I brought the pieces home and set it up. I beat the shit out of that kit every single day for months on end, trying to get the brain-and-hand coordination.

I taught myself "Shout at the Devil" by Mötley Crüe. I got a Buddy Rich beginner's guide to playing drums to teach me more. I give him a lot of credit; Buddy Rich is a beast on the drums.

But before we get into all the drumming stuff, I think there's some background needed to set up my story.

Lawrence is my stepdad's name. Though I've carried this name for years, it really doesn't have any real connection for me. I'm not in the Lawrence family, never was. My birth father's last name is Tocchi. He was and still is living his own life in Italy.

My grandfather, on my mother's side, was an Italian American whose parents were from Italy. I was really close with him. He was the closest thing I had to a father figure. He was a better father than anyone else I had. My nonna came from Italy too. Their last name was Tortora, my mother's maiden name.

So, my son is Orion Lawrence, and he's carrying the name of, well, who the fuck knows, because not only was it not my real last name, but it wasn't even my stepfather's real last name. It's not attached to anything or anyone except until now.

My stepfather's family was Jewish. Their real last name was something very Jewish sounding and hard to pronounce, like "Goobawitz," but I don't even remember it. They had changed their name to Lawrence during the war. They wanted something neutral to not tip off the Nazis, from what I was told. They were in Poland, right in the thick of things. And so now we're all carrying this name that has some heavy history but technically no connection to me.

My older brother went back to our birth father's last name, and speaking of my brother, well, we'll get to him a little later. I need to clear my mind and prepare to dive into those waters. And speaking of waters, I need to tell you about the time I almost drowned.

Some people have religion, some have science, and others follow nothing and no one. I'll talk about my beliefs and spirituality in other parts of the book, but one force that always guides me forward is synchronicity—or maybe you know it as synergy. I believe I am where I am supposed to be for various reasons. Something sends me signs. No other story from my past highlights this belief as much as this one.

And the reason I'm bringing this up right here, right now is I ran into my old childhood buddy Johnny the other day, and he is heavily involved in this story without even knowing it. I also think it'll be a good way to break the ice between us. They say a well-written book is a glimpse into the author's soul, so maybe this will help you see who I am, where I come from, and what I'm all about.

Johnny lived near me when we moved from New Haven to Guilford, Connecticut after my mother married for the second time. Johnny was friends with a lot of the same people from the neighborhood, like Erick Heller, the bassist from my first-ever cover band, Screaming Fetus. After Erick raised his kids and went through most of his life adventures, he has now come full circle and once again plays in my very active internationally touring, classic Black Sabbath tribute band, Earth. Heller was one of the first people to introduce me to marijuana. Except he got all pissed at me the first time I tried it because instead of inhaling it, being inexperienced, I blew out and we lost it all. Erick also owns a cool pub in Guilford called The Country Tavern. It's a small, country-type watering hole where a lot of friends from back in the day meet up on a regular basis. I even hosted a trivia event every Tuesday night there before corona happened. That's where I recently ran into Johnny, and it brought up this memory I hadn't thought about in ages.

Back in the day, my Guilford friends and I had formed a tight knit group. We palled around, and whatever trouble we caused, we did it together. It was the Sachems Head Crew, which was the name of the area in Guilford we lived in. We would hang out in West Woods, drink beer, and run from the cops. Outside of those guys, my older brother and I had other acquaintances, but they weren't a part of that neighborhood friends-type of group. We also had plenty of people we flat out didn't like, who seemed to just pop up everywhere we went. One of those kids was Bob Shuman, who was kind of a bully. My older brother had to put Bob in place once for picking on me, by punching him square in the face, breaking his glasses. After that, we all became buddies.

Guilford is a beach town. One of our favorite places to swim was at the end of Trolley Road, in an area called Sachem's Head, named after a Native American Chief from that area who was beheaded on that land. The area itself is like a niche or a peninsula.

There was a little pool of water that flows out into the ocean. I guess they call it a sluice. One side of the water was our side, and then at the other side sat vacation houses and rental property. We'd take dinghies over to the other side. Over there, everyone was on vacation. They are there to have a good time. We befriended girls who would go there for the summertime, some who we still know and are friends with today. We'd party with them. It was a cool atmosphere to grow up in. You almost felt like you were on summer break all year. You had a constant supply of new people to meet, and they were always in a good mood, because they were on vacation.

At the end of this sluice, there was a crazy current, like a powerful rapid. I've also heard it called a rip torrent. Whatever you want to call it, it was no joke. Throughout the day, the current went into different phases. Sometimes the sluice would be a lot more aggressive, and then at other points, it was more like a lazy river. People would take rafts and inner tubes and just float along to relax. Other people would swim or float down the current. It was a great place to just hang out, swim, and relax.

I wasn't the best swimmer in the world, and I'm still not. So, I should've known going in during a particularly rough time was a stupid idea. The current was aggressive that day, but it hadn't gotten to its full tilt yet. Steady speed for sure, though. Enough that I should've known better being that I don't float; I sink like a rock. There was a group of us all together, and they were going in, so I said, "*Fuck it*," and followed them.

I'd been in the current before, usually in a raft or a dinghy, but this time, I went with nothing. I went through the sluice. As I was coming out the other end, I got sucked down by a whirlpool. Now, I don't know if you've ever had that happen to you before, but you cannot get out of it no matter what you do.

I was freaking out as soon as I felt something pull me down. I started fighting against the current. I struggled to get my bearings. I knew I needed to get up to the top of the water, but I couldn't get there. Within moments, I got exhausted, confused, disoriented, and I felt the tightness in my chest from panic. I'm not thinking clearly, because everything in my head is screaming at once. You can't win against a current like that. It will wear you down. I've since learned that if you ever get sucked down by a riptide or current, you should always just relax your body, hold your breath, and go with it until it eventually spits you out of its grip on the other side. Struggling and working against it will actually make it worse for you. But I didn't know any of that back then.

At a certain point, I made up my mind and literally gave up. It was a conscious decision—one that made sense, because I knew I had no way to escape. I was going to lose any fight with the water. I relaxed my body and said, "Okay, this is how I'm going to die."

I started swallowing water. Drowning is one of the worst experiences you'll ever have. I don't wish it on anyone. The helplessness leaves you feeling so small and inconsequential. I was done. There was nothing left to do but accept my fate and die.

When I stopped caring about survival, a moment of peace and clarity took control. Everything slowed down. I glanced up to the surface of the water and noticed a bright white light shining down through the top of the water onto me. The white light brightened everything around me and had a warming feeling. Sure, the obvious answer is that the light was the sun gleaming through the water, but it captivated me in a way no other bit of sunlight ever had before that moment. They say you see a bright light right before you die; well, whether it was the sun or not, I definitely saw a big bright light.

My soul was calm, at peace. I thought, okay, this is it. It's over. The panic had disappeared. The worry of being too small went away. My focus remained on the light as I welcomed its warmth.

I don't recall when it happened or if I was even aware, but Johnny and Bob, the reformed bully, jumped in the water. They were both great swimmers. They grabbed me and pulled me out of the sluice. I started coughing up water, spitting it all over, as my lungs begged for oxygen. My head spun, my body ached, and everything became instinct. There was no wiggle room. Either air got in and water got out, or I was a goner.

A few people gathered around, offering encouragement. I could hear their genuine concern and anxiety. They knew how dire things were. When I had time to reflect on how others were reacting, I realized I had somehow survived after all.

That was the closest I ever got to dying, and it shook me to my core. Now I'm very cautious around the water. I respect the water, as well as everything in it. Now I often find myself hesitating to just jump in a pool or lake.

Truth be told, Johnny and Bob saved my life. There's no other way to describe it. I got a second chance that not everyone gets and at a very young age. That's a heavy thing to unpack as a kid. Not just the 'almost dying' part, not just the realization I had given in to death, but also the pressure of knowing I have a life debt to pay back at some point. There was no getting around it.

I now had a duty to live life a certain way until I could pay karma back. Well, I started the story talking about synergy, so I don't think it will surprise you to know I unfortunately got the chance.

A month or two later, I went to Johnny's house. We had talked earlier in the day about getting together to hang. He had told me to come by. Man, remember those days? Summer break meant you adventured with buddies from dawn until after dark, in the woods, playing games outside, jamming, whatever. You went to each other's houses and rang the doorbell and entertained yourself without constant stimulation. We didn't have a cellphone or a tablet or the internet. Back then, we didn't even have twenty-four-hour television, and for some reason, I was never a video-gamer. A couple guys had Ataris, but what held our interest was going outside and exploring. In Sachem's Head, we had awesome caves and hiking trails in an area called the West Woods, and that's where we spent most of our days.

One afternoon, shortly after the near-drowning incident, Johnny asked me to come over to his place. I always loved going to Johnny's, because his sister Jen used to change in the window, and all us boys would always watch her. She was hot. Obviously, her brother didn't watch her, but the neighborhood kids did. (Sorry, John and Mike, it's true!) So, that afternoon, I rushed on over, hoping to catch a glimpse, like a scene from the '80's movie, *Porky's*.

I knocked. No answer. I tried again. No answer.

No big deal. Typically, I would've left and continued with my day, but since we had talked earlier, his absence got my attention. I walked into his back yard, (back when you could walk into someone's back yard without the neighbor calling the cops or someone pulling a gun on you). There was a path in the woods that connected Johnny's neighborhood and mine. I figured I'd head back that way in case he had gotten bored and had decided to start walking to my house instead.

Guess who I see laying unconscious on a rock, with blood pouring out of his head?

Johnny Iacobellis. Apparently, he was attempting to climb a large tree, which he enjoyed doing and lost his grip, falling out of the tree and banging his head on the large rock below.

I take in the scene. Blood is steadily flowing out of his head wound. The closer I got, the more worried I felt. He wasn't moving. I couldn't tell if he was breathing. If he was out there long enough and lost enough blood, it would be fatal.

I ran back to the house and called 9-1-1. Before the ambulance arrived, Johnny's dad got home. I took him to where his son was. He got Johnny in the car and raced him to the hospital. Thank God, he made a full recovery without any permanent head injuries. So, guess what? He saved me. I saved him!

How did I get to this story, though? We were talking about naming my son, weren't we?

Now, Orion's middle name derived from his mother Jessica's last name, Spinelli, and my grandparents' last name, Tortora being mushed together. ST-period. We took the first letter of each name. No, it's not Suicidal Tendencies. It's Saint. Orion ST. Lawrence.

Now, this gets weird. My grandparents and beautiful niece Francesca are both buried in St. Lawrence Cemetery. I hadn't realized this when we named Orion. We saw this after the fact, and it blew my mind.

Having a baby changes your life in so many ways. It's very difficult to comprehend unless you become a parent. Part of the reason I wanted to write this book was to help explain to him his history and write out all the various factions of family he came from. I want to make sure that even if it's not the most traditional background, he still has a legacy to draw from, to be grounded. That way maybe one day he can also pass this knowledge on to his own too.

Like, I want him to know about my grandfather. Orion met him as a baby, but I'm sure he won't remember. I'm glad they met. My grandfather was a great man. He was a doctor in the army.

While serving overseas during the war, he met my grandmother. They got married in Italy. He came back to the States, and they had to wait a whole year before she could join him. She came over in a boat, eating nothing but apples. Can you imagine people getting seasick with nothing but apples in their bellies? Throwing up and that smell on board? After that, she hated apples.

My nonna made the best food—meatballs, chicken cutlets, risotto, and lasagna; you name it, she made it the best.

I learned my sauce recipe from her. She barely spoke English, but she was the sweetest person.

After serving in the army, my grandfather became a urologist. I called him Dr. Pecker (I loved Dr. Pepper as a kid). He smirked and laughed along with me, good-natured about the nickname. Dr. Frank Tortora was a Yale graduate, and he remained dedicated to his work until very late in his life. He didn't retire until he was in his late eighties, and even then, he would volunteer at the local clinic. He loved to help. He loved to work. He was a workaholic.

Back in the day, he would do house calls. He helped anyone regardless of race, age, sex and economic situation. So sometimes he'd come home with a bag of tomatoes as payment. He had a bartering system if they couldn't pay, trading his services for favors or stuff, sometimes even unwanted stuff. He lived to be 102.

They established a tradition to gather the family for huge meals on Sundays, which I've carried on until this day, so Orion gets to experience it. usually have our "Italian-style" Sunday with my auntie and cousins. Orion calls her Auntie Nonnie, which means auntie grandma. You know, she's my auntie and sort of still acts as his grandma. Sometimes other people join us like my brother and sister come over with her son, brother-in-law, random past girlfriends of whoever at the time, friends on occasion and whoever else is available. We do pasta, using my grandmother's sauce recipe.

We keep the tradition alive.

So, back to the family names and stuff.

My mom had been single for a while. She was going to school and raising two kids on her own and working. She had a science teacher in college, Mr. Howard Lawrence, who was an alcoholic and much older, but my mom saw something in him. Maybe she needed an *A* in science? I don't know.

Okay, he could be cool at times, I'll admit that, but he was not an ideal partner or husband or father or role model ... Hell, he wasn't really a good person in general. Very smart though and deep down inside, I truly think he had a decent heart.

When my mom remarried, he adopted me and my brother, (or claimed that he did anyway). My mother then converted us to Judaism.

My first name is Christian.

Right?

Yeah, let that sink in for a second.

Got it?

Now picture me in a synagogue, wearing my yalmuka. My brother was there too. Of course, this was before he became an anti-Semite and went off to do his thing. Oh, I didn't mention that about my brother yet? We're getting there, just hang on. I need to get in the right frame of mind.

My brother and I were forced to be at this place.

We were spinning the dreidel during the holidays, and I won a contest. The nice lady running this holiday event announces, "Christian Lawrence," to the crowd, and all these old Jewish women are looking around, confused, wondering what the fuck is going on when a Christian was winning the dreidel-spinning competition.

For a while, we were celebrating Christmas and Hanukkah, so that wasn't too bad. Early on, I remember him taking us to Irish bars to watch bands play traditional tunes, while he would chug pitchers of beer. Afterward, he'd drive us home, clearly inebriated. We'd all be stuffed in his black Toyota Celica as he'd swerve all over the road. He'd slur every word as he told us, "You guys know I love you, right? I love you just like you were my own."

We'd all freak out just watching the world fly by as we swerved left, and then right, and then left. My mom was either gullible or chose ignorance. Or maybe she just didn't care; I don't know.

Howard ended up going back to school and becoming a lawyer. He started making decent money, and he moved us out to Guilford, CT. which is not far from where I currently live now. That's really where I grew up. Howard kept his nose clean, and, at that time, he seemed like a pretty decent guy all of a sudden. We were as close to being a "normal" family then than at any other time. We went on family trips and enjoyed each other's company. It felt good.

I let my guard down for a brief moment and allowed Howard to take on the role of my father. On the other hand, my brother Michael, who is four years older than me, understood what was happening a lot better than I did.

Turns out, Howard was getting into trouble. He was spending money like crazy. He bought a Porsche and a Maserati on fake credit that he couldn't afford, he was constantly cheating on my mom, and there were usually whores and cocaine involved. This guy thought he was a Jewish Scarface.

My younger sister really got messed up by the whole process. She probably got the worst of it, which is why she turned to drugs. By fifteen, she was shooting up heroin. They had her living in a crappy hotel so she didn't have to be at home to get mixed up with all the drama, which means no supervision and no rules. That's a recipe for disaster for a teenager. It was a long, hard road growing up in that house.

I love my mother dearly, but you know, she sort of always went along with whoever she was dating and did what they did. She's too trusting. My stepfather cheated on her. Then the next guy, her boyfriend after my stepfather, had a whole other family hidden. I had to figure it out for her because she had no idea. My mother didn't want to believe me until it was right there in front of her face. And even when he did show his true colors to her, it wasn't enough.

Michael was more resistant to accepting our stepdad than I was. He wasn't happy my mom had remarried. He wasn't happy this new guy was different from our birth father. Y'see, I was about two years old when our dad finally split, so I didn't have any real memories of him. To me, he was an image. He was a photo in an album. He was a guy in a story or memory someone might share with me.

My birth father sent a letter once to check up on us, but my mother tore it up and said we didn't have to think about him anymore. That's as close to a relationship to him as I ever had. Mom told us Howard was our new dad. Again, for me, it was what my mother said, so it must be true, right? Michael knew better. Each rip of the letter tore him up inside.

Michael was older, so he remembered my dad. He remembered his time as a young kid living in Italy. He even spoke Italian at a young age. He had memories with my father. They had a relationship and had bonded. All I had now was Howard A. Lawrence, who supposedly adopted us and wanted me to change religions.

Howard was talented at keeping up an appearance to the outside eye. By that, I mean he was well respected at his school by his peers, though he drank heavily and had flings with his students. He was highly regarded by my mother, even if he went behind her back and often treated us like garbage. No matter how good he made himself look though, he never followed through on anything. He would smile and charm and make promises, but they were mostly empty. Which is why I wasn't surprised to find out recently that he never fully went through with the adoption process for me and Michael. Yes, my last name is Lawrence, and I am not really sure why nor can I explain if I should even carry the name. I don't know who I am technically at times.

The last thing you should do when trying to come into someone's life as a father figure is to put your hands on them. At a very crucial time, getting to know him, our stepdad would slap us across the face if we did something he didn't like. He even felt compelled to do this to other children in our family, like our cousins, who misbehaved.

I didn't know him yet, you know? This stranger came into our house, and I'm thinking I finally have a father figure who cares for me and wants the best for me. To say his actions and abuse were detrimental to my development is the ultimate in underselling the actual truth.

We were confused. Well, I was confused; my brother was angry. He built up resentment early on that grew and developed in unhealthy ways. It snowballed out of control; we just didn't know it yet.

CHAPTER TWO
My Brother Becomes a Duke

We were poor, and my mom was busy, so we ate fast food a lot. I got pretty chubby. If you put two Big Macs, a super-sized fry, an apple pie, and the largest soda on the planet in front of me, it would be gone in a heartbeat. Ten thousand calories for lunch? Sure! I didn't know any better.

We lived on Ferry St. in New Haven, which is now one of the scariest parts of the city. You don't want to walk down that street by yourself at night.

Every day, we'd go out to the bus stop for school, and my brother and I would have to fight these Puerto Rican gang kids. They fucked with us endlessly. No joke, we're trying to go to school, and these kids are throwing rocks, and chasing us with sticks. Eventually, they brought BB guns and would shoot at us. It was silly. Eh, silly isn't the correct word. It was ludicrous. Then one day, they were threatening me with shards of broken glass, and my brother flipped and beat one of them up bad.

Between the Puerto Ricans picking on us and my Jewish stepfather beating us and treating us like crap, my brother withdrew. He got into hardcore and punk music and dove deep into that world.

He wouldn't hang out with me or our friends. Basically, by age fifteen, he was out of the house. Aside from coming home once in a blue moon, my brother became a stranger. He started leaving the state for concerts. In NYC, he met a group of skinheads at shows and clung to them.

He got a gig as a roadie for the band Agnostic Front, a legendary hardcore band. During his time touring with them, he befriended a violent group of skinheads. Drugs were prevalent in that social circle. My brother was doing acid almost daily, from what I heard. I am not anti-drugs, but if you're mixing them with racist, overthrow-the-government, radical ideas, you have a severe environment that can prove dangerous. He was young. He didn't have a father or a stable home life, so this group became his family. I felt like he was getting brainwashed.

It was hard to add it up in my head, because my brother is smart—maybe too smart for his own good. I didn't think he would fall in line with the chaotic views and narrowmindedness those skinheads were about.

He started feeling like he needed to fight and save the white race. Michael was the only family I felt I could trust. He was the closest person to me, but I didn't understand this path he was taking. I mean, we came from a mixed family, and we grew up around many different cultures and races and backgrounds. I mean, I guess we are considered white but very Italian.

It didn't matter. He was so smart that he was acting dumb. He was blinded to the truth of our situation by a burning desire to be accepted by this group and to be a part of something bigger than our lives. It didn't matter to him that the things he preached would conflict with reality at times. Now those new friends were his new family.

I dove into music, some that he had introduced me to, and moved on with my life, while my brother became considered one of the most dangerous, notorious, racist skinheads in the country. He was a founding member of the Hammerskins down in Texas. Back then, they were called the Confederate Hammerskins. They used a symbol from Pink Floyd's *The Wall* movie as their calling card. Remember when Pink is rallying everyone into hysterics and there are flags flying with two crossed hammers? Yeah, they took that shit literally and made it real.

He was a foot soldier in this group that started to have tentacles all over the world. He would chase Black and Hispanic people out of public places, like Robert E. Lee Park in Dallas. Him and his crew would terrorize synagogues, smashing out windows. They painted graffiti of racist symbols around cities, and I'm sure much worse. I wasn't in contact with him at this point, so most of what I know was through rumors and stories that had been retold through the grapevine a dozen times before I heard. I didn't know what to believe, and I still don't have clear answers.

One specific story about my brother was one time he got into a fight with an Indian gentleman who owned a bar or nightclub, and their argument got so heated the guy shot my brother in the ass with a salt rifle. My brother went back later that night and threw a Molotov cocktail into the establishment after hours and burned it to the ground.

He would resurface, usually when he got into big trouble, and to try to recruit me. He handed me pamphlets about his cause and about the injustices done to White people by other races. I was scared of him. Terrified. I remember one time he came home after I had started to hear some of the stories of what he was up to, and I slept with a knife under my pillow, just in case.

I always thought the whole gang thing was silly, pathetic even. I would think about the group who had beat me and my brother up at the bus stop. These were all kids who were too weak to stand up for themselves. They needed a group of people to feel strong and to handle their business for them. They didn't want to think for themselves; they wanted to be told what to do. Gangs prey on the weak-minded or the damaged kid and convince them there's a different, better way.

Look, I get it, some people come together as a family to fight for common beliefs or to make their neighborhood safe. Sometimes, the gangs start out with noble intentions, only wanting positive things, but it goes too far. People get drunk on the power. When a guy realizes he can command a group to do something for his bidding, the whole thing gets corrupted. It's no longer about the community and the members of the gang; it's about the ego and power trip of the guy at the top. I strongly believe each individual should have their own identity, even when involved in group activities. I've been in many bands and tried to make it a group thing. I want everyone involved and each member to add their quirks and history and vibe to the sound and images we share.

My brother spent ten years in a federal prison for crimes he had committed. I went to visit him once. At the time, he was in a prison in Oklahoma, and my "then" girlfriend's parents lived nearby.

I hadn't seen my brother in years, so I thought I should check in and see who he had become as a person, as an adult. I never knew him as one. To me, he was a teenager who had disappeared from me, just like my dad, my stepdad, and a string of my mom's boyfriends who came in and out of my life. I expected to meet someone like Charlie Manson, but that wasn't the case.

The prison was out in the middle of nowhere. It looked like a fortress with massive towers and armed guards. I had to go through three levels of security to get in. That whole experience shook me.

Around the time when he got released, one of the people he founded the Hammerskins with was killed. Apparently, when you attack and threaten people and do a bunch of stupid, crazy, mean-spirited shit, there are consequences. People were fighting back. He and his group were being hunted, and I believe he was afraid for his life. There was also a feud between rival skinhead gangs, which played a part in all of this.

Whatever the situation, I think being on the other end of the violence helped my brother realize he isn't immortal. I don't want to say it calmed him down, but he certainly had a different perspective on what he had done and where he was at in life.

He left the Hammerskins and defected to a group called the Volksfront—a skinhead group from Portland, Oregon, also prone to violence and hate. I believe my brother was on, or at least mentioned on, the show Gangland years ago as a part of his involvement with the Volksfront crew.

Now, if you met him, you'd never believe the stuff I'm saying. He's sort of like a grumpy old man, similar to Archie Bunker. He may still hold some of those beliefs, but he has turned to religion. He is a devout Greek Orthodox Church member. Every conversation is about Jesus and God, but I feel like they mask racism through religion. At one point, I think he even became a minister.

The whole thing is crazy. This is my brother. I played in the streets with him, went to the same school, got beaten up by the same people, and yet, we couldn't be more different.

He isn't a foot soldier anymore. He's now looked at and considered to be this legendary figure in the white supremacist movement. He's regarded as this hero. Part of that was him being on the forefront and starting a big group, but also, in his ten years in prison and through all the times he got caught up in trouble, he never threw other people under the bus to get a lighter sentence. He served the most time from the incident he was arrested for.

He married a woman named Danielle, who was also mixed up with the skinhead shit at the time but isn't any longer. Danielle met my brother while he was in prison. She actually sought him out. They had a kid together. My niece, who's "Nickelhead" (Nicholyn), is cool as hell, and even though my brother tried and tried to inoculate her with all his beliefs and bullshit, she recognized how foolish he was. She told him to fuck off, and she went her own way. She is a proud lesbian, which probably makes my brother furious, because it goes against his way of life. She's also an awesome guitarist/musician as well.

My brother and his wife split, and he quickly remarried. I didn't know any of this part until after it had all gone down, but come to find out, his new wife is the daughter of David Duke. No lie.

So, I am married into the Duke family, which is ... uhh ... uncomfortable. From what I hear, she is estranged from her father though and doesn't follow him or his beliefs, which is good.

She and my brother had a kid, so I also have a nephew, Alex.

David Duke is my nephew's grandfather. That is hard to process. It's insane. Think about it. Me and my brother are one hundred percent Italian, and I was born in Rome, but, at one point, I was Jewish. My mother also has kids who are half Italian and half Jewish, my other brother and sister. I have first cousins on my mom's side who are half Italian and half Puerto Rican. My sister's fiancé is Black, and they just had a baby boy. My own son is 25 percent Jewish and 75 percent Italian.

Imagine that family reunion. My family tree is a beautiful mess, but I'd like to think if we all got together, we'd get along.

It's hard for me to look at racists and not think they are dumb. We all bleed the same color. We all breathe the same air. We all poop. There's no golden poop. We all need to eat. We're all going to die. I don't know how someone can be blinded to that fact and fall for the obvious bullshit that these hateful people project. You're simply either an asshole or you're not.

Anyone who thinks differently is oblivious.

When I was a kid, I didn't have the best guidance, so I sort of sought out my own truth and blazed my own path. While I'd like to think I generally made the correct choices and steered clear of most trouble, I do look back at my brief attempt to explore black magic as a weird misstep. I still get chills down my back thinking about some of that time.

As a kid, and being in the 80's, I was neck deep in metal and the lore that came with it. I was fascinated by the backstory and the imagery and the lyrics. I wanted to find out for myself what was real and what wasn't.

When I was nine or ten and my brother was just becoming a teenager, we found a book. We were at a small mom-and-pop bookstore and saw the book sitting by itself on a shelf. It was a creepy-looking book, so obviously it caught our attention and piqued our curiosity. The binding was pitch black, and it had a skull on the cover. I don't recall the title, but it said something about black magic.

We got the book, and inside, there were legit spells and shit, like a guidebook to start doing black magic. What to use, what to say, what might happen—this book spelled it out.

Of course, we had to fuck around with it to see what we could make happen. To this day, I don't know if some of the stuff worked or if it was my imagination or if I'm remembering details incorrectly, because it's been so long, but it felt legit and scary as we tried to follow the steps in the spells.

The one spell in the book, which seemed easy, was— man, I'm getting creeped out just thinking about all this old shit. I'm all paranoid now, looking out my window and shit, or maybe I'm just stoned. Anyway, the spell, if done correctly, could make it rain. We needed a broom, ocean water, a few other items, and we had to say certain words. We lived right by the ocean on the Long Island Sound, so getting the water was easy. We mixed it up, said the chants, and boom, five minutes later, it's pouring.

Yes, I know it rains a lot there especially during spring and that it could've been a complete coincidence, but it felt like we had a hand in the weather that day.

Another spell we tried was to help us deal with a guy who bullied my brother. Well, we got a strand of the guy's hair from a brush or something, I think, and we tied it to a piece of grass. Then the book told us to put it under the doormat at the kid's house and to think about whatever we wanted to have happen to him while chanting the spell.

A day or two later, the kid got into a skiing accident and broke his leg. We were floored. It was the weirdest, creepiest thing ever. I started to feel like we had made a mistake in testing out the book.

Then one day, the book was gone. My mother had overheard us talking about it. She found the book and took it. I don't know if she burned it or threw it away or hid it, but we no longer had the book. Not having the book and getting to finish what we started made us want to do it that much more. You know that feeling?

My brother and I knew the author and title of the book back then, but we couldn't find it anywhere. We started to believe it didn't actually exist.

Another time, my buddy Kai Blackwood and I were messing around with a homemade Ouija board. These stories never end well, so I'm sure it won't surprise you to know this is a freaky story too.

We asked if there were any spirits around. It answered, yes. We kept going and getting weird responses, and then out of nowhere, the hand control thing flew off the board and across the room. I was already uneasy by that point, so I flipped out.

Kai took me to discuss our thoughts with a priest. I told him about the black magic and the creepy, uneasy feelings it brought up in me as we had tried to conjure magic.

He told us, "If you open yourself to these types of things, you're giving them permission to seep into your life and your heart."

He warned us not to open that door or allow that inside of our souls.

Kai was also there when I tried to shoplift a cassette tape from an older chain store called Bradlee's.

According to Kai, "We were at a department store with a couple buddies. Opus decided to steal *Headhunter* by Krokus. He slid the thing in his pocket, and we turned to leave. We got to the door, and there were security guards waiting for us. We all got banned from the store for, like, a month or two."

I'm not sure why I chose that tape, but the song "Eat the Rich" comes back into the story later.

CHAPTER THREE
Christiano Who?

Anyway, we're not writing a book about me to make me look bad, so let's get back to the family. We've talked about my stepfather and a bunch of random boyfriends for my mother, but to know me and my situation, you need to know about my birth father as well.

When my mother was younger, close to eighteen, she was dating a guy, and it wasn't going well. I think he was actually married or something. I don't know the details, but she got suckered into a weird relationship. My mother's parents decided to send her to Italy to finish school and to get away from all that drama. After all, that's where they were from, and they thought maybe getting her away from this man and the town would help her get a fresh start. They wanted her to concentrate on school and straighten herself out.

Shortly after getting to Italy, she started working at a casting company. You know, they help find actors and actresses for movie roles.

Here enters my father. His backstory could be a whole chapter. Luigi Tocchi. I want to say he's, like, ten or twelve or maybe even fifteen years older than my mother.

He had been cast as a background actor in *Cleopatra* with Elizabeth Taylor. He was a Roman warrior guard.

My mother was working the desk at this casting place—you know, answering phones and whatnot—when he came into the office for something, and they met. They hit it off right away.

My grandparents' grand plan for my mother getting done with school backfired. She met an older guy. Soon got pregnant. And then she got married young.

She had my brother Michael when she was only nineteen or twenty. They stayed in Italy for a while but eventually relocated back to the US, where she got pregnant again. I'm not sure exactly why, but while pregnant, she moved back to Italy again, and that's where I was born. They somehow, again, ended up back in Connecticut before I was one. My grandfather paid for him to go to school to become a hairdresser, and he opened a little shop in New Haven down the street from our shitty little apartment on Ferry St.

After that, my parents' relationship dissolved quickly.

It was the '70s. A different era. Rumor had it that my father spent a lot of nights out at disco clubs like Studio 54. He experimented with various drugs and more than likely had sexual encounters with both men and women as well. He'd come home to my angry mother.

It ended badly.

After they split, my mother, once again, moved back to New Haven. Now though, she was a single mother going to school, supporting us, and working two part-time jobs.

As a kid, I remember one day when this man came to our place. This was in our old apartment in the ghetto of Fair Haven. My mother was upset. She tried closing the door on him, but he put his foot in the door. It was my father. I looked up at him, and he was holding this giant teddy bear he had bought for us. He was trying to come get one more chance, but my mother wasn't having it.

She yelled at him to, "Get the fuck out of here!" And eventually, he left. And that was his last grand effort to see us. This was probably my last and earliest memory of my real dad.

She was furious. She was a woman scorned and bitter. So, she told us that our father was literally dead.

Flash forward a few months; my brother and I were at the famous Pepes Apizza in New Haven, CT. My brother points to a man across the dining room and says, "There's Papa." (Which, ironically, is what my boy calls me now.) But, yeah, sure enough, there he was. Our father, resurrected from the dead, eating out with another girl at a pizza joint.

I was confused. I asked my brother, "I thought he was dead?"

Apparently, my mom had gone crazy and went a little overboard. She had tried to get him deported. He did eventually move back to Italy.

I didn't know or understand any of this back then; I was two or three years old, so from that time until I reached my midtwenties, I had no desire to meet or talk or have any type of relationship with my dad.

As I got older, I realized I had only ever heard my mother's side of the story of their relationship. She always told us how my father never wanted to be with us, how he wouldn't fight to stay in our lives. I wondered what his version of the truth sounded like. There are always, always two sides to every story.

I had also developed a passion for music and had no idea where it had come from. I couldn't help but wonder if it was from my father's side.

Jump ahead to when I was about thirty; my friend was going to go to both Oktoberfest and Amsterdam and asked if I wanted to go. I told him I was down as long as we could take a detour to Italy and surprise my father—just show up at his doorstep and see what he did.

My aunt helped me track down my father's address without him knowing. He was in Rome, about twenty minutes from the Colosseum, and had continued styling hair, gaining some attention as a well-known male hairdresser. I got the information on where he worked before the trip.

Now, mind you, it was wintertime there, but to me, coming from Connecticut, it felt like spring or fall. Everyone in the city was walking around all bundled up, freezing. Whereas I was wearing a kilt, a cut-off t-shirt, and my hair all spiked up. My tattoos were showing—remember, this is many years ago, when tattoos weren't as acceptable as they are now.

I was outside the piazza, banging on the door to his hair salon. Now, I didn't realize it was during their daily siesta time. I didn't even understand what that was.

So, I bang on the door over and over.

This guy started yelling from across the way, behind me, "Whoa, hey, what the hell?" He approached me, so I faced him to see what he was going to do. He was wearing black leather pants, short spiky blond hair, and from what I could tell, he looked to be in his mid to late sixties. He started speaking Italian. "Who are you? What do you want?"

As he got closer, it dawned on me that this was my father. I could tell it was him, and I could see, from his expression, how confused he felt.

He repeated his questions of, "Who are you? What do you want?" in Italian.

I said, "Christiano." Meaning, "I am Christian."

He asked, "Christiano, who?"

I said, "Christiano Tocchi," using his last name.

He turned white as a sheet of snow and said, "Holy shit." (In Italian of course!) My father grabbed me in a hug and said, "This was a good day."

In Italy, they walk everywhere. Walk, Walk. Walk. He dragged me around town, telling everyone that this was his son from America. I was trying to keep up with this older man almost three times my age. I was huffing and puffing behind him. This mofo was walking so fast.

Over his shoulder, he was telling me, "You're too fat. You gotta lose weight."

First time I've seen this guy since I was a toddler, and he was breaking my balls about being a fat American. Ever since he left the States, he'd never had a desire to return. He blames a lot of that on my mother and her efforts to deport him.

After his siesta was up, my father had to finish work. He invited me over for dinner.

My brother Zach, who is technically my half-brother, happened to be in Rome for school, as part of a study-abroad program. He spoke some Italian, so I invited him to join us. It seemed weirder for Zach to be there than it was for me.

We met up with my father and found out he'd had another kid, who he brought along to the dinner. His name was Alex. This was weird, because not only do I have a nephew named Alex, who is my older brother's kid, but now all of a sudden, Zach is also meeting another half-brother of mine.

The dinner was great. We all got along and had wonderful conversations. We were both in a relaxed, good mood, so I decided to get to the point.

I asked, half-joking, "Does your dick still work?"

He had no issues, and he told me, "Fuck 'em all—long, short, fat, or tall." Super stellar parental advice.

That's the kind of character he was. He had other expressions like that, but while it's great to get advice from your dad on important topics, I had some genuine questions to ask. I wanted to know about his health.

He told me he was healthy but that his lower back had started to hurt. Being a drummer, I could relate.

My father had a few photos of me and my brother displayed at his house. I don't know if they were always there or if he had put them up last second, but it felt good.

We parted ways, but he invited me back. He said, "Come back again. Stay longer. You can stay at my house for a week. I'll take care of you. Bring your girl. My treat. All expenses paid."

I decided to take him up on it a few years later. This was just to hang out with him and get to know him more, not part of a larger trip.

My girlfriend at the time and I were together for seven years, and we are still fake friends, but I was going through phases, trying to date too many people at once. I feel bad talking about her because I never treated her the way I should have.

Anyway, we went to Italy, and she met my dad. He was definitely a pervy old man. You know? Like, he started making comments about her large breast implants at dinner, asking, "Are those real?"

During dinner, I asked him, "Did you ever play any instruments?"

He told me that he used to play the flute. At first, I thought he was joking, but he was totally serious. So, he was a musician and an actor, which made a lot of sense to me. It helped me understand where I got some of those desires and talent.

While I was there, he and I dug into his relationship with my mom, and I quickly realized he was spinning a much different version of the story that I had grown up knowing. Here was this man, my father, crying as he was reliving those moments.

He said, "I was never gay. Your mother overreacted." He had pleaded his case, the story from his point of view. He felt he wasn't in the wrong. He felt like we had been split apart.

The trip ended, and again, he implored me to keep in touch.

When I returned to the States, I was pissed at my mom. It was ugly for a while between her and me. I couldn't understand why she had forced my dad out of my life, why she had lied about what happened and about the man he truly was. He seemed like had wanted to be involved. He wanted to be in my life.

I wanted to keep in contact, like he had said, but I've had a hard time doing that with people who aren't close by or in regular contact. Out of sight, out of mind. It was hard to find the right place for him and his new family in my life.

He called me around Christmas for a couple years and sent happy birthday wishes sometimes, but I started to see some of what my mother had always said was true.

But I still wanted him in my life.

Many years later, I did a tour with Flotsam and Jetsam, as a tech for drummer Jason Bittner (Shadows Fall, Flotsam, & now Overkill).

Eric AK, the vocalist of the band, said, "What I picture, when I think of Christian, is watching him come out of the hotel with a bright white mohawk and wearing Elvis glasses, a camo onesie (with the butt-flap), and bright orange shoes. This is how he spent the day with us. He may be embarrassing to some, but people never forget him."

One of our shows was only an hour away from my father in Italy. I invited him to come grab lunch and meet up, but he had no interest, like he couldn't be bothered with seeing me. He had been out of my life for thirty years and yet didn't want to meet up. That was a real red flag.

The more time that went on, the less and less we spoke, and I understood he had seen my last trip to Italy as enough, like he had made up for never being there.

I felt like his tears and big display of emotion had all been an act. He was playing a part, not connecting with his long-lost son. It was fake.

I still thought he could be a part of my life. After the birth of my son, I had wanted to get dual Italian American citizenship. Having an Italian passport would make touring overseas easier, and, as a bonus, the citizenship would pass down to Orion.

Since my father lived in Italy, I asked him for help in securing my citizenship, as that fact made the process way easier. Instead of being excited or, at least, supportive of it, my father freaked out. He thought I was making some weird attempt to attach myself to his last name and to his family, like I was sneaking my way further into his life. I think he thought I might want to get something out of him, an inheritance or whatever. My simple request for him to assist me with some simple paperwork had him convinced that I was trying to pull one over on him, like I had this whole conspiracy planned.

He showed me his true colors. It was worse than out of sight, out of mind, really.

All the things my mother had told me since I could remember were true. My dad was a piece of shit. He was self-centered. He was vain. He didn't really give a shit about me or my brother or my mother.

Now I have a son, who I'd love for him to meet and get to know his grandfather, but we never really talk anymore. Similar situation with my brother, Orion's uncle except even he is way better than our father. When you're so distant, the longer and further your paths diverge, it gets harder and harder to forget the past. All the issues. All the lies. All the emotions tied to those memories.

But I digress. We were talking about how I met Jessica and the birth of our son Orion. He was born in NYC, but Jessica wanted her kid to grow up in a nice area. I mean, New York City for a little kid can be tough, especially with Jessica's TV job keeping her working insane hours each day. She felt like she had to give up her career after he was born. She pretty much gave up her life and her job for me so I could do music and so she could be a good mommy.

Now she's teaching videography, and she's a writer too. She's doing things she likes. She's using her degree. She has written for a bunch of magazines and websites and has written/ghostwritten several autobiographies for people. After leaving TV, she has carved out this second career. She also sometimes still shoots incredible music videos as a hobby for me and others when she has the time.

She's allowed me the freedom to pursue my dreams and passions with music which I'm super grateful for. I leave for weeks at a time to tour, and when I come home, I get to be a fulltime dad. Even though I'm gone for long stretches, I still see my kid more than most of the 9-5 dads I know.

Orion is now seven, and he thinks he knows it all. He's also way too comfortable bossing me around. He's got this crazy advanced vocabulary. He's in first grade but reading at a third-grade level and beyond. That comes straight from Jess. She reads a lot of books.

He loves to draw, like I did. That's why I went to art school. I grew up as a huge Spiderman and Hulk fan. Orion loves to draw superheroes, like in comic books. Even at seven years old, I feel like he's way beyond where my talents ever were.

He's a goofball. Sometimes he goofs around too much, you know. He loves attention. Not sure where he got that from, ha! He likes to show off like I do too.

Orion lives life on his own schedule, which conflicts with me, since I'm the same way. If he's in the middle of something but I want to leave, he fights it until he's done. This sets me off because I want to stay on schedule. When it's time to go, it's time to go.

My son takes Tae Kwon Do lessons from the same guy, Mr. Cuddy who I took them from when I was in high school. I was taking Orion each week, so I thought, hey, I might as well get out my old green belt with blue tip and start training again.

Jessica, Orion, and I all tested last week. Now I'm a red belt black tip. Jessica is a green belt. Orion earned a green belt. He's breaking boards and memorizing all his patterns. And so now, because of him, I have my eyes set on the goal of achieving black belt status at almost age fifty.

Orion's lively. He's vibrant. He's full of energy, a bit hyperactive, like I was as a kid. I tell him he can turn that into a huge positive if he sets his mind on a goal to achieve.

I often talk about how music saved my life. Whereas some people get into music, then get hooked on drugs and spiral out, go to jail, or die young, I had the opposite experience.

Yes, I tried some drugs. I experimented, but cocaine made me feel awful. I mean, I was already too hyper when I was sober. I puked after taking a lude. I remember the food looking exactly the same as it had when it went in. It was the weirdest thing. I had other bad experiences with various other pills and quickly realized I couldn't take them because I would always get sick. I was afraid of going to jail. I was super afraid of needles, so that kept me away from certain things.

Eventually, I realized I was in it for the music itself. I honed my energy and focused on the creative side, as well as the promotions and marketing side. I knew what I wanted. I had a specific goal. I worked toward that goal above all else.

Other musicians, even bandmates or friends, were out in the woods, smoking crack or whatever, while I was at home, practicing my drums and booking shows. It kept me out of a lot of trouble and brought me satisfaction when I reached my goals.

Orion hasn't shown much interest in music yet, but then again, neither did I at first. I was probably ten or eleven-ish by the time I got really into it. The problem is at six, he already thinks he can play anything on the drums and do it awesome, but he can't. It takes practice. It takes patience.

I hope Orion understands my point and learns this lesson. I want him to focus. I want the best for him. I want him to have a better life than I had. I hope he follows my path, but, of course, I'll support him in whatever he chooses to do. It doesn't need to be music; it can be anything. Just as long as he gives it his all.

It hasn't been easy. It hasn't been quick. It hasn't been free of drama, but I am proud of where I am at.

CHAPTER FOUR

Music is a Violent Industry

I followed a fairly common path into music. First, as I mentioned earlier, I joined a cover band from the neighborhood called Screaming Fetus with my buddy Erick Heller when I was twelve or thirteen. That led to playing originals with some friends under the moniker, The Putrid. We were a punk-rock trio that kickstarted my music career in many ways. We did a demo at an awful place called Trod Nossel Studios and played out, but it was short-lived.

My older brother played me a KISS record, and I fell in love with them instantly. I found myself listening to a lot less punk. I loved punk, and as I got older, I appreciated it a lot more. Gang Green, Black Flag, Sex Pistols, and all those bands wrote killer songs, but their recordings sounded like a mess. Even The Misfits. The quality was low. I'd go as far as to say 'yucky.' I grew up on AC/DC and Ozzy and was used to a certain quality, so it was hard to go backward to those old punk bands and to understand it.

Around this time, I met Kai Blackwood, though he had a different name back then. He was a drummer interested in trying his hand as the front person for a band. He wanted to be James Hetfield. ("I certainly wanted to be a James Hetfield-esque person," Kai clarified.)

He and I would go to underground record stores and check out all these imports from Venom, Metallica, Destruction, and all these other new thrash bands. We talked a lot about writing music in that vein. He wanted me on drums so he could sing and play guitar. He showed me some of his techniques to expand my horizons.

I was in a band called Safyre. Yes, the name sucked. I asked Kai to join us on guitar, but he wasn't interested.

Kai said, "I wasn't a fan of their old singer. He did the high-pitched-wails thing that I wasn't into. I did go to practices. We'd play a couple Metallica tunes, but I would have to sing them, because the other guy's voice was too high. He was a good dude but just didn't fit the style. Eventually, he left, and they asked me to sing. I agreed as long as we changed the band name."

We switched our name to Violent Industry. We gave up our spandex to embrace jeans and explore thrash.

Kai said, "On stage, Christian is an animal. He is the best drummer I have ever played with. He also helped me understand what a drummer goes through at the back of the stage. When we played, I would scan the crowd and soak in the emotions and response the crowd offers. Opus told me, 'All I see through the set are three asses.' I never thought about how his view was limited by sitting behind the rest of us. That still makes me laugh to this day."

Violent Industry opened doors for me. Some contacts I made were super positive, like when I gave our music to Munsey Ricci from Skateboard Marketing. Munsey has thirty years' experience pitching metal music to commercial and college radio. I knew if anyone could help Violent Industry get some spins, it would be him.

Munsey didn't add us to his roster. I was young and bummed, but he explained that without real distribution or a record to sell in stores, a radio campaign, even if successful, wouldn't help us as much as I thought. He easily could've taken our money and pushed our song and potentially wasted our time and resources, but he was honest and sincere. That's why he is still in the business all these years later. Also, he is a fellow Pasian, which is a plus. Here I am, now running a label, with great distribution channels, explaining to the bands that they need to wait on radio until they have a full length to promote.

As I played more shows, recorded, and networked, I realized for every Munsey, there are dozens of dirtbags. Yes, you have to put yourself out there and sometimes deal with unsavory characters, but some doors are better left unopened.

Ever since my brother played them for me, I became obsessed with KISS. The music, the showmanship, the theatrics, marketing, and the mystique all fueled my love for that band. They were what rock stars should be, but, as they say, never meet your heroes. I've interacted with two members from KISS—the two who got booted from the band—and I can tell you both moves were justified.

Ace treated me like an annoyance. I approached him at a show at my hometown venue Toad's Place to sign some stuff, and he made it obvious he saw me as an unwelcomed distraction. He made me feel so small and inconsequential. I'm sure he has his moments, everyone does, but it felt like shit. I can justify his attitude, but when it comes to Peter Criss, we almost fought. Straight up. We came close to a fist fight.

A promoter I knew, Lord Bishop, who I'm still close with, who went by the name Suave back then, booked Violent Industry to open for Criss, which was Peter's solo band right after he got kicked out of KISS. He had gotten a group of nobodies together to play the other parts. They were all Italian goombahs from NYC.

Lord Bishop said, "From the first time I met him, Opus was so full of enthusiasm, drive, and had power behind the kit. He was always thinking and working and working and working. I knew he'd do big things if he stuck with it, and it seems like he's on his way."

Peter was such a huge influence on me growing up, so I was beyond excited to get that gig to open. We sold fifty or so tickets, which represented about 95 percent of the crowd who showed up.

Peter arrives in this busted, old jalopy of a gray limousine. He's waving to the fifty people that we brought, like he's some dignitary gracing them with his presence through the top open sunroof window. I thought it was cool at the time, but that was short-lived.

We played our set, and I added in a drum solo, which might've been the first and last time I did that. I was just beyond excited, ya know?

Lord Bishop said, "The way Opus got his band the slot was by him calling me over and over. He even called my mom, who ran Capricorn Sisters Presents. Opus's drive was charming. I arranged to get him backstage to meet Peter, because I knew he was such a huge fan. Peter was one of his heroes."

I brought my drumhead with me to meet Peter, and I asked if he'd sign it.

I was polite.

He looked at me agitated and said, "Get out of here, kid."

I was shocked.

I said, "Dude, you're a dick."

He shot me a pissed-off glance. "What did you say to me?"

His guys jumped up. They were all huge. My guys jumped up. We're not as big, but we're young and scrappy, and there were more of us. There was about to be a brawl backstage.

I can't recall how things settled down, but they did.

Lord Bishop remembered how it ended. "We had to drag Opus out of there. It was a real rockstar moment."

Ever since then, I talk as much smack as I can about that guy. I know he has seen it too. I tag him every time I mention that in an interview.

What a dick.

After my time in Violent Industry, I took a big leap forward by forming a band that would shape the rest of my life.

CHAPTER FIVE
G-Soul is the Goal

In the late '90s, I formed a band called Gargantua Soul, a mishmash of styles and attitudes, rooted in various Eastern philosophies. At the center of the band was our vocalist, Kris Keyes.

At the time, I was still in Violent Industry, and Kris sang for a band called Blind Justice. They were getting some buzz around the city as a band to watch. They played to packed houses. I mean, this was a local band who was selling out shows a couple times a week, sometimes even back-to-back nights.

Blind Justice was so innovative, ahead of the curve. They knew they had to get outside of our area to grow, so they toured and played other cities and colleges a lot. Their sound was also fresh. They mixed rap with rock before most others. You could say they were sort of pioneers in that style. There wasn't even a real name for it yet. Like, way before nu-metal, Kris Keyes was doing "rap-n-roll"—at least, that's what he called it. The same style became what ended up being labeled as rap-rock.

It wasn't just the music that set them apart either. I'd hear these stories about the crazy stuff the singer from Blind

Justice said and did on stage and off. I wanted my band to ride a wave of chatter like that, and I was committed to making that happen. I hustled. I booked shows. I networked. I did the dirty work that no one wants to do. So, when clubs wanted to book us, they called me. If a 'zine wanted to interview us, they called me. I was usually the point man for the band.

After many years, Violent Industry finally got our shit together and recorded a CD with Jeff Cannata, who was known for his solo work, along with the band Arc Angel. After we had a solid CD, I took trips into NYC to drop copies off with labels/managers/media and anyone else who might help get us to the next level. I was hanging with label scouts and executives and making great contacts.

My bandmates seemed to take it the wrong way. They got suspicious of me—jealous, even, at times. There was talk that they thought I was stealing the spotlight, and worse, I was even accused of stealing from the band. Bro, we had no money. There was nothing to steal.

I knew all the guys. They were my friends, so it stung the way they acted around me. We had been together for eight years, and now they thought I was betraying them? They were young and delusional, and soon, animosity built. They conspired against me behind my back and started treating me like shit. Eventually, they became convinced that I "wasn't healthy" for the band, and then they literally threw me out of my own band.

Kai's recollection is a bit different. He doesn't remember being jealous. "We did think he was stealing, but none of us thought he was getting all the attention. I think we were all getting sick of playing with each other. I mean, we were like nine years in at that point, and Opus just made himself the easiest target. He is always so nonstop. I think it was about the money and about control. Why would I worry about him getting attention? I got plenty of attention. I was the fucking singer."

Look, we were all inexperienced and kind of dumb to the business at that point. I get it, and we're cool now, but at the time, it was a big blow, and I was pissed!

Joe Delaney, a producer and a musician I've worked with for years, put it into perspective for me. "I think people in Connecticut thought he was going to screw them over at the shows he promoted, but that's just smalltime, local ignorance. Dealing with the business side of the industry is work, and work deserves compensation. He needed to get paid to make shit happen. I respect that, but sometimes other musicians don't get it. Club business is fucking brutal. Opus was always fair, especially compared to any big-city fuck-over."

After being disappointed, I became angry, but I didn't want to just sit around and feel sorry for myself. I could've just tucked my tail between my legs and ran away from the problem, but, in a way, the guys had lit a fire under my ass. So, I made a plan and followed it. The plan was concocted after I smoked a big, fat joint, sat back, and stewed over the whole thing. I felt a little lost—only because I saw a clear path for the band to get bigger, but the other guys weren't on the same page, and some didn't have the same hustle and drive as I did. I wanted to be a rock star, man. I reached out to them and tried to explain my side of things, but they weren't having it. I got even angrier and resentful ... and then I got petty, and thus, my plan unfolded. I decided I would form another band and make it bigger than they ever got. Revenge is sometimes a great motivator. It worked.

Around that time, Blind Justice broke up. Shortly after, their drummer, Pete McNeal, moved on to play with all sorts of amazing bands, including Cake and Norah Jones. Unfortunately, his demons and addictions got the best of him, and he ended up charged for some dark crimes involving children, faced a few lawsuits, and is currently doing time. I didn't follow how it turned out. I don't know much about it, but I know I never liked the fucker, and I'm a pretty good judge of character. So is my mom. I must get it from her. It's too bad, because he was a very talented groove-based drummer. I should've known he was a prick when I tried to work together once in the early days of VI's career. I actually contacted him to try to network, and basically, he told me, "No thanks! You guys are metal, and we don't play with metal bands." Back then, all the concert bills were diverse, and I know he was just blowing me off and being a cocky dickhead. But anyway, enough of that crap. I knew of Kris Keyes, as our bands had played some of the same local clubs, and everyone in the scene just knew about Blind Justice. But up until that point, it was just from word of mouth; I didn't really know him personally. I heard all sorts of weird stories though and thought if I could bring together one of the best vocalists in the area with me, two hungry musicians who were driven, the rest would fall into place and become history.

Joe Delaney knew Kris. "Kris Keyes is a world-class front man. The guy is a human cartoon character."

Kris was the biggest, baddest dude around, and he had a buzz growing about him. He also had a mystique. We were all way younger back then, just a couple local musicians trying to learn the game, and yet, he had developed an identity, an aura that preceded him. It rippled outward from him in all directions. I've only seen an effect like that a few times, and it doesn't come without a lot of creativity and planning.

According to Kris Keyes, "The first time I remember painting myself, I was like nine years old. I always had these ideas, even when I was a kid. Then, with Blind Justice, I decided to explore, you know? I wanted to test out the ideas and see what worked and what didn't work in a concert setting. I always wanted to push the boundaries to see how far I could take it. Maybe not as far as I was willing to go, but how far the crowd was willing to follow me along the way before they got uncomfortable."

I had logged a few years in bands in the area and had a following of fans and contacts that would come out to support us too. It was the start of something cool, I could feel it, if I could get Kris to say yes.

I then proceeded to stalk him. It might sound less creepy to label it reconnaissance, but let's call a spade a spade. I asked people about him for info. I dug around for more information. I don't recall how, but during all of this, I got his home address.

One day, I worked up the nerve and knocked on his door.

He had no idea I was coming. I don't think he even had any idea of who I even was, aside from maybe seeing me at some local shows.

He answered the door in a green-and-white-striped robe, and he was brushing his teeth. I could tell by his expression and body language that he was a little confused, caught off guard and a little apprehensive about finding a stranger at his door.

I smiled and said, "Hey man," like we were old buddies.

He looked at me funny, suspicious and wary.

I continued, "I'm Opus, from Violent Industry."

He pretended like he didn't know who the band was. I'd like to think it was because our bands were sort of rivals in the scene. Or maybe he just didn't really know us, like I had assumed.

I could feel nerves kicking in, telling me to get out of there. The plan wasn't going well. Instead, I just spilled my pitch to him.

"I know your band is done. I just got kicked out of my own band for nonsense. I think if we worked together, we'd have a winner."

He didn't say much; heck, he barely even reacted at all. I wondered what his problem was, so I just kept talking. He never expressed anything to me about wanting to work together or appreciation for the compliments, or even really admitting he knew who we were. Finally, I gave him my number and took off. I was kind of bummed that he didn't jump at my idea.

In fact, his lack of enthusiasm or reaction had me wondering if the whole team-up/local supergroup plan had been foolish. Did I want to waste time in a band with a guy who couldn't string together a couple coherent sentences?

A week or so later, he called me. He *had been* listening. "Hey, man."

I knew it was him right away because he has a very unique voice. He is a big, brawny guy, but his voice is sort of high-pitched, soft, breathy, and welcoming, like Ozzy mixed with Anthony Kiedis, a touch of Seal, like a heavy-metal Michael Jackson. I don't know ... thin at times but in a higher register. His raps were lower, loud, mean, powerful, and had an old-school hip-hop street style to it. You would never expect his voice to sound like that if you saw him first. I still have a hard time believing it.

He said, "I've been thinking about your idea. How about we get together, go to the gym, maybe, to work out and discuss it further?"

I took him up on it, and as anxious as I was to just go full steam ahead, the workouts turned out to be a healthy thing. Kris taught me ways to get more out of exercise. He also introduced me to a breathing yoga he had learned from an instructor with an almost cultish following. Hmm, maybe instructor isn't even the right word. The guy was well-known and respected all over the world. He was like a ... a guru. His name was Ravi Shankar, but he's not the same sitar player who hung out with the Beatles. Anyway, he was a leader in teaching Sudarshan Kriya.

Not only did I get in better shape, but it forced us to take a calming breath and lay out a plan of action. Kris didn't want to just form a band; he wanted to start something cool and all encompassing. Yes, he was spiritual, into martial arts, yoga, and healthy eating, but he felt like all those things had a place in the music and on stage as well. We wouldn't just be a rock band. We would be a movement.

I bought in, and we continued our journey together before actually getting into the music. We talked a lot, and he explained his lack of response when I sort of "cold called" him at his house. He lives his life by following his intuitions and instincts. He believes things happen for a reason and that it's all connected via spirituality and being clean. He wanted to listen to and observe me that day to help him decide if he thought a team-up made sense.

Kris Keyes said, "In many ways, my personality has been shaped by depression. If it's true that we are reborn, over and over, I've had many lifetimes of sadness in me. I never cried as a kid. I didn't know how. I was taught at a young age not to cry, to be a man. I remember when my mother died, and everyone said how strong I was, because I didn't cry at her funeral. I was an orphan. I lived in a detention center, so by the time I became a teenager, I acted out violently. I had had nothing but violence around me. I started to party a lot. I'm an alcoholic. Eventually, I knew I needed to find an inner peace, because no matter what I tried, I was sad inside. I went on a spiritual journey. The human body is made up of earth, air, water, and aether. I am a physical being, but there's another part of me that I can't explain. I don't even know what the fuck it is. Some people won't even acknowledge it.

That thing is really the biggest part of you. Spirit, soul, mind, whatever it is, when I finally understood it was there, it needed acceptance and exercise, just like my physical body. And that's when things started to become clear for me. Maybe not exercise ... that spirit side was hungry, and it needed to be fed. You can't just concentrate on your physical body and expect to find a balance in life. You need soul food. So, I left on a quest to restore what was missing from my life. I dabbled in various ideologies. As I dipped my toe in, I started to get a clearer picture of my path. I lived in a Buddhist ashram, and then a yoga ashram, and the more I learned, the more I realized how big the hole inside of me had grown. My spirit had been neglected so long there was entropy and decay at an alarming level. I soaked in all the knowledge I could. I felt myself coming alive. Parts of me that had been dormant my whole life tingled as they were reborn. I understood that I didn't miss drugs and alcohol and pussy and fighting and partying mindlessly. None of that was filling me up; in fact, they left me feeling emptier. Look, beating the fucking shit out of someone, being the biggest guy on the street is a rush. After the fight, you stand there and growl and feel so tough and powerful, but when that wave of excitement is gone, if you have any conscience at all, you realize you could be next. That same guy could beat you and make you hurt. You have to realize that, unless you're a psychopath and enjoy the pain. So, you step back from that fight and think, what type of energy am I putting out in the world? What did my actions do to improve life on this planet? You look around and realize anyone who saw the fight is looking at you in fear, not respect. What I did just put a negative vibe into everyone. I let off awful energy. Every fight, every fuck, every drug. None of it was a positive for me. What my body and mind and soul missed was this enlightenment. What I found interesting is that practicing martial arts was the opposite of fighting. The more you learn, the more responsibility you have to use that knowledge in a positive way. I liken it to Spiderman's mantra of, 'With great power comes great responsibility.' Each of my martial arts teachers became my spiritual guidance. I found comfort in the more circular martial arts. My teachers showed me how to focus on my breathing. That was a big key. I understood what a huge impact breath support had on not just kicking and punching, but on all aspects in my life. My temperament could be changed with a simple inhale. This led me to explore meditation, which, in turn, opened the door to yoga. This is a long-winded way to show you where I was at when Opus knocked at my door and asked me to start a band and why it was so important to me that he and I didn't start just any other rock band. We needed to be more."

Funny Kris mentioned about having to be a man and taught not to cry, because that was also how I was sort of brought up as well. My grandfather, who was basically like a father to me, was very old school and also came from the outdated mentality that men do not hug or kiss (even on the cheek) to acknowledge each other, never mind show feelings or crying in public, so I can definitely relate to all that.

Anyway, Kris and I continued to talk and discuss and develop the band, and, at times, I felt frustrated moving so slowly. I worried that he was leading me on all in the name of recruiting me into Ravi's yoga-cult thing. He was a stanch advocate, much more than a foot soldier. Kris was like a warrior for them—a spiritual warrior, in a sense.

And let me say, I got jacked. I was stronger, faster, and there's no debating I was in the best shape of my life at that time, until now. It was frustrating, because I started out defiant to the whole thing, like, aren't we forming a band? Why are we spending all this time in the gym lifting weights and all this other crap?

But I waited and got encouraged as I saw the pieces slowly coming together. We were building a foundation. Our band wouldn't be just sex, drugs, and rock-n-roll. We incorporated spirituality, yoga, theater, mystique, and a purpose into all aspects of what we wanted to do.

Kris Keyes said, "I want to name the band Soul Man."

I liked it as a name. It was cool, but I didn't think it was the right fit for this project. It didn't seem to give any insight into our sound or our attitude. It wasn't ... hard. We weren't heavy metal, but I thought the name should at least give an impression of rock. Soul Man fit, you know, a soul or funk kind of band.

According to Kris Keyes, "Soul to me meant I was having an awakening in my life. Whereas before, I was only relating to the fame and the trappings that came with it; now I was interested in spiritual things. Even now, there's so much I don't know or understand, and even that I can't comprehend. I've had a lot of spiritual experiences and one paranormal experience I don't think I'll ever be able to understand."

Kris was really into the name, so I didn't want to just dismiss it offhand. I went home, puffed a joint once again, and thought about the name. While sitting around, I heard the word *Gargantua* somewhere on a radio ad commercial, though I can't remember how/when/where. It struck me as a cool and unusual-sounding word that you didn't hear very often in daily life. It sounded big, and we wanted to be a big band. I suggested we combine Gargantua and Soul. Boom! And there it was. Every band that develops a fanbase and sticks around seems to also develop a nickname. For us, we became G-Soul, which I think is dope.

CHAPTER SIX

Our Sound Was Our Name ...

Gargantua

Kris Keyes said, "Our sound was our name: Gargantua Soul. It was a big soul. Massive. We started a street team when no one else was doing that. We had a website with a very active chatroom before most other bands."

Our website was designed by a fan who became a great friend and now label partner, Gary Sandler. Who Kris Keyes nick named "G-Rock." We were so lucky to have a guy who knew how to design a website back then ... at least that's what I thought, until we spoke to Gary for the book.

Gary said, "I didn't know anything about web design at the time, so I went to the store and bought a beginners book on web design."

It worked.

Gary explained why he learned how to build a website and why he offered to do it for us. "There was a very deep connection there for me. I knew the world was heading in a troublesome direction, and Kris Keyes was talking about the same thing. We both had felt a sense of being robbed of our true essence, our true nature by powers that were working to suppress us. We both had a burning in our hearts to try to educate and empower others, our peers in particular, through the message and music of the band. It literally became the only thing I cared about, 24/7, for years."

I had just gotten out of college where I took courses in art, fine arts. I thought we should invest time and energy and resources into the visual side of things too. I took inspiration from sports teams, even though I can't stand sports or the typical gang sports mentality that goes along with it and decided to give the band "colors," like we were a brand, or a gang even. Sports teams have mascots and logos and stick to a color palette, so I thought we should as well. Again, it was something we thought might help separate us from the hundreds of other local bands playing the same circuit. If you can stand out, be memorable, it goes a long, long way.

If you want to simply play music and rage at the bar and play "The Trooper" or "Paranoid" over and over, go right ahead. I'm not saying that's wrong or you're a failure if you do that, but I wanted this band to be special. We wanted to go mainstream but also be respected as real artists.

As we explored color schemes, I decided to focus on two contrasting colors. Kris wanted orange, and I wanted blue, so that worked out well. Everything we did, we incorporated those two colors. Our logo, our fliers, our t-shirts, our album covers, our stage show and attire, and anything we could promote ourselves in, we strived to add our "team colors."

Orange was Kris (which was the color he also decided to mostly paint himself). I was blue. Two opposites working in tandem. Yin and Yang. Kris said we were like chocolate and peanut butter. Both are good on their own but stellar when you combine them.

Kris chose orange because, "In India, when a person renounces worldly existence, they are called a renunciate. The person paints themselves orange, and they cup their hands, which is the size of their stomach. They'll go to someone's house, and the person will give them a handful of rice and nothing more. I consider myself a spirit in this world. I am a world traveler. Many people call me Nomad."

While the foundation of spirituality and our name and image formed, we brought in my longtime buddy Pat Garcia to be the behind-the-music writing piece of the puzzle. Pat has helped me start almost every band I've been in. He also helped create some of the band's biggest songs. He has a large family and had a lot of real responsibilities at an early age, so touring and steady gig work has never been in the cards for him long term, but we've managed to do cool stuff together. He later helped shape the first Dead By Wednesday album with me and did some of the band's first major tours. More on that later …

I started to find my own path out of Kris's teachings and my own spirituality to meld into our band. I connected with Native American culture and beliefs, and as I channeled more of that, it strengthened my understanding of Gargantua Soul for what it truly could become. I read more and more about shaman ideologies and allowed myself to explore a part of my soul I had kept guarded for years without realizing it.

I ran into Marc Amendola at a concert at Toad's again and mentioned the band to him. He was in a cool local band called Spoonfist at the time.

Shortly after, Marc joined the band on guitar. According to Marc, "I knew both Kris and Christian wanted to make a noise, and I did too. We focused on our strengths as a group. Stylistically, we had hard-rock guitar riffs, big drums, and Kris provided both rapping and harmony vocals. Beyond the music, we took time to discuss and develop our stage layout, theatrics, and our showmanship."

As we started to play shows and develop, Kris dealt with a lot of the doubters who didn't understand what we were trying to do.

Kris Keyes said, "One time, we played at Toad's Place; this was in the early days of the band. I was painted orange, wearing a swimsuit and some Doc Martens, and riding a skateboard. I remember roaming around through the crowd and seeing all these sideways glances and scowls and disdain from young kids who were punks, just like me. I had just been doing it longer. They wore the same stuff I had worn when I was fifteen, but now I had lived life, and I was onto something they had never seen before. We got up and played with conviction. The crowd changed as they understood what we were doing. They left buzzing."

Within a short period of time, the buzz started to grow.

Gary remembers how we started to grow as a group. "I was completely blown away by the G-Soul live performance, in particular by Kris Keyes. I didn't know what he was singing about yet, but I loved the energy. There was something about his attitude, his confidence ... his style. It was really something I had never seen before but that, for some reason, resonated with me. It was like he was on a mission. Their music was so creative and unlike anything anyone else was doing at the time. Opus was a huge part of G-Soul. He had the hunger and the street smarts to keep things moving in a forward direction. He had a wide range of musical influences and the discipline to be on point at shows and keep getting better."

Joe Delaney helped us get into the studio to produce our first demo. He was instrumental in developing the band beyond our early limitations.

"The band sorta sucked a little," Joe Delany remembered. "They were good but definitely not great. I saw the potential in Kris. I knew he could be big time with the right production and some calculated strategy. I could hear Opus was developing from being a straight, old-school metal drummer into a guy with a solid groove, but he still had more to learn. I thought the guitarist's work was lacking. The riffs were very derivative and unoriginal. When they added Lou Jaque to the rhythm section, that made a huge difference. He and Opus locked in, and the band got ten times more powerful."

We continued to write even as we recorded.

Joe Delaney said, "I think some of the other musicians thought they were Kris's equal, but that was not reality. It led to issues with misplaced egos, bad business decisions, and picking the wrong leadership. It also allowed for some shitty songwriting. So, I took charge and brought a song to the table. I wrote the music and the arrangement. Kris wrote the verses. It became their song, 'Rattpak.'"

We wanted to make a statement with our demo, though you still have to maintain the rest of your life while doing it.

Joe Delaney said, "I remember Opus cooked a huge pasta dinner for everyone when we recorded on a Sunday. It was so Opus to feed everyone like that. I also recall him leaving the studio to 'do something' which ended with a phone call from the police to bail him out."

We knew we were doing something right when we started to get attention as soon as we released our first demo. Our bassist, Lou, who was also a very well-known and respected tattoo artist, passed our demo on to a close female friend of the tour manager from Rage Against the Machine, Ford Englerth.

He started asking around about us. At the time, we didn't know he worked for Obi Stienman, who, if you look up most any '80's hair-metal band, was probably their manager and had a lot of contacts in the business, especially on the West Coast.

The two of them took us under their wing, and that opened a lot of doors. We were the only unsigned band to play Woodstock '99. We shared the Emerging Artists stage with Two Skinny J's, CC Deville of Poison, and a bunch of others from that era. Some are still around, and some, like us, are not.

Though Marc Amendola pointed out, "Technically, the band is still on hiatus."

We named our second full-length album, *The First, The Last, The Tribe*, followed by the album, *Impact*. It came out on September 11, 2000—the first of three of our albums to come out on the eleventh day of September.

By this point, we had expanded our roster. We had bongos, keys, bass, multiple guitars, drums, a DJ (RIP Budzy!) and vocals. The audience was also a part of the band. We got them involved in our shows far more than simply asking them to get loud a few times per set. Hell, we had so many members, it felt like a sold-out show almost every night on stage. You'd look out at the crowd to see several people flashing us G-Soul tattoos or boobies or both and taking the time to talk to us after the shows, not just about music but about life and philosophy, spirituality, and all kinds of stuff.

Kris would get the crowd chanting at the shows. "G-Soul, G-Soul, G-Soul, the soul is the goal!" or "The Tribe is alive in '99!"

Kris came from a theater background. He wanted to draw from that experience, as well to set us apart from other bands. He was confident that our music would have a certain level of quality, but he wanted the audience asking, "What will crazy Kris do next?"

Kris is a wild card. It is his greatest strength and his greatest weakness at times. He has the passion and punk soul of some of the old-school guys, like Henry Rollins. He was unpredictable, he challenged each moment, and the guy is very hard to direct. With Kris, you just open up the gate and let him loose. Sometimes you get gold and other times sour grapes, but no matter what, you can believe he'll bring something interesting to the music and the performance that moves the crowd. There will probably be a mess to clean up afterward too.

His vibe was the key to how the night would go. Sometimes he channeled this Jim Morrison charisma, and he'd have the crowd eating out of his hands. I remember a night we played a festival, and he was able to command 3,000-plus crowd members to all sit down, and they obeyed him. I would watch in disbelief as he controlled the set and owned the stage and the room. I mean, owned it. He could take things to a spiritual level, seriously. The room would buzz, and the crowd would lose themselves; hell, I lost myself a few times, for sure—like we all tapped into some higher thing, a hive-mind, and we were connected by the music, by the lights, and by our fearless front man, Kris Keyes.

One night, he climbed up a pole about sixty feet high, and he balanced at the top on one leg. He started doing yoga poses up there. Then he was holding onto the pole and sticking horizontally out from it. Mind you, he had a wireless microphone, so he was singing the entire time. He had a knack for those moments. It was a miracle that he never got severely hurt. He would push boundaries and create unique experiences for the concertgoers on any given night. You don't often see performances like his anymore: risky moves and unpredictable, unrepeatable moments.

He thrived at making his entrance onto the stage at each concert. One time, he was carried on a platform by four dudes, one being one of my best childhood friends, Eric Morton, dressed as medieval knights with real lit torches. You could never get away with that nowadays. And if you've ever seen photos of Kris, you know he would paint himself head to toe, so he already looked like a wild man up there. Almost alien. Another night, he got a troop of female African dancers to perform an elaborate tribal dance to start our show, and the whole time, he was tucked away in a coffin on stage. At the right time, he revealed himself, and we started to jam.

Kris pulled optical illusions, even. He would sometimes get a friend to dress up and look like him, and they would each move around the club so the Kris clone could take the stage and would get everyone to look at him, but then the vocals were going, and the guy wasn't singing. Then Kris would reveal he was in the back corner of the club with his wireless microphone, and the fake Kris would magically disappear. Sometimes he'd start parading around the club, and the clone would go somewhere else to set up another illusion. It even confused us at times.

He pulled a trick once where he dressed up as if he were homeless and messed with people in line getting tickets, as if he were trying to get into the show. Kris had to get started super early to transform himself with different clothes and do crazy things, like literally stuff his cheekbones like *The Godfather* to change the appearance of his face. Then came the makeup, wigs, or whatever. You had no idea it was the singer of the band you were paying to see messing with you. Sometimes I didn't know who or where he was on a given night until he just appeared on stage. Nerve racking and fun all in one.

So, he would harass the people in line, make fun of them, whatever he could do to get a rise out of them. It got to the point where people were threatening to call the cops or to fight him, but he wouldn't break character. Then he'd get on stage, in character, and tear off the costume, and the audience would be dumbfounded, laughing and shaking their heads, like, "Hey, that's the annoying homeless dude from outside."

"Look," Kris said. "Before a show, it's all hurry up and wait. You rush to load in, and then wait to soundcheck. You rush through soundcheck, and then wait for doors to open. You scurry to sell merch as the people come in, and then you wait through a few bands until it's time to play. This leaves large gaps of free time, and it lends itself to predictable rituals: drinking, drugs, smoking, etc. I didn't want to fall into that trap, so painting my body became a way to fill the time, along with some of the other preshow stuff and elaborate intros."

He put all of himself into the show. He brought theater and melody and intensity and spirituality, and it set us apart. He was a maniac. He risked his life several times in the name of music. It created such a cool atmosphere, because you never knew what was coming, even if we played the same songs.

But ...

The flipside of that coin was that Kris was also sometimes a loose cannon. One night, we were all taken to a higher plane of consciousness and connected on a level that cannot be explained in mere words, and then the next night, he leaves the stage, rushes into the kitchen at the bar, and disappears. We're mid-song, and I can't see my singer. The crowd is looking away from us, and I can hear people calling out in surprise. What the hell was happening?

Well, Kris found some potatoes and some heads of lettuce, and he decided to start firing them out of the kitchen at the crowd and even hit our bassist Lou in the head with one. He was pissed! Kris was pegging people with raw potatoes in the face, while we were trying to impress them into buying our merch. Sometimes it just backfired. And there were many times like this. It's hard on the road when all you want sometimes is peace and quiet after the gig. There is no real downtime or peace and quiet with Kris a.k.a. Diggum.

He would be laughing, having the time of his life, completely oblivious at how inappropriate or harmful his actions may have been to the crowd and to the band even. Another time, during a Halloween show at this small bar near my house we played often, he knocked over a giant barrel of raw peanuts while wearing a real carved-out pumpkin head. Midway through the first song, he took off the head, smashed it on the bar floor, and started swimming around on the ground in the smashed pumpkin and peanut mixture, all while performing. But these are also the fucked-up things people remembered and talked about with their friends. People wanted to see this shit for themselves, so they came to the next show with their friends. And that's how it grew and grew and grew.

He is creative. He is artsy. But he is also a bit what you call "koo-koo." (My nonna used to always say that when I walked into the room for some reason too?!). But the ups and downs with Kris are extreme, and there's no avoiding them or keeping him even keeled. All you can do is damage control.

Sometimes it was amazing and other times it went too far.

I recall stopping at rest stops around five in the morning on the way to the next gig and walking into the store with Kris. Now, a few hours earlier, he had been painted head to toe in makeup and thrashing around, getting sweaty on stage. That stuff doesn't just wash off, and a lot of the times, we didn't have access to a shower post gig, so he would be walking around with various colors smudged all over him. He looked kind of crazy to me, and I know him and the situation. Just imagine a stranger grabbing a cup of coffee and gearing up for work on the farm, then coming in contact with Kris like that at that hour of the night. That was just a few of many of these types of similar situations.

Needless to say, we got a lot of weird looks.

Kris didn't always let that slide. He is a performer. He feels the attention, and it fuels him. He thrives on getting a reaction out of people, right? It doesn't matter if that reaction is complete adoration or if the person despises him with a passion; it's all the same to Kris. So, no matter how odd or out of place it was or how exhausted Kris was, he put on a show. He needs to be the center of attention most of the time in the room. I get it.

Kris jumped behind the counter at the convenience store, grabbed the intercom, and started singing and pretending like he's taking people's orders. The girl allowed it but was baffled. I'm surprised he never got arrested.

He's a bigger dude, with a solid frame and crazy-looking eyes when performing. He was painted half orange, like a giant Oompa Loompa, singing at five a.m. to people who had already judged him when he'd bounded through the door. Pure madness. Exciting, hilarious, and disturbing all at the same time.

I can picture farmer Jed getting asked about his morning and retelling the story, moment by moment, only to be told by his farmhand that he needs to cut down on the caffeine.

Another time, we were at a Chinese restaurant in Boston, trying to eat in peace, and Kris jumped up on the table with no warning or reason and started singing and dancing. He scared the shit out of everyone there, including us. Some of the band were so road-worn by that point and tired of the antics that they got up and left midway through dinner.

Kris basically said, "Look, I love it, and if I want to do it, it's going to happen. I don't care what anyone thinks. Most people in the crowd are followers. They just want to hear 'Free bird.' I'm a leader, and I'm the one on stage with the microphone, so I'll decide what we're doing. If you don't like it, oh well … It's my five minutes of fame."

As his bandmate, you see these things daily, and it becomes routine. You learn to deal with it and love him for who he is.

Kris said, "Opus is gung-ho too. He's the same way. You put us together and all bets are off. And that's how rock music has to be. The second you start asking the crowd what they want, you're a cover band."

After a while, it can drain you, because even when things are going good, you know you're never more than one moment away from potential disaster. Now that I'm doing my own thing and I can watch from a distance, I appreciate Kris Keyes so much more. A lot of what he did was funny and heartfelt. The stuff coming out from him is genuine. He isn't slanting his art to appeal to the crowd. He isn't begging for worldwide acceptance. He is saying, "Here the fuck I am, and this is what I do. Take it or get the fuck out of the way."

I can respect that, especially when I'm not the guy calming down pissed-off promoters or clubs. And there were definitely a few.

Now, I can't pretend Kris was the only wild dude in the band. We all had our moments. Mine came in many forms, usually sexual in nature, but one time in particular that comes to mind was when we approached the Canadian border while on tour. We weren't playing in Canada, but we were way up in the Northeast and had a show in Traverse City, Michigan. Going through a stretch of Canada was going to save us hours of drive time and plenty in gas. The only hassle was getting over the border.

This was right after 9/11. Before that awful day, crossing the border was no issue, so we didn't even think twice about how things might've changed. Change, they had. You may or may not recall, but their border patrol sort of took the blame for allowing several of the terrorists into the country, so they were understandably upset and on edge.

I had no idea until after we left that we were going into Canada, and I had brought four or five joints of weed with me for the ride. When we had gotten on the bus, I fell asleep almost right away. By the time I woke up, we were getting close to the border, and I had no idea what was going on. I was way too close to ditch the weed. Not that I wanted to waste it anyway, but it might've been an option had I understood the situation earlier. If I dropped it then, they would definitely have seen it on the ground. So, I was stuck between a rock and a hard place.

This wasn't just regular old weed either; it was super stinky and strong, dank buds. If I smoked half of one, I'd probably be wasted, let alone four or five. They were meant to last for the whole trip.

I tried to get other people on the bus to help me get rid of the weed. I even asked our keyboard/percussion bongo boy, Tommy Hetz, a.k.a. "Tommy Salami", who kind of already had half a brain to begin with, to help me out and eat one, but he was smart enough to refuse. I honestly don't even really want to bring up his name, that's how low of an opinion I have of that guy.

Hmm, for the record, I don't hate him or wish him any ill will, because I don't really hate anyone, but I guess I can say dislike and would rather not mention him either. Unfortunately, he was always hanging around so I kind of have to. He did so many shitty things over and over. I gave him chance after chance, and he would pretend to be my friend, only to screw me over and over, again and again.

It was never about the music for him, just about status, parties, and piggybacking ladies off me. Thinking he was a friend, I brought this guy in and got him involved in almost every music project I've been in up until DBW, because I finally got smart and realized what was going on. Sometimes shedding deadweight really helps lighten the load off your back. But that's enough about him; I've already wasted too much space here on him.

Anyway, we're coming up right to the border, and I'm freaking out. I asked Tommy to please take one again, and he literally told me no and left me hanging by myself to deal with this situation. Of course, he had no problem smoking all my weed all day, every day, but when I asked him to eat some, all of a sudden, he's too scared to help me out.

I figured even if I had a good hiding spot, border patrol could inspect the bus and find the joints, so I just ate them all. I knew I would be wrecked, but all I needed to do was get past the border, and then I could pass out, puke, or both until we played.

Except they pulled all of us off the bus to talk. Of course, they did. The process wasn't quick either. By the time they singled me out and led me into an interrogation room, I was feeling the effects of the weed spiraling out of my comfort zone. The room was spinning. When I walked, I would zigzag. I was freaking out, assuming they had to know how fucked up I felt. Everyone's words sounded like they echoed from another planet.

I was stoned to the bone.

The Canadian border patrol can check your background and reserve the right to deny you access to the country due to anything they deem suspicious. It could be something you did twenty years ago; it doesn't matter. They don't care if you have reasoning or excuses or whatever. And they are very hard on people with past records, big or small, and look down upon anyone who has even one DUI, never mind anything major. Luckily, I don't have any DUIs, because driving while drunk is completely irresponsible and stupid, but I did have some other older weed-related bullshit still on there, and it was an immediate red flag for them. Especially post 9/11. Once they say no, that's it. You're toast.

I got so paranoid about getting busted. They picked up on it. They must have because they were peppering me with questions and watching me super closely.

I imagine I was letting off a real fucked-up vibe. I certainly felt that way. And I knew I hadn't even peaked yet. It was just getting worse and worse and weirder and weirder by the minute.

They asked, "What are you guys doing here?"

I told him, "We've got a show in Traverse City, Michigan. We aren't even planning on staying in your country, just passing through." Thinking that this would actually maybe help our predicament. Well …

"Nah," he said, shaking his head. "You want to go to Traverse City, Michigan, you guys go around the lake. You don't get to cut through Canada."

Wow, what a dickhead!

Before I could protest, he pointed to the door. "Now, get outta here."

We had to turn around and readjust our route, adding several hours in the process. Unbelievable, but at least we got out of there, and no one was arrested or detained, but that was a close one.

Marc Amendola remembered that day. "He was sick, ill. We had to pull over so he could throw up. That was no fun."

Within an hour, I was shaking, sweating, and throwing up. I couldn't stop shivering, even when we got to the gig. I could barely play that night. I have always hated when musicians get too drunk or whatever to play. That's not how I roll, so I was pretty pissed.

Kids, if you're reading this, understand that what you do now affects the rest of your life. What may seem like a simple, harmless decision today could come back to bite you in the ass down the road. I know this all too well for many reasons. Trust me on that.

Gargantua Soul was way ahead of the curve when it came to bad decisions ending with disastrous results. I mean, even the theatrics I just described, which helped get us quick and intense attention, also ended up hindering us from finding a label to partner with to take the next step forward. We were hard to pigeonhole and stereotype, looked at as more of a gimmick and less about our actual music. How do you label a band who defies labels? We didn't want to be confined to a certain space and sound and look, but that's exactly what managers and labels and MTV and the tastemakers wanted. We were playing insane shows and getting great feedback from the crowds, but that wasn't enough. For better or worse, we started discussing changes to our look and even to our sound. Why not? We got one foot in the door, the hardest one to get in, and some of the band thought we owed it to ourselves to adapt and see if we could pivot this thing into a million-dollar deal.

What did we need to change? Well, for one thing, the recordings we had done didn't have the same quality as some of our peers. I remember when Disturbed broke into the metal mainstream with their first hit, "Down with the Sickness," and everyone thought it was us. We had a lot of similar elements, but our sound and look were different enough that the comparison surprised me a bit. They had a way more polished, tightly produced sound, whereas our latest record was raw and rough around the edges. It lacked the punch and edge of the records coming out at that time. We had played with Disturbed a couple times actually, around Illinois, while we were on tour. They were local to that area. Promoters started hitting me up and asking about all the recent radio play; that's how much people thought it was us.

And don't get me started on the band Motograter who came out after us and their stage show basically mimicking ours. They painted their bodies, talked about meditation, and even called their fans "The Tribe." It was hard not to think we had been copied and that it was possibly even an inside job. Whatever the details, it worked for them for a short period. They, as a band, committed to the whole schtick; whereas, we had a few guys in our band resisting a single image. They didn't want to get painted up or dress a certain way or match or grow the mystique. Too many cooks, as they say, spoil the meal.

Years later, we found out that at least one of the founding members from Motograter actually went to school in New Haven (our back yard) at the height of G-Soul, so there's a good chance they saw us and took the gimmicks we had built and expanded on them times ten for themselves. They were also connected to a few bigger label & band people, one being No Name Entertainment who I knew all too well, so there were two "coincidences." Even our own fans were telling us about them. Some were so adamant about it that they would angrily hit them up and accuse them of robbing us, kind of like the whole Slipknot/Mushroomhead conflict.

We took the stage at Woodstock '99, and I remember looking out at the crowd, a sea of people. For some odd reason, I chose to play this show in my tighty whities. I felt like I had to poop from nerves but, as usual, couldn't. My legs were shaking. We played right before Limp Bizkit but on a different stage. Biggest show of my life that I've played thus far, but I want to do better. I always do.

Kris said, "For four days, I walked around without sleeping at Woodstock '99. I didn't have a shirt, and my whole body was painted orange. I wandered around, speaking with strangers, meditating, dancing around bonfires and drum jams, and soaking it all in. I performed my rituals. These are martial arts routines that I still practice today. Boxing, kung fu, Tai chi, muay Thai, and chi gung are all things I've practiced since I was younger. My photo ended up on the cover of, like, 150 newspapers. I feel like I was there, but I wasn't there, almost like an out of body experience. I'd get up on trashcans and chant as people followed me around. It was a trip. Woodstock '99 was a rip off. That's why they burned that place down. We got the hell out of dodge right in the nick of time. Eight dollars for water?! People were knocking over the Porta-Potties. Unlike the original Woodstock, this one wasn't about spirituality and unity and coming together, a calling of the spirit. The vibe was off. Way off. The whole thing was a tourist trap. It was a dark, muddy pit, which was poorly lit. Everyone looked miserable, evil, and drugged out. I remember they had MTV VJs up in these booths on stilts. I saw Kurt Loder in one above the main stage, and the kids in the crowd were shaking the bottom of it. Kurt was scared out of his mind."

Luckily, we had use of the golf carts, being one of the main acts on the Emerging Artist stage, so we were being driven around and had access to the bottled water behind the band stage. I felt legitimately sorry for most people there, and we even started secretly handing out water to others. Talk about a reality check, the next day, after just playing in front of thousands of people, we played some dump bar with a leaky roof literally dripping on my head, a crowd of about fifteen people somewhere in West Virginia. True story! Just goes to show you that one minute you're up and the next you're down in this whack-o biz.

One year later, we were named the number one underground act by Hard Rock Café through a national music contest sponsored by the drink SoBe. Every night at shows, people would show us their Gargantua Soul tattoos, and I would watch people mosh, dance, and sing along to our stuff.

We then landed a SoBe sponsorship because of the win, and they flew us out to Colorado to open for Papa Roach. We performed in a giant heated tent on a ski slope in front of a crowd made up of industry people. A&R reps, DJs, suits, and models were everywhere. It was crazy. All expenses paid. Beautiful hotel overlooking the mountains. We were treated like kings. It started a snowball effect that also got us casted in a VH1 movie as part of their Movies That Rock series. The movie was called *At Any Cost*. You can still pick it up online but only on VHS, heh. There's a good reason it hasn't made the jump to DVD, Blu-ray, or, as far as I've seen, any digital platforms. It stands as probably one of the worst movies ever produced.

The cast was cool. James Franco plays a junkie. It was one of, if not the first role in a movie he'd had. I don't even think he lists it on his résumé. I wouldn't either if I was him, but the experience for us all was amazing. Gene Simmons is in the movie as a label rep too. We played a fictional rap-rock band (how ironic) who was in the process of getting signed. The manager who was signing us was played by Glenn Martin Christopher Francis Quinn. He was the Irish kid in *Rosanne* who wore a leather jacket all the time. He was also in a show called *Angel*. He passed away. I don't want to speak ill of anyone, especially someone who is not with us any longer, but we saw obvious evidence that mounds of cocaine were being blown in his dressing room. He was a paranoid mess and looked pale. He actually flipped out at one point and yelled at one of the band members, actually it was Tommy Salami because the Glenn kid thought he was staring at him. He said he was trying to do his lines but that he couldn't concentrate with all the eyes on him. It was funny but not funny all wrapped into one. All I remember was after being yelled at in front of everyone, Tommy's entire bald head and face turned bright red. He was pissed.

We filmed in Houston, Texas. They flew us out and put us up in a five-star hotel. They paid us around 10k and gave us part of the royalties. Looking back, I know now how ridiculous that amount of money is, especially considering what we brought to the table. There is so much more money in the movie industry than music that they have no idea what to do with it or how it should get spent. They could've asked us to drive to Texas and stay in our van, and we probably would've said, "Sure!"

Marc Amendola added, "There I was, at twenty-seven years old, filming VH1 movies, playing the biggest shows, meeting and playing with my heroes, and maybe the topper on all of that was playing at our hometown coliseum."

There was a huge venue here called the New Haven Coliseum where, as a kid, I saw all the big acts: Iron Maiden, Dio, AC/DC, Ozzy, Metallica, KISS, you name it. If they were awesome and on tour, I saw them at the New Haven Coliseum. During a Judas Priest show there, I saw a riot. People started ripping out all the seats, and the place was pandemonium. When I got into music, I dreamed of playing that stage. The more I got into bands and the business, I realized how difficult that would prove. I respected it more. It made me want it more. It was that dangling carrot just out of reach, you know?

So, the drive to play grew, and the legend of the venue grew. I realized that few bands ever reach the point where they get to play places of this size. I mean, Maiden is legendary. Dio is freaking mythical.

We got a call.

Gargantua Soul got an opening slot on a bill of, get this: At the Drive-In, Gang Starr, and Rage Against the Machine.

Now, sure, you can say, you guys played when the doors just opened, and the lights were still on in the Coliseum, while people were taking their seats. You can say it was so early the place wasn't even full or ready for music yet. You can say this and that, and you know what I say?

I played the New Haven Coliseum, and it was glorious. It was a dream come true. I had a goal that, at times, felt unattainable, ridiculous even, but there I was. You can't take that away from me. I stood behind my kit, staring out at the crowd. I remember seeing shows there as a kid, and the place felt enormous. Now, it all seemed so much smaller from that point of view on stage, but it felt better than I had dreamed. The crowd, even at half capacity, was buzzing with excitement. They knew we were local cats getting a chance of a lifetime, and they were all sharing it with us, so they were in for a special night.

A few years later, the Coliseum closed its doors, and the building was knocked down, along with dozens of childhood memories. They cited safety concerns and building code violations and whatever else. Pieces of the roof kept falling out of the ceiling. But it was awful to see it go. I understand things change and neighborhoods adapt and all that, but concert halls, good ones, are a piece of history, like The Rat in Boston or CBGB in NYC—which I am also very lucky enough to say I've had the honor of playing both of those famous shitholes several times with my past acts. We need to appreciate venues like those for what they are, warts and all, and embrace the magic heard inside the four walls.

We got to know the RATM guys a bit as we interacted with them and shared Ford, their tour manager. Tim, their bassist, was a no-frills guy. He's an athlete who loves playing various sports. He wasn't into the flashy, weird '90's clothing styles of the time or anything like that, whereas I embraced everything that was hip back then. I wore goggles. I had platinum-blond spiky hair. I wore a kilt. I went full-tilt rock guy, trying to get attention. I wasn't famous yet. Tim was.

So, we're hanging out, and Tim is breaking my balls.

He asked, "Why do you dress like that?"

I tried to answer, but he shook his head.

"No man," he said. "You're constantly crying for attention through your clothing, attitude, and persona. Let the music do the talking, and the rest will fall into place."

I scoffed. "Easy for you to say. You're already famous. I'm trying to get seen here."

We went round and round, but neither of us convinced each other of our own perspective. That's not to say that he didn't change my life in any way. I credit Tim with not only introducing me to sushi, but also teaching me to care more about my craft as a musician and less about "the show." Prior to hanging with him, I had never had sushi, and he was shocked. He basically forced me to try it. He called me a pussy and shoved sake and spicy tuna down my throat one night while we were over in their neck of the woods in California. I've been hooked on it ever since.

Gargantua Soul did a showcase in LA one night, and we ended up partying at the Viper Room after the gig. It's LA, so you know you'll see some famous people somewhere, no matter what. Everlast, who was pretty popular at the time, was there at the bar and a couple of other people I recognized.

Tom Morello was holding court at a circular table with several attractive females. I wanted that kind of attention. It's one of the many things that kept me striving and grinding. Since Tom was aware of my band through Ford, I thought I'd ask him his secrets, see if he had any wisdom he'd be willing to share.

I whispered to him something along the lines of, "Damn, Tom. Look at you. How do you do it? You're like a pimp."

He grinned and replied, "Nah, Opus, you're the real pimp."

I laughed hysterically and was humbled by his kind and generous words.

Brad, the band's drummer, and I connected over some video games before a show. Turned out he was a drum gear nerd and had a huge stockpile of vintage drum sets all tucked away at his storage unit.

His collecting helped me out one time. I was flying to California for a showcase without enough warning to arrange for a drum kit to come with me. Ford asked Brad to help. Brad opened the doors to his collection and said, "Grab something. Whatever you want to play is yours to borrow."

I'm telling you; the place was wall to wall full of top-notch gear—a drummer's paradise. And all classic stuff, like Gretsch & Ludwig drums.

As a band, we did do some things together of which I am very proud of. Kris and I would go out to share fliers of our upcoming gigs. We would hit up every telephone pole, bulletin board, bar, or anyone we passed along the way. Other guys in the band helped out as well. Not just helped. There were nights when all seven members hit the streets all gung-ho and ready to go. We split into small crews to hit different areas. Some guys would hit up shows happening that night and hand our stuff to people leaving the show. We would put stuff on cars, on street signs, or wherever else we could manage. When we took over, we took over. We hounded the local radio stations. We got onto TV shows that weren't for independent bands. It was almost to the point, locally, that some people got sick of hearing and seeing us everywhere. We had a collective energy we shared with each other on and off stage and with our street team, fans, and whoever else came to the shows. We were genuine, not some manufactured bullshit thrown together by a label or management group. We evolved organically, while still following many of the initial foundational ideas Kris and I had developed in the gym together.

Kris said, "When it came to promoting, we went full steam ahead."

To find success as a band, you have to operate like a motor. All parts need to do their job in sync to keep the momentum driving forward. We had seven guys in the band at one point. There was a DJ, a percussion/keyboardist, two guitar players, a bass player, a singer, and a drummer. Ridiculous when you think about it. Sometimes it could be a mess live on stage with too much going on, but when it clicked, it clicked, and either way, we were entertaining.

The difference between a local band that can't get anywhere and a local band who refuses to stay put all boils down to putting in the work. Do the things you have to do, no matter what. Make the sacrifices. We were about as big as you could be without mainstream success. We were known in many circles, and we heard all the time about how it was crazy that we didn't have a major deal with a label yet. Although we had some indie labels helping us out mainly with distro, like Wonderdrug Records in Boston, it wasn't the type of deal our management wanted for us but Ken at Wonderdrug was a great dude.

We shrugged it off because we all believed a better deal was coming. We saw our peers getting big and making money and doing cool things on bigger stages and tours, and we all knew—or, at least, thought—we were next. It felt like fate. We had put in the work, and we were about to be rewarded for our extra hard work, dedication, passion, and belief.

Only, the big deal never materialized. We inched closer and closer, a shark circling chum in the water, but weird things got in the way. Just as we followed fate and instinct to get there, that same philosophy sometimes stood between us and our break.

The conversations with different A&R people kept coming, but no one pulled the trigger. We were rubbing elbows with the biggest names, playing big shows, but we hadn't found the person to champion us to the next level yet.

Marc Amendola said, "I took out a loan for the band, but looking back, I wonder if that was a mistake in that maybe it scared off someone else from taking a chance on us."

WCCC The Rock 106.9FM, a now defunct local rock commercial radio station, took us under their wings. Even as an independent band, they had us in regular rotation. This was a weird period for music. Corporations had taken over a lot of the stations around the country, but deregulation hadn't allowed them to turn them into one station run by a couple of consultants who only wanted to play fifteen to twenty songs on the charts from the biggest labels to ignore everything else. Rock radio found an audience, because it was fresh, wild, unpredictable, and constantly embracing new sounds, major label or not. The DJs don't have that freedom anymore, and the audiences know it. FM radio keeps wondering why they don't get listeners anymore. Well, maybe it's because those consultants you pay millions to are dead wrong. Listeners do want DJs with personality and personal opinions. Listeners don't want the same songs played over and over, hour after hour, day after day. Your station is stale. Try something different. Take a chance.

WAAF in Boston, MA played our stuff too sometimes. They were tastemakers. They were the East Coast trendsetters. All the other stations watched what they played each week, and then usually followed suit.

Our shows grew, and we grew as a band, for good and for ill. Internal changes forced adjustments to our sound and attitude.

We would meet with label people, and they'd say, "If you stopped rapping in your songs, we'd be more interested."

We'd talk about it, and then write a few songs with no rapping.

Nothing.

Next guy would wine and dine us. He'd talk us up and get us all excited.

Then he'd say, "If your singer stops painting himself, we'd be more into it."

So, we'd meet as a band and discuss. If you go through that process enough times, you realize a few things: one, you're willing to change almost anything to get that contract; two, the labels and managers don't have your best interest at heart; three, once you start making wholesale changes, you can easily reach a place where your music is missing the very elements that got you to the table in the first place. You've lost your identity. You've become a mixture of half-baked ideas from a guy in a suit who has no idea what your band is actually about or what your fanbase loves about you.

If you learn this too late, you alienate the people who helped you get started: the fans. When that passionate group leaves, it's really hard to keep momentum. The focus and drive is gone. It's like we imploded from the inside out by suddenly second guessing ourselves and our style.

Marc Amendola said, "In hindsight, I can see where and when the band lost its footing in the music industry. Why didn't G-Soul break through? That's the million-dollar question."

Networking is key. Stop worrying about protecting your little circle or clique and start realizing that whatever you put out there comes back to you. Think small, stay small. The more you help and do for others, the more you find success in more ways than one. You'll also find success and satisfaction from within. It's a simple concept, but so many people do not see or understand this. The world would be a better place if we followed that advice together every day.

As a band, we experienced a weird synchronicity that proved both positive and negative to our careers. Sometimes opportunities came exactly when we needed a boost, but others, well ...

We released an album called *Impact* that had a cover image of a meteorite crashing into New York City. It came out on September 11, 2001.

Give it a second ... yeah.

Talk about weird, awful timing. The world got flipped upside down, and no one wanted to see anymore images of mass destruction even hinting at damage to NYC.

Gary, who helped with a lot of our designs, said, "The album titled *Impact* showed on its cover a meteor striking the northeastern United States. When I was working on updating the website to reflect the new album art, I distinctly remember getting a call from Marc, the guitarist, whom I dealt with mostly on business matters. He told me the album release date would be moving back from an earlier date in September, to September 11, so I had more time to work. I was relieved. Little did I know what that September 11 would bring. It was the infamous 9/11 date. The first song on the album was called 'Calling My America,' and the first line of that song is, 'Now I pick up things like radar,' which to me is a reference to Kris's psychic abilities. Additionally, there is a hidden track on that album called 'Tuesday.' Nine-eleven was on a Tuesday. These might, of course, be mere coincidences to the coincidence theorists out there."

We had a song, "Drive," from a previous record that had won us some attention. If you go back and read the lyrics, they are just as relevant now with what's going on in the world then they were even back then. I don't know if it was because Kris was so spiritual or if it was all due to his meditation and his willingness to let the universe flow through him, but he seemed like a portal of information at times. That's why I think we had so many weird coincidences happen to us. It was like he knew what was coming, because he took the time to listen and open up to the universe.

These events and our spiritual journey helped give Kris the nickname of the Prophet of the Fire. We ended up writing a song by the same name.

Gary was able to see these things from the outside of the band with a better perspective. He said, "Kris saying he was the PoF was a serious proclamation. He wasn't just giving himself a name, like Lil baby or Killa-G or whatever. At first, I thought he was just being silly or that he was pretending to be like a superhero or something, but it soon became apparent it wasn't just a gimmick or nickname. Look, if anyone is the prophet of the fire, it's him. I don't know if he still is or if that was a period in his life which manifested strictly during the G-Soul days, but he certainly professed it with much conviction and as you can see by the many events which he wrote about coming true. It does make you wonder."

Kris calls me, Earth—which is ironic, being that I also started a successful Black Sabbath tribute band that tours internationally called Earth (which was Black Sabbath's original band name).

Kris Keyes said, "Opus is the Earth. He's grounded. He's the foundation. Having Opus around is healthy for me.

Even more so, it's comforting to have him in my life. He handled a lot of the leg work stuff. I am the air. Shifting, unpredictable, spacey. I am creative, artistic, and weird. I'm not saying Opus isn't creative; he totally is. He can tap into that side, but he always stays grounded, which I can't."

Gary added, "Christian is definitely someone in life who found their calling. He was absolutely meant to play the drums. I think he knew that instinctively too. He has a tremendous amount of talent and even more drive and determination. He has come a long way since the days of G-Soul, but even back then, he was very much a major part of the band himself, writing some of my favorite songs by them. I think he was a bit taken for granted actually. He knew what Kris was going for, and he knew how to execute it in a way you can't teach; it's just either in you, or it isn't. It's as if he was chosen for the band or chosen to work with Kris so he could bring his message forth. Opus is very similar off stage as he is on stage while playing—loud and booming and aggressive. What you see with Opus is what you get."

Kris and I complimented each other, aided each other, pushed each other, but it wasn't about being opposites or at conflict with one another. We had common goals, and we used our differences to make each other stronger.

For a while, we had solid bookings, and we had started to get some buzz. Our slow implosion started to put us on the outs with our manager, Ford.

Gargantua Soul was in a weird spot, having done some great things independently, but we hadn't inked a deal or broken out into the mainstream. In a way, looking back, we had already had our heyday, our moment in the sun, but we didn't know it was over yet. Ford never said anything about splitting from us; he just did. But there are no ill feelings though. He's a great guy. Chalk it up to bad timing.

Bottom line, we were looking for new managers. David Ellefson's name had come up, because we heard he was starting to manage bands and launch a music company. He had left Megadeth, and he was doing a bunch of other jobs. He was an artist endorsement guy at Peavey, and he also started Ellefson Music before the EMP, a label he would later create. Ellefson Music was basically just him trying to figure out what he was going to do with his life after Megadeth.

He wanted to help other bands, manage bands, and see what doors he could open in the industry. There wasn't a label yet; there was nothing. It was just Ellefson Music. Just him, managing bands and helping other people while doing artist relations for Peavey.

So, we hit him up. We had a couple conversations that went really well. One was when we were on tour with Union Underground and Soil. The meetings went well, and we thought he might have interest in managing us, but at the time, we actually decided not to go with him. Why? Well, our style wasn't really his thing. He was more of a metal guy, and we were more of like a Faith No More, Red Hot Chili Peppers, Rage Against the Machine kind of vibe, you know what I mean?

So, although it probably would've worked in the long run, we didn't go with David. Again, Gargantua Soul, we were our own worst enemy. If we could think of anything that was wrong with someone or something, everyone would talk about it, and we would choose not to do the deal or whatever. We lost at least two or three legitimate deals because of our own stupidity. Because, you know, a lot of the guys in the band were overly cautious. They were what I call 'no' guys. They would always say 'no' first instead of 'yes.' I've learned you should always say 'yes,' and then figure it out and worry about it afterward.

Kris Keyes said, "Opus and I spent so much time and energy trying to convince the other guys to say yes. I knew Opus had my back, but I also knew the rest of the band didn't. Opus and I were constantly doubted, even by our own bandmates. They didn't even want to admit to being in the band until we were selling out clubs."

We were approached by Flavor Flav's manager with a proposal for one of the best-known hype-men ever to join our band after his long departure from Public Enemy.

Kris Keyes said, "We won a battle of the bands, and then we were approached by Public Enemy's camp. Professor Griff came in the studio and re-did one of our songs with us, and then they pitched having Flavor Flav be in our band."

I mean, Public Enemy?! C'mon, I grew up on that shit. We all did. He had been at the game for decades. He had experience, character, connections, and would've added another layer to an already eclectic group like Gargantua Soul. An eighth member!

We discussed it at length. Some guys were worried about how he would fit; others thought he might be too political. They wondered if he was still doing drugs. Half of the band had several reservations. I fought for it.

I remember saying, "It's motherfucking Flavor Flav! How can we just dismiss this?"

In the end, we couldn't come to an agreement. Our band dynamic was pretty much a democracy by then. We decided things together, and on this, we couldn't get everyone on board, so we passed on the opportunity. And now you understand why there's more than one reason the first Dead By Wednesday album is titled *Democracy is Dead*.

Kris Keyes said, "There was talk about us touring the Bahamas as Jay-Z's backing band, another thing we reluctantly turned down. Of course, another band got the gig. They were called Lincoln Park. I mean, that one decision alone would have sent our lives in a totally different direction."

Shortly after that, Flavor Flav was all over the media with a string of reality shows on VH1, like Flavor of Love. In the blink of an eye, he was a superstar. It was hard not to look at that as a big swing and a miss. Could've, should've, would've ... oh well.

I know that stuff doesn't always translate over. TV markets are very different from music scenes. But the media attention that came with Flavor could have raised our awareness and opened some different doors for us at a critical time. Not to mention, I'll bet he would've been an interesting person to work with, good or bad. Character and uniqueness stick out in entertainment. Flavor has those oozing out of him. He's got a cool energy and charm that seems impossible to ignore.

Another time, Gargantua Soul went to NYC to meet with a huge entertainment lawyer. This guy had a long track record of getting huge deals for his roster. He was as plugged in as they come. Even mid and lower-level bands that he worked with had gotten deals and opportunities. We had a buzz building, so he came sniffing around. Something we were doing attracted these people. They saw money to be made. He invited us to his place.

You've heard the saying, 'Too many cooks spoil the soup.' (Yet again)

The whole band came to the meeting. Had it been only a couple representatives, maybe things would've gone down differently. I don't know.

Kris Keyes said, "That was a defining moment for us."

The first thing you saw as you walked into his office were gold albums on the wall. The furniture and decorations and the whole vibe was flashy. We were a collection of rock dudes from various levels of low to middle class, so we were fish out of water for sure. We played shows at places where the backstage area doesn't have working water or heat, you know. The walls would be covered in graffiti, and the preshow rider would be a couple drink tickets and a bag of chips at best.

The secretary had designer water and talked to us in a pleasant tone. We were so used to getting weird looks wherever we went, so it was just a mindfuck to be treated well and with respect. We couldn't help but feel pumped.

I was looking at my bandmates, and they were all starry-eyed. I was googly eyed, I'm sure. Come on, could you blame us? This was all new and exciting, and we thought we might be walking out of there on a path to breakout/mainstream success.

We sat at this massive, elaborate roundtable and listened to his pitch.

I got some vibes from him, like maybe he was slimy. I felt that right off the bat, but maybe that was my own defense mechanisms firing. I have seen enough bad deals and have heard disheartening stories from other bands to know many musicians get taken advantage of. I didn't want that to happen to my guys, no matter how much we all desired success, so I was watching him closely. I was double checking his words, sniffing for bullshit. I was almost actively looking for a reason to say, 'Fuck no,' and storm out, but overall, what he said had promise.

And to be blunt, if the guy got shit done for us, I didn't have to love him. I probably didn't even have to like him. He had a job. He appeared to be excited and aggressive and good at his job, so maybe he'd be a great teammate for us.

At one point in the meeting, he said something like, "Look, you guys should be huge, but you need the connections. I have a throughline to the people who can make things happen for you."

He had a Rolodex of labels, producers, booking agents, press, and anyone else needed to launch a successful album release. No deal is ever perfect. No album is ever guaranteed a successful shelf life, but it helps to have a champion in your corner who knows everyone.

He wanted to add us to his client list. He was clear about that.

He had the means to open doors we never could on our own. He was clear about that.

So, what he would do is shop our band to major labels, and then if/when he got us a deal, he would be paid for his efforts.

All he needed was to negotiate some reasonable terms.

The sticking point? He wanted a bigger percentage than most other agents ask for.

We had talked to other agents and attorneys who only asked for 10 percent or fifteen. Some wanted publishing, while others didn't. Some wanted partial control; others felt we needed to be ourselves. There's good and bad in every deal. It's a give and take, right?

Well, if I remember correctly, he asked for 20 percent of everything and with other stipulations.

The attorney was cocky. He was good at his job. To him, time was money. I get it, but it still felt cutthroat when he laid the papers on the table and said, "I need an answer in forty-eight hours, or the deal is off the table."

We went home, and we hemmed and hawed.

There were reservations on my end as well. I wasn't, like, gung-ho, wanting to jump at the deal, but I wanted to see it play out. The terms were in his favor, no doubt, but that's how negotiations work, right? A lot of bands would've signed the deal and asked questions later when it was too late.

Did we want to give this guy a controlling interest for a long period of time? No. Did we think he should have his name over the copyrights and some of the other stuff he asked for? Hell no.

Half the band felt like the percentage was just too much, regardless of any of the other terms.

I argued that 20 percent of nothing, which is what we had at the time, was nothing, but 20 percent of a million dollars is … well, who cares how much he is making as long as we get ours. I felt like if our band was able to break into the mainstream, we could bring in big money. We were entertaining. We had crossover potential. We had character and … soul. Our audience was a mix of races. Our audience was male and female. We had a message instead of being just another cock-rock band singing about chicks, booze, being depressed, or partying.

But in the end, we ended up passing, or we took too long to decide; I don't exactly remember. The deal went away. Just another kick in the dick. I think that was a huge mistake. We passed on more things, but that might've been one of the worst ones of them all.

I'll always look back and wonder again what could've been or what should've been, but even knowing that can be unhealthy. You've got to keep going. You've got to stay in the present and work toward your future. I've had another twenty years under my belt of hard work since then, so I recognize what an absolute misstep that turned out to be for that band.

Saying no to too many of these opportunities was the downfall of that band in my opinion.

Kris and I started Gargantua Soul, but as we filled the roster, we tried not to neuter the newer guys, so they were a part of all the decisions. This turned out to be a bad decision when certain people were added to the band. There were just too many de facto 'no' guys.

It wasn't just saying no a bunch that is the issue. It is when it becomes a knee-jerk reaction every time before actually listening and giving it an honest shot. Each opportunity should be discussed or weighed individually.

Soon Kris and I started feeling as if we were losing control of what we had started together. Other members didn't want to consider if taking an unpaid gig might lead to something else cool, or maybe by taking some unknown chances, other things can happen. You know, sometimes doing a favor can open a door. Play a charity show, and you hit it off with the promoter. Show up early to a radio interview and meet the program director. There are a lot of opportunities that come without a paycheck. It can be a tough pill to swallow. It became more about "money, money, money." It started to dilute the things that had made us special when we had started. We were being pushed away from being heavy, and with less rap and more rock. I didn't think that was the way to go.

I tried to look at opportunities as a whole and not just by percentages and dollar bills. Music is a business, so I get it, in a sense. All musicians want to succeed, but there's more to it than a black-and-white contract. You pay your dues. You scratch a thousand backs until you find the one who can scratch yours. Network, do favors, and hope it comes back to you.

There is a saying in the music business that when you get an opportunity you don't simply say yes; you ask, "Yes, and …?" Bite the bullet by maybe playing the occasional free show, opening for the bigger band, but ask what's next. Angle the conversation to find out what other opportunities you can be involved with. Keep your names and faces and music in front of decision makers constantly.

If you stand still in the music industry, it's worse than being stagnant. You fall out of the picture really fast. You're forgotten. There are way more bands than there are opportunities. In fact, it's oversaturated, so if you get a reputation for saying no, the powers that be will cross you off their call list in favor of a band or person willing to go the extra mile.

Now, look. Flip all this around. If you say yes to everything, you also might be taking a risk. Maybe the free show sucks, maybe the promoter doesn't take care of you, maybe the compilation CD doesn't get promoted like they promised, maybe it was a waste of time. Sure, it happens, and it sucks, but I've got many years in this industry, and I don't look back on any time I said yes with regret, except for a few social dates.

Did I waste a few Friday nights? Yeah, sure, maybe.

Have I built a network of contacts and experiences and memories doing what I love? Definitely.

Don't say no.

Don't even say yes.

Say, "Yes, and …?"

We knew things were serious with the band. Labels and managers were snooping around. They smelled blood in the water—or, better yet, they smelled money in the water. Our shows were getting bigger; the buzz was getting harder and harder to ignore. We were on the radio and TV. We got all kinds of opportunities thrown our way, and the press even picked up on what we had going on.

Of course, I wanted to take the next step and get signed to a major and have a big-time manager and get a taste of real success, but I didn't think the band should have to compromise to make that happen, even after repeated calls for us to do so.

One of those times was a literal phone call from the one and only Avery Lipman, the head of Universal Records. He got my phone number somehow and just hit me up out of the blue.

He asked, "I'm hearing all about Gargantua Soul, so why don't you tell me what your band is all about."

My heart jumped in my throat. Forget wondering how he got my number or why he called me personally, I needed to figure out what to say and fast.

Bands, I implore you—and this goes for every member in the group—have your elevator pitch ready at all times. Figure out what your band is about and really who you are as a band and why you are a band. Labels want to make money, sure, that's the number one thing. They want bands who can appeal to a wide audience, a band who can stand on its own, but part of figuring out how to make that happen is determining the best way to market and package your band. Where does your record sit on the shelf at a store? What bands are your influences, peers, and who looks up to you, and why? What three bands would yours fit with to make the perfect tour? What part of the lineup do you fit in? Are you the opener/warm-up, direct support, co-headliner, or headliner of the night?

If you get a call from someone who can open doors, make sure you have smart, planned-out, educated things to say.

Me? I stumbled over my words, trying to recover from the shock. My attempts and playing it cool were anything but smooth.

Of course, you can try to tell the president of one of the largest labels on the planet that your band is too unique to label or that your mission is to be the next Rolling Stones but with a social conscience aimed at saving the world. You can tell him you're too cool to put in the time and effort it takes or that you have many other outlets for your creativity, and then see how that goes over. My guess is that by the time you're done talking, all you'll hear is a dial tone in response.

You need to live music. Breath music. You need to get uncomfortable. You need to invest in yourself, in your band, in the industry, and it's a bumpy rollercoaster ride of ups and downs, so you'd better put on that fucking safety belt.

The call led to a meeting with all-star A&R rep, Sinji Suzuki. At the time, rap-rock was waning in popularity as the next wave of metal and hard rock took over. You had Godsmack and Breaking Benjamin and Staind getting all the spins and attention that nu-metal had been getting the last few years.

I sat face-to-face with Mr. Suzuki, unsure what he wanted, but obviously, I was hopeful he wanted to partner with Gargantua Soul.

He said, "We've been watching your career, but what do you think about this band Hatebreed?"

Hatebreed was just starting to make their mark and was from my area back home.

Now, I knew the guys from when they had been in other bands, and I had seen how their singer Jamey Jasta handled his business. In fact, when he was a kid just starting out, I had been in the game for a while already. He reached out to me about booking my previous metal band, Violent Industry.

Being older and feeling more experienced, I was like, "This little baby-faced kid wants to book my band?! Who the fuck is he?"

He was eager and passionate, and my ego was out of control. There are times I wish I had swallowed my pride and taken him more seriously. Years later, I was selling Hatewear merch at the Mayhem dates for him and got to know him.

Since then, our paths have crossed many times. I always seem to be nipping at his heels.

Back in the day, MTV had a TV-show contest called *Wanna Be a VJ?* that was eventually won by Jesse Camp. Remember that weird, skinny, druggy-looking dude? Well, I went down and threw my hat in the ring. They picked me out of the crowd due to the way I had dressed. (So, take that, Tim!). They took me into a different room to do an audition for one of the current MTV VJs. I killed it. Straight up, I introduced Eminem's song, "My Name Is," exactly like a VJ would, and they ate it up.

The crowd loved it. It's still up on YouTube if you're curious to see how I did. You can see me stutter a bit at first, fighting nerves—but c'mon, tell me I didn't own that shit once I got started.

So, before I can even congratulate myself, I've got someone from MTV saying someone wants to talk to me upstairs—meaning management, meaning the people who actually make decisions and who can bring me on staff.

I get shuffled into another room to do another intro and talk a bit. This one was private, off the air. They had me read something right away as a second audition.

I'm thinking, shit, I did something right.

The whole studio is set up with all these secret doors hidden behind two-way glass mirrors. After I did my readings and auditions, this guy comes out from behind one of them, like I'm on some weird gameshow. He talked to me off the air.

He said, "Hey, I'm so and so, a producer, and I handle this and that. I don't think you're right for this competition. You don't really fit what we're looking for in the next VJ, but ..."

Turns out, MTV was looking for the next host of *Headbanger's Ball*, which they were bringing back but that they hadn't announced yet. He told me I was great, and I was what they were possibly looking for. He asked if I would be interested in that, to which I obviously told him I was a metal fan and would love to be a part of it.

I was pumped. I was live on MTV, and they think I might be a candidate for their metal show. My phone is blowing up. I went home electric.

I never got called.

A month or so later, I heard Jamey Jasta got the *Headbangers Ball* hosting gig.

Anyway, back to the meeting with Mr. Suzuki. I loved Hatebreed's first record, *Satisfaction is the Death of Desire*, so I said anything positive that I could to pump up some local guys who I knew and respected.

I said, "Jamey hustles his ass off. They are an incredible band that is blowing up, not only in our area, but all over as well. Their shows are intense. They are the real deal."

Well, guess who got a deal after that meeting I had with Sinji over at Universal and who didn't? A million-dollar deal on the table went to Hatebreed, and we got a big fat dick. Obviously, I'm not saying I personally got Hatebreed signed, because obviously, I didn't. He did it himself with all his hard work and perseverance, but I'm sure my two cents didn't hurt. They told us they liked what they saw in Gargantua Soul and that they'd keep an eye on us, but that was the last meeting on the subject between us and them.

As time went on and deal after deal fell through, I wondered if this was as close to super stardom—or, at least, the big leagues—I'd ever get. Gargantua Soul had done so many cool, positive, big things. We had proven ourselves worthy of a shot but also prevented ourselves from accepting the chance.

Kai Blackwood joined the band after we released *Impact*. He saw the writing on the wall. "The band was backpedaling. Instead of putting out these great full lengths, they were scraping together EPs and being pushed by the currents instead of steering their own ship. We were directionless. I started writing more stuff for other projects and eventually left Gargantua Soul to do my own stuff again."

You never go into a project thinking you'd mess it up, but at that point, it was hard not to see it that way. Just as quickly as our window of opportunity opened, the industry moved onto the next big thing. We were instantly un-fresh, uncool, out of touch, and maybe worse, out of step with current musical tastes. When we started, it had proven difficult to get attention outside of our shows, because our music didn't fit neatly into any categories. We were sort of like a Faith No More-type band or Fishbone even, you know? We were just weird enough to give labels pause and to confuse mass audiences. We didn't fit into the established boxes, a bit of an oddity of a band, if I'm honest. We didn't have a set direction, and we didn't want to have one. We wanted to see where things went and ride along. The problem with that is a person who hears one song and loves it might hate the next tune he gets from us. Meanwhile, another music fan might have the exact opposite reaction. That makes it tough to get a consistent crowd who sustains the same energy throughout your whole live set. These were the end days for the CD single, remember. The digital file-sharing revolution had already begun in the shadows, but Napster was coming, iTunes was coming, Amazon was coming, MP3.com, and a million other sites would sprout up in the coming years, changing the rules of the game. We were either a couple years too late or perhaps a decade early, and unfortunately, Lars Ulrich was right.

Now, I say we were too weird, but certainly, we got enough attention to show we were doing something right. You spend all your time and energy chasing your own tail. We would've been better off sticking to our guns and steering the ship ourselves. Fuck the outside noise. Fuck second guessing ourselves.

It was interesting to watch, because at the time we were all still so full of hope, and we carried that feeling of destiny inside us. You know? Like we had put in the work, so it only made sense that we'd reap the rewards. We tasted success as we chased glory. We knew a breakout opportunity was so close, just around the corner. The signs were everywhere. Our sound was being copped by other bands. Our look was being copped by other bands. Our style could be heard on mainstream radio. We were no longer an outsider/alternative band. We were the mainstream. All we had to do was keep hustling and not get in our own way.

Of course, there's a reason I joke around about my Native American name being Almost. I almost hit it big. I almost got that gig playing drums. I almost got that insane tour slot. I almost got a real acting career going. I was almost a VJ on MTV. I almost did this. I almost did that. I got so close with Gargantua Soul. Almost!

CHAPTER SEVEN
Reality Bites, but I Bite Back Even Harder

My first foray into reality television happened when I was playing with Gargantua Soul in New York City. My friend's sister, Lara Morton, who's now more of a family friend, was a huge supporter and fan of G-Soul and became my neighbor for years. At that time, she had a friend who worked in TV. They were doing this new reality show where two strangers would go on a cruise before meeting each other.

The show was called *Shipmates*, and it was hosted by Chris Hardwick, before his stardom with *The Talking Dead* and other shows. The show aired on UPN. It was a new type of dating show. The woman and I didn't know each other beforehand, so our episode could've turned out interesting, romantic, hilarious, stressful, or even uncomfortable to watch, or it could have fallen flat.

The crew of the show followed us everywhere with cameras, 24/7, unless I went to the bathroom. That got old really fast. After about four or five days, I was over it all. Imagine doing that for months on end for some of these other shows.

I realized right away that our interactions were going to make for an extremely boring episode if I didn't do something horrendously fast to add something interesting and spicy to the dynamic between her and me. Because the first day we got to know each other I was so bored, I knew it would be worse to watch for the audience. We had no connection or chemistry. I realized I would either have to try to fuck her to give them something to use in the episode, which I didn't want to do live on TV—that just seemed disrespectful—or I could be funny or a total jerk. I thought I could avoid her and hit on other chicks to mess with her. I decided to go the latter route.

I embraced my role. I mean, I sort of had that reputation back then anyway. And this is back in the '90s, by the way. I want to share my story, and that era is part of the narrative, but I'm not very proud of it. I don't feel good about it. For a while, I was considered a womanizer.

A lot of guys who were in my position who could do it probably would, you know? This is going to sound cocky, but it's not meant to be, I mean it as the truth; I think if I dedicated all the time I spent juggling women, almost a fulltime job, into my career, like I'm doing now, I'd be so much further along. But what else could be expected, sex was a common theme throughout my entire life, even in school. My principal was Mr. Pleasure in Cox Elementary School. Then I went to Middlesex Community College. Seriously. I was doomed from the start.

I'll say it; I was too concerned with my dick. Looking back, I think it was a direct result of growing up the chubby kid. In high school, girls never looked my way. My nickname was fat tracks, because I was overweight with braces, and 7-Up, meaning "never had it never will." This initially started to change when I first lost some weight toward the end of high school. Not only did being in a band help my mission with attracting women, but I had a dancing phase. My buddy Tony Valle taught me how to dance, and we'd go clubbing and dance our asses off. Knowing how to dance not only helped me attract the ladies, but it also helped me with my rhythm for drumming. But once I had a taste of being the center of female attention, I became obsessed.

I wasted so much time and energy on that one aspect of my life. Juggling women, juggling drama, and, in the meantime, I put everything else aside, or at least low priority. There would be women in and out of my place, Monday through Saturday, and I would force myself to take Sundays off to rest and recover. Plus, I would go over to my family's' house anyway for my weekly "Sunday Funday" Italian dinner. It got disgusting at times, to be honest.

Some days I would have someone over in the morning, another in the afternoon. When the night shift arrived, she was typically the one I liked the best at the time, and she would spend the night.

The rotation switched each week. The lies grew and grew. Now, don't get me wrong. There were a lot of great moments, and damn did I have some wild times, but eventually, feelings got hurt. I mean, that lifestyle and schedule sounds fun, but it's so full of drama and bad karma. I was selfish.

Anyway, back to the show, *Shipmates*. So, I decided to be a fucking total misogynistic prick. A dick. I strolled around the pool deck like I owned the place, and I flirted with every girl on the cruise. Just a guy hanging out and having the best time in the world. I made myself the popular guy, the rock-n-roll guy who was ready to party with anyone.

So, the show aired a few months later, and I felt kind of guilty. The girl who I was supposed to film with was crying. She was asking why I had to be such a jerk. She wanted to know why I was the star of the show. She went nuts. They had paired me with a lunatic. I think she just didn't get it. If I recall correctly, she was from Alaska or somewhere far, and maybe she didn't understand why I played my role the way I did.

From that show, I got two other offers for productions, and a bunch of other opportunities popped up. I wanted to take advantage of the situation while I could. Those windows close quickly. I started doing all these different shows, and even more importantly, I started pitching ideas to them. Capitalizing on the moment and striking while the iron is hot.

I found some success on a brand-new game show, which was all a marketing ploy for Kmart. For you younger readers, Kmart was a popular discount box store years earlier, but they had been wiped off the map by newer stores, like Target and Walmart. This show was a last-ditch effort to appeal to a younger audience and boost sales enough to keep going.

The show aired on the Gameshow Network, and it was called … what the hell was it called? Man, it was so bad that I can't even remember what it was called. I'll bet no one else remembers it either. Anyway, to get on the show, you had to audition at a local level. One morning, I went on the FOX affiliate at 7 a.m. in NYC., and I had to showcase a weird skill. I chose to make a sandwich while blindfolded and playing my drums. I got picked.

They flew me to California to appear on the show, and I won first place. The prize was Kmart points, no money, so I had a year to spend $76,000 worth of Kmart points. I was wheeling and dealing with friends and family. They would pick out a $500 TV, and I'd buy it for them and charge half-price so I could make something from my win.

The problem was—and this is probably why they went under—the products were all cheaply made. A lot of people who bought stuff told me the stuff didn't last long. TVs broke after six months, and by then, Kmart was bankrupt, and no one could help them.

I did get a nice hot tub, a new bed and a bunch of other random stuff, but most of it was garbage.

I got a makeover on the *Rachael Ray* show. That was another way to promote my music career. Rachael was very cool to work with. She made the experience fun and easy.

I rode that "reality" wave for a good ten years or so, and then I pitched an episode idea to the DIY Network.

At the time, I lived in a duplex, with one of my dear friend's mom and his sister Lara, who I mentioned earlier next door. It was like a little commune—well, maybe not quite that, but it's kind of like this little complex out in a suburban area.

There was, like, a whole circle of people who lived in the same area, almost all on the same property. We all smoked bud, and it's a really cool set up. It's a real neighborhood. There's just a group of friends around who are all attached in some way. Yeah, we joke around and call it a commune, but realistically, I basically just lived on my buddy's mom's land. The house in front was on the same property, and we shared the driveway. There was a little apartment where my friend from high school's son had lived before me, and his grandfather stayed next door. We all partied and hung out and stuff. We had bonfires and just enjoyed each other's company.

So basically, I loved this property.

I had a vision. I wanted to turn the dilapidated, shitty garage into a band room, which I knew would require a lot of money.

I was already privy to several different reality show application submission process options, like websites or email groups, that I learned about through years of networking. In between music projects, filming shows, and whatever else I got into, I made sure to stay up to date with what producers and networks were looking for. These trends change fast. Shows come and go. You need to keep your eyes peeled so you don't miss opportunities, and you need to stay prepared to strike quickly.

One show listing desired people who wanted to renovate rooms and stuff. Pretty straight forward. Who doesn't need a new bedroom, bathroom, or kitchen in their house, right? The show could help out almost anyone who saw it, but I would always think of ways to try to mold the episode to work for me.

The show was new, but they wanted the same-old boring kitchen-redo, bathroom-update bullshit, you know? I filled out a reply, but I suggested that instead of the typical kitchen or bathroom, why don't you come to remodel a garage to allow two rock-and-roll dudes to practice and hang out? I threw out my own hook on a line to make this shitty garage into a soundproofed, band room/studio. Mix it up for a change. To my surprise, they actually bit.

They sent two producers to scout me and my buddy Eric. At the time, he played in local bands, so we both needed a space for us to jam with whoever. His mom is the one who owns the property.

We did a great test shoot. We had a blast. Shortly after, the show came back, and the powers that be said, "Hey, we want to do this show with you." They offered to pitch in x-amount of money but said, with the budget, they needed us to match a bit to complete the project the way we all felt was the best way. We agreed, and they went off to make some plans for it.

In the meantime, we hit a snag, because the house was in a flooding area, so we had to put in some extra work to raise the floor. In the end, I got a totally awesome studio out of the deal. It was soundproofed. It had cathedral ceilings. It was small, but the space worked well for what I needed it for.

This girl Jessica was one of the producers of the show and was there for the filming. We really hit it off. Again, I was like this Playboy dude, and she saw I had a lot of girls coming and going and stuff, but there was something about her. I really liked her.

We stayed friends.

We weren't fucking around or anything. In fact, she was married at the time. We were friends. She liked my style. She liked who I was. She liked my band and that I did the whole band thing.

At one point, she expressed an interest in taking a stab at doing music videos. She had a background in TV, and we had music, so she saw it as a natural fit. She pitched an idea for a video. She figured the budget could be free. She would help us by giving us a new thing to promote that looked slick, and she could use us to help kickstart her demo reel. She did our very first video, featuring zombies before zombies were popular.

It's for the Dead By Wednesday song, "Godlike Feeling," off our album, *The Last Parade*. The band members play zombies attacking people. We had fake blood and body parts, and there's a gang faceoff between zombies and humans before all the zombies gather to watch us play the rest of the song.

The shoot was a blast, and the video came out great; in fact, it still gets steady views online. If anyone from *The Walking Dead* camp or any of the offshoot shows needs a zombie or someone to scream and run from zombies, please hit me up. I am not doing the whole reality thing much anymore, but for The *Walking Dead*, I'll make an exception.

Jessica and I kept working together on stuff. She would find me little parts on shows.

Like, she got me on this show, *Oddities*, which was a show about this store in New York City, Obscura Antiques and

Oddities, who sold weird shit. The episodes aired on Discovery for several years. The premise was simple. People come in to look for stuff you can't find anywhere else, and the store owners search for it, and then barter with the customer. Jonathan Davis from Korn was on an episode, and he bought an old embalming kit. I mean, you'd see people selling jars full of toenail clippings, shrunken heads, and fossilized dung from ancient Egypt.

To make the most out of my segment, I pitched it as myself looking for a specific prop for a music video for Dead By Wednesday. I said I needed a giant skeleton. They allowed me to plug and promote the band. It was really cool. We got a lot of airtime, even though it was all fake, like most everything else in reality TV. We had everything set up beforehand.

Jessica got me other shows, and I made connections that saw me cast into more and more stuff.

One aired on the Science Channel. I was involved in a human psyche test for the show, *Head Games*. The premise of the show revolved around putting people in odd social situations to see how they would react.

My segment explored the question, "If you found twenty bucks in a pile of dog poop, would you pick it up?"

We also got into whether you'd offer it to someone else if they were standing there, you know? Like, do you give them all of it? Do you split the money? Are you honest? Do you leave it in the poop for someone else?

Then, through her, I did a show called *Nightmares: Death and Zombie Dreams Decoded*, where you go and reenact a nightmare. It was another zombie thing. I played a zombie trying to attack a family in an old farmhouse.

Cash Cab was another fun one to add to the resume, though I did terribly on it. I didn't win a single dollar. I was in New York City with my buddy Steel Neal, who did a show with Anthony Bourdain at one point. The show was a total set up, but I didn't know I was going to be on it. The video is online, and you can see how goofy we were and how we didn't take the show or ourselves seriously.

One time, I was on a show, and my job was to go into a diner in Jersey, break a vase, and act like a total asshole so they could tape people's genuine reactions and see how they handled the situation. There was a certain employee who the producers were testing to see if she could keep her cool. I think that was on the channel, *Vice*. Now that I think about it, these shows asked me to play a loud asshole a lot. Hmmm.

I was an extra in an episode of *Law and Order: SVU*, and as cool as any of this sounds, there's three times as many opportunities I missed out on. For the *Law and Order: SVU* episode, it was a full day of filming, and yet, you can't see me at all. I was in the background with a group of other people. I did get to meet Ice-T and some of the other cast, which was awesome. And I got paid.

I was getting calls on a steady basis, but as you get older, they don't need you as much, unless they want me to play a criminal or a musician or a biker gang guy. I also sort of "grew out" of it. It's a pain-in-the-ass grind, and if you don't live in NYC or Los Angeles, you fall prey to out of sight, out of mind. You need to be at it, hustling, every single day for those roles. To take a train two hours into the city, sit around all day waiting, and walk away with $100 takes a commitment, and acting was never my main focus. I did it to promote my music. It's one thing to get a spot on a reality show or a part on a drama that showcases my personality and gives me some time in the spotlight, but to be in the background, eh, I am over that, I think.

For a short time, I was a nude model for art classes to paint and draw. While I was certainly in the spotlight at those moments, I did see enough of the finished products to know the majority of them were not flattering. I didn't care; I was proud of myself and comfortable in my own skin. It was just a way to make a few bucks and feel alive.

What I learned about reality TV is that about 75 percent of what you see isn't reality at all. It's scripted and acted and produced and edited and directed, just like another sitcom or drama show you watch. The producers and directors put you into situations and coach you in ways to help make happen what they need and want to happen on screen. They will even feed you lines, get you emotional before you go on camera, or any number of tricks to ensure the results match the script. That format has seeped into all media these days, even the news. I saw that firsthand in my experiences.

If I wasn't so focused on the music, maybe there was a career for me in reality television?

David Ellefson agreed. "Christian is not a guy who lives life by a script. I think that's what makes him so good at reality television. He doesn't have to stay true to someone else's words. And that spirit is also what makes him so rock-and-roll. That's what I love about him too. He lives in the moment. He can improvise on the spot. He can pivot quickly when needed. It makes him charming and fun out on tour together."

Jessica continued to work in TV, on shows like *Chopped*, and we did a few more videos.

A few years pass, and I find out she's getting divorced. The process presented challenges. Even changing her name back to her maiden name became a big issue.

We talked more and flirted a bit online. I mean, we'd go to lunch and talk business still, but there was a different vibe, a little room for more social talk.

I had convinced her to come out and spend a day together, and I took her for some New Haven pizza. (By the way, if you want real pizza, you come to New Haven. We've got the famous Pepe's and Sally's, both known worldwide. People think of New York City when they think of pizza, but I'm telling you no matter what Ron 'Bumblefoot' Thal tries to tell you, New Haven, CT is the mecca of pizza.) But it was still platonic.

We would usually talk some business, and then one night, after a while, business turned to pleasure. We had one too many glasses, or should I say bottles of my homemade red wine, and then it just turned into something, you know?

It all happened so fast.

One day, I got a phone call from Jessica. She said, "You motherfucker. I'm pregnant."

I was stunned. "Whaaaaaa …?"

She was pissed, and I understood. I felt bad. I mean, she was separating from her husband, and then immediately got pregnant.

It was like, "What the fuck? Holy shit. What do we do?"

After a rough patch where we didn't talk much or at all, one of her good friends stepped in and helped her put it all into perspective.

Jessica and I decided to give the family thing a try. The only way she was having that baby was if we did it together.

I was never really sure. Look, I hate to say this, but I had other situations in the past when I didn't keep the babies, but this time I felt ready. It felt right.

I didn't want to live that old way anymore. I wanted to protect this life and do the opposite of what my own father had done with me.

I wanted to be there for a child. Do it right. Give him everything I didn't have.

So now that everything was settled, and we were preparing to welcome our child, we had to name them, right? We were told it was a girl. I was happy, because I was big on the name Arya for a girl, pronounced A-ra-ya, like Tom Arya from Slayer, not the character from *Game of Thrones*. And she liked it as soon as I said it. Easy.

And then we found out it was a boy. Turns out, his penis was hiding during the ultrasound.

Jessica turned to me and said, "How about Orion?"

She liked it because the whole star constellations thing (she is Wiccan) and just the whole astrological angle. If you look at the history of all the stars in Orion's constellation, there are a lot of weird theories behind that. I've read up on it since, but at the time, I didn't even know any of this stuff. So, there's a lot of synergy with his name.

So, I was intrigued as soon as she suggested the name Orion. It was close to the name I wanted.

I said, "That's perfect. Great."

She said, "Okay. cool."

And that was it. The easiest naming ever. We named him right there within seconds. Orion. Boom. That was his name, and we loved it. After all, now there'll be little "O" for Orion and big "O" for Opus.

So, the funniest thing is, back then, I played in a Metallica tribute band, and obviously "Orion" is one of their old-school songs, right? It's a cool instrumental.

Jessica ended up needing to have a C-section after Orion refused to come out naturally. Well, the anesthesiologist found out I played in the Metallica tribute band Alcoholica and was a metalhead himself. Knowing his name would be Orion and knowing about the band, he wheeled Jessica into the operating room while he blasted *Master of Puppets* and continued to let it play once we were in. So, she delivered Orion via a C-section to *Master of Puppets*, and the anesthesiologist was rocking out during the procedure to the song Orion.

Fuck. It was the weirdest, funniest thing ever.

And then Orion came into the world. We were in New York City at the time, so right after he was born, I cried, and then I went downstairs and immediately bought a few slices of pizza to stuff my face.

After our son was born, Jessica said, "I want to give Orion your last name."

In New York, however, there is a law that stated that since she was still technically married (the divorce was long and drawn out), they wouldn't allow my name legally to be on the birth certificate.

I had to do a DNA test and fight to get on, which I did. I mean, it seemed silly, since we knew the child was mine. Everyone involved knew; heck, even her ex knew.

So, it got straightened out, but for her to change her name as well became a hassle. Total hell. We discussed the whole thing, and both decided marriage was an outdated tradition, and it didn't fit within our lives and priorities. We live together as a family, and it works for us. That's it.

CHAPTER EIGHT
Dead By Wednesday

After Gargantua Soul ended, I was a bit lost and unsure of my next step. There was no doubt that I needed to keep making music, to keep pushing forward, but with whom? What would we sound like? The previous few years were spent on the inside of the industry, chasing the big fish, and it left such a bad taste in my mouth. It was hard to remember who I was and how I had gotten into this situation.

A few years before the band called it quits, I started to notice how the business was shifting in a direction that would forever taint it. Big booking agencies started doing something called "buy-ons," where bands that wanted to open for larger acts would have to pay money to go on tour with them, instead of actually getting paid for their time. So now any Tom, Dick, and Harry with money (or rich parents) can open for Metallica regardless of their talent, when there are some amazing bands who just can't afford to get a shot. One of the originators of this awful (still current) trend was a complete scumbag, trolly agent, who was a known for pedophilia and traveling to Thailand to solicit young boys. Everyone he knew hated him, but they dealt with him because he was one of the top agents in the metal world. My experience with him during the G-Soul years involved him offering us major tours if he could fuck my then girlfriend. Thinking I did not need him, I proceeded to tell him to "fuck his mother instead." Needless to say, he didn't like that. He went from a calm and cool tone to completely snapping. He threatened to blackball me from the industry. I dusted it off as nonsense, not actually realizing the weight behind his words. For years following, he childishly went out of his way to stand badmouth me, and bully people into not working with me. He ruined many, many opportunities for me. When I got signed to Jasta's label, Jasta reached out to him, without me knowing or knowing anything about the situation, and this agent flipped out at the mere mention of my name. Karma is a bitch though, and years later, he finally got what he deserved. People finally started to stand up to him and speak the truth about his ugliness. He is finally insignificant in the business.

Regardless of that major asshole, over the years, I've been able to work with amazing and talented people who produce music, like Nicky Bellmore, Zuess, Joetown, Enoch Jenson, and even a dude named Mike Z. in the early days. I also found mentors early on in Jeff Cannata and Vic Steffens from the Horizon Music Group, but at that moment, I was on my own. I needed to make a decision.

Luckily, I had my family. My first cousins, Ceschi and David, who were heavily into music, super talented and I respected their input a ton. I passed them some demos and got more than feedback in return. It was the start of Dead By Wednesday. Both Ceschi and David Ramos played such a huge role in those early days of the band it might actually make more sense to let them take the lead for a bit.

Ceschi said, "For me, personally, Dead By Wednesday started at a pretty complicated time. I was the main music writer for a band called Toca out in LA who were gaining a lot of traction. We were signed to Snoop Dogg's management team. We were selling out small shows and starting to feel the buzz around us. That band was connected more to the progressive rap & rock scenes that I've been a part of for years. DBW started during a period of limbo for Toca. We were waiting for the label in LA to get us into a studio to finish our record. That ended up taking years, and the album didn't come out till 2007. Toca quickly dissolved after that. So, for me, juggling all the promises that were being made out in LA, along with work as an elementary school Spanish teacher and my solo music, became a bit of a hurdle. Me and my brother call Christian, Big Bully, sometimes, jokingly, because he's our big cousin, and there were times when he would nearly drown us in the neighbors' pool and toss us around when we were small. We've also seen him be unnecessarily harsh on people a time or three, so that name stuck. Christian can be a knucklehead and *cavone*, as we say in Italian, but I jumped at the chance to make music with him. It started organically with some demos my cousin sent for fun. His band, Gargantua Soul, was sort of fading out after an incredible decade-long run, and Christian was trying to get back to his metal roots. He started laying down riffs and drum tracks on a 4-track. I remember he wrote 'Code Red' on the tape he gave me to check out. One night, my brother David ended up going to Christian's house for a small get together and ended up laying down some speed-rap-type vocals over one of the demos. Shortly after, I went over and knocked out a song or two with them. David and I enjoyed the energy of high-speed, heavy music from our youth. My brother and I were heavily involved in hip-hop, experimental rock, and jazz-fusion stuff, but this flashed us back to the days going to hardcore, punk, and metal shows. DBW provided a solid outlet to get out our aggression and scream about radical politics. My brother and I had both missed the environment of heavy music, but I don't know if either of us had realized just how much until we had it back in our lives. Finding the rest of the band proved easy. Pat Garcia had a long, long history with Christian. They had a demo project called Leech, I believe. Then Pat joined as an original member of Gargantua Soul. He ended up going to prison for 'intent to sell' a small amount of marijuana. It was a fucked-up situation. Pat had been a principal songwriter on that band's indie hit, 'Drive,' but his bullshit imprisonment never allowed him to taste the fruits of his creativity. It made sense that Pat would join Dead By Wednesday. He and my cousin always got on well.

"I honestly have no idea how Mike Modeste (bassist) was found. My cousin has this knack for finding amazing players, and Mike was no exception. One of the best bassists I had ever seen. Christian found Ross Ragusa (guitarist) somewhere somehow through metal circles. He was super young. He looked like a child back then, but he could fucking shred with the best of them. He had a unique approach to soloing and songwriting also. We rehearsed a few times, and it all clicked. We were still in it just for fun. We didn't have a masterplan. We took it a show at a time. It was also at a time when George W. Bush started endless wars and was forcing "patriot acts" on us, so we used heavy music to critique the socio-political situation in America from a radical stance. Christian had more of a vision than the rest of us for where he wanted things to go from the start. He's always been the band leader, which can be a tough position for a drummer. When he's on stage, he's set up behind the lights and the band and his kit, so it's no easy task to be seen and heard. He always manages to make sure the crowd feels his presence though. My cousin is maybe the most outspoken person I've ever known. That mouth and fearlessness has gotten him in trouble and rubbed people the wrong way a few (hundred) times, but the dude has the biggest heart as well. He cares a lot about family. If you're family to him, he'll always have your back. Aside from being the leader, he is also a stellar drummer. He's always been influenced by John Bonham and Dave Lombardo, which I think shows in his combo of groove and ferocity. I think he's a thrash drummer at heart though, so I could see him with bands like Megadeth, Slayer, or Metallica. He's definitely a better drummer than Lars anyhow. Then again, he is versatile and can handle Black Sabbath stuff, which has a jazzier feel, and I've seen him nail brutal death-metal stuff, straight funk, hip-hop, and he'll even sing and play soft acoustic music when the mood strikes. So, we played and developed. Like most other bands, this took writing songs and playing to really find what we wanted to sound like. Eventually, we would call ourselves crossover, because we had a lot of elements of old-school thrash metal and hardcore, but back during the first album, we had a lot more speed rap as well. At first, DBW sounded like political rapcore, which was not very fashionable at the time but stuff my brother and I grew up on. Downset and Madball were big early influences. Musically, it came from a lineage of thrash metal though. I can now admit we were almost cartoonishly radical with our lyrics back then, on purpose, like the ultra-violence found on *Democracy is Dead*. It was partially done out of our strong conviction, but my brother and I also thought it was hilarious. Once we realized DBW was a real thing, we made a much more earnest album with *The Killing Project*. I remember when we landed our first tour with Scum of the Earth. There were grumbles from some of the band members about it being a disaster, but I knew better. I told the guys, 'Just watch. My cousin may talk a lot, but he is a man of action. He's gonna get us on some big stages.' He proved me right, though touring wasn't always pleasant with him. Christian used to get all pissy about us not cleaning the van. It got so heated the band almost broke up a couple times because of stupid shit like that. Don't get me wrong. I'm super grateful for my time on the road with Dead By Wednesday. Over the majority of the last decade, solo music has been my bread and butter. In the hip-hop world, people are super spoiled. No amps or drums to carry. A couple solo artists in a small car with a laptop can make five times the amount a band does. Touring like that is soft and sweet compared to the DBW-band days. Seven sweaty dudes living in an old fucking van that may or may not break down at any minute. Ten-to-fourteen-hour drives through bum-fuck nowhere, day after day. One night, DBW may play to three meth heads somewhere in Indiana, and the next night, we'd open for Insane Clown Posse in front of thousands. In fact, DBW won some underground Juggalo contest through ICP's label Pyschopathic Records which landed us several large festivals including The Gathering of the Juggalo's among other events and even full tours with the clowns. That grind taught me a lot. It taught me to lower my expectations and be surprised and appreciative when good moments come. That type of touring builds character and strength, even if it also sucks at times. My cousin is a solid, overly honest dude in a music world full of snakes and leeches. He's just trying to survive and make art, living outside the lines, and seeking his own version of freedom. At times, his shamelessness when it came to promotion would make me cringe, but it's the same promotion that built an entire scene from the ground up. You kinda have to give all the fucks and give no fucks at the same time for people to pay attention. The older I get, the more I understand what we did, why, and how much effort it took from Christian to make it happen."

Thanks, Ceschi, but let's get back to talking about me, okay? This *is* the Opus book, after all.

We were touring a ton in those days, but David had to sit out more and more shows. Our grandmother had fallen ill, and it hit us hard but him harder. He hated being away from her without enough care being taken. He's a very sensitive caring person, but he wasn't only taking care of our nonna to appease himself, he did it for all of us. His sacrifice and selflessness allowed Ceschi and I to keep going out there on the road.

We liked having the two-singer dynamic, so we found a replacement to fill in when David had to stay home. The singer's name was Marc Allan. At the time, he was fronting a band called Cold Read. He had a similar look to David, and he had a great scream, making the transition easier. Yes, it was easier, but not seamless, as their skillsets were quite different. Ceschi took over a lot of David's parts live.

As Marc got integrated into our shows, Pat Garcia and I discussed bringing in a second guitar player. We always wanted to push boundaries, you know? Get louder, allow for more layers and riffs, harmonies and to find new ways to punish the crowd.

Enter Ross Ragusa, a young guitarist who I had recently brought in to play for my Metallica tribute act, Alcoholica. That band played all the classic stuff and was a labor of love which had my buddy, Ron Zombie (not Rob), who is also a wrestler, and Kai Blackwood, my lifelong friend, in our lineup. Ross had been brought in as our Kirk Hammett.

Ross was recommended to me to try out, but I was skeptical. I mean, he hadn't even been born when most of the Metallica songs we played were written and released. He looked really young. Kai and Ron shared my doubts, and you could see it on their faces the first time we set up to try Ross out.

The doubts didn't last long. Ross could jam. He started belting out the solos, note for note.

I remember Ron dropping his jaw in disbelief and saying, "Holy shit! Where did you find this kid?"

After Ross had proven himself in Alcoholica, it didn't take long for me to start thinking of him as a solid candidate for the second guitar position in DBW. He joined us without much fuss at tryouts.

Well, that's not entirely true. I thought it went one hundred percent smooth, but Ross told me later I was mistaken. Turns out, when he showed up to try out, he was scared and intimidated by Pat Garcia. I laughed. Why? Because while Pat stands six feet tall and was wearing a hoodie and bandanna and scowling a lot, he is the kindest, most soft-spoken teddy bear you'll ever meet.

The fresh blood and positive energy from adding Marc and Ross propelled us into recording our next album, *The Killing Project*, which was released on Chris Poland's label, Eclipse Records.

Pat started a family and eventually told me he couldn't tour as much, if at all. He and I had fought through so much over the years, driving the tour van and grinding, show after show, so it was a huge blow to me.

We had just established a new singer and had added a second guitarist, but, in the end, we really had just transitioned to a new guitarist as we lost our old one.

A booking agency reached out with an offer for a two-month tour. It was the perfect way to promote our new album. Two months is a long time, so even us guys who were all in and excited had our reservations. Think about your life right now. Could you step away from it for two months without a lot of planning, arranging, and sacrificing? And could you afford to do it?

I decided not only could I find a way, but I had to.

Marc decided not only that he couldn't, but he had to quit.

New album, new singer, new band photos—all rendered old news before any chance to have a life of its own. *The Killing Project* was dead in the water as our band was left standing with our dicks in our hands.

I just wish Marc would've quit before we put his voice and name and face all over everything. He had gotten a solid job at a cymbal company in Boston, I believe Sabian, that he didn't want to lose. I can understand his situation and why, but after leaving the band, he got fired literally a few weeks later for making cymbals shaped like a penis, making the whole episode a joke. Marc is a good dude, but he became just a small blip in the DBW story.

We had to pivot quickly to replace him for our major tour coming up.

I scouted area bands to find someone who could scream like Marc but who could also contribute more, now that we knew they would be a fulltime member. I caught a band called Naga Cult, whose name had something to do with snake worship or something, if I recall correctly.

Their singer, Joe Morbidelli, was younger and seemed to have his shit together, and he had great rhythm, which is important in DBW. He had a good scream/rap sound, like a Vision of Disorder or Biohazard but different. Rawer. I recruited him by saying I wasn't stealing him from his band but that I just needed help on this big tour.

He was blown away and humbled and agreed to jump on right away. In the beginning, he had a great attitude, which sadly didn't last long. This is a common theme with musicians, and to a degree, I get it. We all start out with delusions of grandeur. We all think we are the next rock star, but when that doesn't happen, each person has to decide whether they're in it for fame or to create and share the music.

Joe pretended at first to want to play nice and listen, but quickly his true colors shined through. He was one of those trash-punk dudes who didn't want to listen to anyone, especially me. He had some weird dad complex, so anytime I tried to offer criticism or direction, he lashed right back out. It got worse as time went on, and that was before he started to get addicted to multiple substances.

But he was talented, so we put up with a lot. Joe never contributed to cover costs of recording, practice space, equipment, gas, or anything else. He didn't drive, so someone always had to always pick him up and drop him off. If he had a great attitude, I would still be happily paying his share and babying him along, but it all got annoying when he acted like a jerkoff.

His time in the band was painful for me, but we created some great music, including the album, *The Last Parade*, and the EP, *Death of the Rockstar*.

As we recorded that EP, however, Ross was realizing he couldn't continue on with us. He was miffed because we had decided each member would pay for their own recordings to own them. This was in response to me and Mike always showing up to the studio prepared and knocking out our stuff quickly, so it seemed silly for us to pay to sit around and watch the other guys write their material and test it out while paying by the hour in the studio rather than showing up with a plan. Ross couldn't really afford to record like that or just didn't want to, so it was way easier to quit. He had a girlfriend, and he was sick of being broke. He wanted a real job and knew with our show schedule it couldn't happen. He had lasted longer than just about anyone in the band aside from Mike and me, so it hurt to see him go, especially with how good we were sounding.

Having someone leave after a record is recorded sucks, but Ross left halfway through the recording process, which felt even worse, because we needed to find someone to try out, join, and finish the tracks all at once.

Charlie Bellmore—who now plays with Dee Snider and Kings and Liars and has also played with Alcoholica, Jasta, and Toxic Holocaust—stepped in as a hired gun to finish the recordings. I walked him through what we were looking for on the rhythm side, then we cut him loose to do some leads how he wanted. The collaboration and record came out great, and it's still one of my favorites.

Charlie was too busy to join us, so we immediately started looking for a replacement guitarist for us for the Shadows Fall tour. A few friends recommended I reach out to a young guy on the scene named Joey Concepcion.

I called him up, and he said, "No."

I was bummed, but I had a list of people, so I moved on.

Twenty minutes later, he called me back and said, "Listen, I talked to a few people, and I think I might've made the wrong call. I'd like to give it a try."

Joey is a guitar virtuoso. I mean real deal shredder. But, as with many virtuosos, he tends to live in his own world. He's a good person, just a little bit of a space cadet, which, for an anal guy like me, can be difficult to work with on the road. Creating wise, we work great together. But while playing shows, I would find myself getting frustrated. I'd be lugging my drum kit up three flights of stairs to the club and I'd see Joey just staring at his phone, unaware of the world around him. Regardless, Joey is one of my favorite people on the planet. Give the kid a guitar and he can shred to the point that you just know it's what he was put on this Earth to do. You've probably seen him on stage and heard his recordings with a plethora of other established metal bands, like Lost Symphony, Dark Tranquility, Armageddon, Sanctuary, Once Human, The Absence, Jasta, and has even filled in for Arch Enemy.

Touring and recording are expensive propositions for the biggest of bands, and it's a huge mountain to climb for independent bands. We needed money. As much as I've talked about DBW being a family thing, sometimes you just need a little help from your friends.

So, a close friend of my family was involved in a big ring of nonviolent people who transported marijuana from California to the East Coast on a regular basis. A couple years back, he got my cousin busted with one hundred pounds of pot after being set up transporting it across the country from California to Connecticut. The bust happened near the end of the year, so the marijuana had been lovingly wrapped in gift boxes with holiday-themed paper. I don't know all the details, but from what I was told, the driver got pulled over on the highway in Illinois. The authorities followed him to his destination to bust the people buying the weed. I think they call it a controlled buy or something like that. The driver might've even been forced to wear a wire. In fact, I'm pretty sure he did. I wasn't there. I'm just sharing the details I got when they looped me in. I will say the police were overly eager, jumped the gun, and acted too fast. The cops were violent and very rude to some of my older family members who weren't involved. One cop even held my grandpa at gun point just because he was there. Their aggression and hate caused the police to make a lot of mistakes.

Marijuana is being decriminalized more and more. It is widely accepted outside the last few religious and conservative groups who see the "Devil's lettuce" as a one-way ticket to Hell and lump it together with other manmade hard drugs, which isn't the case. In fact, I consider it medicine with many benefits, including stress and belly relief, helps with sleep, and much more! The driver got in trouble, but after snitching, he got off with a very light sentence, no time, and has now disappeared. On the other hand, my family member was given a two-year sentence, but after good behavior and doing a ton of rallying around him, he only ended up serving six months in jail. Don't get me wrong, six months still sucks, but with one hundred pounds of weed, I could see a much longer stay on the inside before recent law changes.

So …

You're wondering how I fit into this story. Yeah, I get it. Don't feel left out. A few band members, friends, and family are about to find out right along with you. Part of me says to shut my mouth and keep it a secret, but I am not writing a book to hide skeletons in my closet. I want my son to pick this up someday and know the truth about his dad's life before he came around and when he was too young to remember. He isn't going to love this whole book and all the stories, but I hope he can at least appreciate, laugh, cry, yell, and understand who the hell I am and what I tried to do (mainly for him) and how I've changed for the better. I also want him to not make the same mistakes or poor decisions I made, so if reading this helps, that's great too!

Every person has their moments, good and bad. Some people strive for perfection, while others find themselves on the wrong side of the law with little effort or luck or both. I am sort of in a grey area, because, while I follow my heart and while I believe things happen for a reason or in Mother Earth and the spiritual side of life, I … Okay, no more stalling.

I was a mule for these guys. Yup. One time only though.

No shit. Straight up. I agreed to transport fifty pounds of marijuana when it was still very illegal across the United States of America. Am I reckless? Am I crazy? Was I playing too footloose and fancy free? Yes, yes, and yes, but they offered me $30,000, with all my expenses paid on top of that money, which was pure profit.

Ah, that got your attention.

So, how does a drummer from New Haven, CT transport that much weed without getting busted?

Well, Willie Nelson style, that's how.

I booked a real tour from Connecticut to California and back. I front loaded the itinerary, confirming fifteen to twenty shows or so as we headed West but intentionally only a spare couple gigs on the way home, being that I wanted that weed on board as short of a time as possible. I also wanted the tour to be and look as legitimate as possible just in case I needed a real alibi. The tour was dubbed "The Make it or Break it Tour" (seemed appropriate). I either made it or we wouldn't and then probably break up.

So, I had 30k, but nothing is ever that straight forward. There were a variety of hidden fees and extra gas costs, but at least la familia dropped 10k to rent a tour bus for us. We had always traveled by van, so the band was shocked at the upgrade all of a sudden. Oh, did I fail to mention I didn't tell anybody what I was doing? My bad. But in situations like this, the less you know, the better off you are. Tell no one and keep your mouth shut.

And just as a disclaimer, don't try this stuff at home, kids. Authorities have caught on to this method, so your chance of success is way lower than mine was if you try this now. Don't do as I did; you do you.

If I got busted, the punishment I'd face would certainly break up my current family, my band, and my future. Not worth it.

Before we left, I shipped an old eight-by-ten Ameg bass cabinet to California. It was gigantic. The contacts of my associates unscrewed the back. They left the speakers in, so it looked good, but they planted fifty pounds of marijuana, all vacuum sealed.

When we did our last show in California, a guy met us and our bus. I had been telling the guys along the way that I had done a bunch of work on endorsements, which was true. I mean, I'm always trying to work any angle I can. We had endorsements with liquor brands, equipment companies, and anything else I thought could help keep us going.

So, he shows up, and I say, "Guys, this is the Ampeg promoter I told you about who I've been in touch with. He has an amp he wants us to test out, and it could lead to some cool promotional opportunities down the line." Basically, a white lie, but I hate to say it; it's still a lie.

I made sure they knew the amp needed to get loaded under the bus and that we couldn't mess with it until we got home. We didn't want to break it or drop it by accident, right? Everyone fell for the bullshit except for my guitar player, Ross. He knew something was up and something weird was going on, but he didn't question it much.

Why did everyone go along with it?

Everyone was getting paid, we were super comfortable on the bus, and the tour had actually gone great. By then, everyone was ready to get home. All we needed to do was drive a few thousand miles and play a couple quick gigs. At one point, we did turn on the amp, and it worked just fine. I was glad. I thought if we got searched, that might be enough to distract and appease the curiosity of the inspectors.

As we drove home, I was shitting my pants. I was in full freak-out mode, but I couldn't express that in front of the other guys. No one knew. With every stop and every bump felt from inside my coffin-like bunker, I was shaking and a nervous wreck the whole time.

Turns out not telling anyone proved to be the correct choice, because at one point, we got stopped at a cultural border checkpoint. I'm not sure if you've ever dealt with these places, but they are found on the California and Texas border. The people ask if you have any plants, fruits, or vegetables that you plan to bring over the border.

I had way more than a plant and some seeds, but I wasn't about to tell them that.

A few officers boarded our bus to speak to us individually. They wanted to look in our eyes, watch our reactions to their questions, and look around.

They asked, "Do you have anything in here that we should be aware of?"

Gulp. "No."

"Have you been asked to transport anything by anyone?"

"No."

I am shitting my pants. They know something. They had to. How else would they know to ask that? I was going to get busted. I was screwed. I could feel the sweat beading on my forehead. The officers were looking around the bus. Could they smell the weed? Could they smell my fear?

I glanced around at the other people on the bus, and they all looked calm, bored even. How the fuck were they playing it so cool?

Oh, that's right, they didn't know. I was the only insane person trying to hold it together and hide fifty pounds of marijuana in a bass amp. I told myself that if worse came to worst and they found the amp, I could say it was on the bus before we took it. Y'see, we never told the driver that we had added the amp, and the driver ended up being kind of a dick anyway. We had just loaded it in an empty compartment and kept it quiet. I'd hate to push off the trouble onto the bus driver or the company, but they could turn around and blame the last person who had rented the vehicle.

If they busted me, I'd claim, 'I had no idea the amp was in there or that it was there when we got on the bus.'

If they didn't buy it and pressed further, I'd shrug and say, 'Hey, we rented this bus, but we don't know the driver. We also don't know the company. Shitty right? Maybe the bus line was into some funny business that we weren't aware of.' But from experience and from speaking to my brother Z-Man, who is a criminal lawyer, when dealing with police, it's always best to plead the fifth and say nothing at all. Whatever you say can be used against you in the court of law, well … it's true! Less is more. Say nothing at all except be polite and give them your name and ID so you don't get killed, and that's it. Then they have no leg to stand on and no information, which is what they want and need to arrest you.

Without anyone truly having possession, what could the law enforcers do aside from burn the weed? Hell, they'd probably confiscate it, and then maybe sell it themselves.

In the end, I didn't need to lie or deflect or plead ignorance, because the officers cleared us, and we got on our merry way. It was like a weight lifted off my chest.

We played one last show. I was shitting my pants the entire time. Every stop, I was freaking out, at the edge of my seat, hanging by a thread. Finally, we got back to Connecticut. I fucking kissed the ground. I got the amp out, looking all around, hoping not to get surrounded, but I fucking brought it home, and everything worked out, thank God!

It was a one-and-done deal. I did it. I was able to do it. Balls of steel. I got away with it, but I'll never ever fucking do it again!

That last story is an aberration of touring life. In fact, a typical day on the road is not exciting. That's not to say it's not great or that there are no exciting moments, but touring is sort of mundane.

The lifestyle is a grind. When I was younger and before I had traveled, there was a lot more to look forward to. You saw amazing sights, you tried different foods, you met people with fresh faces and different attitudes. On the road, you can learn so much and bring it home with you. After a while though, you've seen the waterfall, you've binged on the world's greatest pie, you've heard why people in North Dakota and South Dakota refuse to become one state, and you find yourself thinking about being home more and more.

Not on stage. Not after the show when you're buzzing and selling merch and riding that high, but when you pull into that truck stop on Route 80 just outside Gary, Indiana for the fifth time in a month, nothing could be sweeter at that moment than hugging your kid and girl and tasting a home cooked meal.

No matter how many times I tell people that life on the road is boring, they get shocked and ask about all the sex, drugs, and rock 'n roll that happens. Look, we've all heard the stories, and sometimes that stuff happens, but this isn't the freewheeling '60s or the hard-partying '70s; hell, we're thirty years removed from the outrageous '80s. Things have changed. The industry is such a different animal than it was. Not to mention the fact I've got a family, I don't drink, I don't do drugs, there's "cancel culture," and by the time our set is done, and we load out, I'm not in the mood for much more rock or roll, let alone anything else. As an aggressive, older drummer, I need real rest in between shows.

These days there is less money to earn and more competition to deal with in the touring circuit. Plus, people have less money and time to spend and way more distractions and choices for entertainment than they've ever had before. We play some clubs that the average person doesn't want to look at when they drive past, let alone go inside, pay for entrance, order a drink, use those bathrooms. To go to an indie metal show requires a certain level of love and dedication. It's not something you dip your toe into.

Same goes for forming and touring with a band. You've got to remain willing to put up with some bullshit and make sacrifices with few rewards or perks. Now don't take this as complaining; I'm all in and proud and happy with what I'm doing. In fact, later in this chapter, I have the joy of typing this, while touring as the opener for Flotsam and Jetsam ...

FUCK YES.

That is a dream come true. I had known those guys since way back and always loved their shit. I respect them as musicians and people as well, which made the tour all that much cooler.

Here's how it goes for an opening metal band on tour: You start your day waking up in a bed (if you're lucky), a floor, a car, or wherever you crashed the previous night. It takes you a few moments to remember where you are. A hotel? A fan's house? A truck stop? Then you try to recall what city and state you're in. Next, and more importantly, you need to figure out where you're headed and how long of a drive it will take to get there.

Actually, I take that back. If you're in a hotel or motel, you need to first figure out what time they stop serving breakfast to see if you need to get your ass out of bed and run as fast as you can to the lobby to grab shitty coffee, the last stale bagel and expired yogurt. Don't even try to think about expecting orange juice to get any hint of vitamins into your body. They seem to always clean up and close the juice machine first. So, you grab your untoasted bagel and use it to scoop out the old yogurt, because the hotel either ran out of spoons or cleaned them up before you got there.

You need to eat the bagel while walking back to the room. Why? Because three out of the other five guys didn't wake up, and they will attack you for your food. Since they missed breakfast, there's a chance they won't eat until after soundcheck, which will be later than dinnertime. If the club or promoter doesn't provide us with any food or a cool fan doesn't offer to pick something up, they might not eat anything today.

If you do wake up and have time before you need to rush off, force yourself to do push up's, stretch, or take a walk, hit the fitness center, or even just a quick fifteen-minute jog. Do something to stay active, because most of the rest of your day is going to be cooped up in a van.

After everyone is up and you have your itinerary for the day—and by itinerary, I mean you've drawn straws to see who will drive first while setting the GPS to the club's address—you rush to pack and hit the road. You now have eight hours on the turnpike, staring at nothing through the Midwest. Nothingness for hours on end. Fields. The occasional tree. Corn fields. If you're lucky, a body of water somewhere to look at. You might get to see a dust storm or a fire or tumbleweeds, but day after day, you'll see the same sites. I think part of the drab feeling is how still everything is out there. Nothing is moving. Not much is happening. Go stare at a Bob Ross painting for eight hours while smelling five guys' farts and listening to your belly gurgle.

The bulk of your day is spent driving from city to city. And from one shitty watering hole to another, unless you play the occasional classy venue. There's no way around that, especially on a full US tour. There are huge gaps with no cities big enough or willing to host metal events, so you play, and you drive, and you drive, and you drive.

Most major tours are built with tour buses in mind. You hire a driver, and the band can rest, write music, rehearse, conduct interviews, or whatever during the ride. Us? We are not at that level. We can't afford a bus. We can barely afford renting vans. So, we drive. That starts to wear you down.

I'm a good driver, but I fucking hate driving. I loathe it. There is a passion in my soul that burns red with a fiery dislike of sitting on my ass for hours on end, watching the idiots on the road and staring at nothing. Never mind hitting traffic jams or congested areas. I think I might even have some minor road rage. I can't ever get comfortable. Anxiety bubbles at all times, because I can't check my phone to see if the club or promoter is reaching out. I can't promote and post about our show to drum up awareness. Driving long distances is painful, but I do it because that's where the industry says I have to be.

Selling albums is virtually impossible unless you're on the road. People have so many options to spend their money on, so unless you're right there, shaking their hand and in their face, they'll choose something else. It's not exaggerating when bands say they are out there winning over fans and selling records one fan at a time. That's it. That's the model we all follow. We'll lug five hundred vinyl and one thousand CDs (well, now download cards) and a few hundred t-shirts and stickers and patches and whatever other merch we have so we can find a few fresh faces to help us sell enough stuff to afford to get to the next city.

This isn't a get-rich-quick scheme; hell, it's not even a get-rich-slow scheme. It's a strategy to slow down bankruptcy as long as you can in hopes that a label or management sees a way to make enough money off you that they front you a piece of the pie eventually. There are a few truths I've learned in my time in the industry. All bands have an end date. All music has a shelf life. All music is valid and has a chance to sprout big enough to make you some money, but you need the band to go on long enough and function for that to occur.

I've been in the game for enough years that I have seen personal opportunities sprout up. I wish it was for our band, but my job now is to follow those opportunities and find any way I can to make them extend to the band or my music career in some fashion. To use my connections and any clout to bring the band up, expanding our visibility and trying to get us heard in as many living rooms as I can.

The industry is small, all things considered. Once you start meeting people and opening doors by proving yourself, you enter a web of intertwining musicians, producers, managers, labels, and bands. Chances are if you don't know someone or haven't worked with them yet, you know someone who can get a hold of them. Reaching out to strangers might seem a bit odd, but we all share common experiences that tie us together. We've shared the same truck stop bathrooms, we've dealt with the same sound people, we've been stiffed by the same promoters, we've felt the same judgment from family and friends, and we've spent our lives striving for acceptance and acknowledgment that we belong inside creating music and memories rather than merely watching from the cold, vast space of independent musicians out there.

I could expand on this thought, which ran through my mind as I drove, but we just got off the highway, and there's three guys shouting directions at me.

You get to the club, and you're almost always late. Why? Because when you travel hundreds of miles per day, you have a great chance of hitting some sort of delay or many delays. Construction, car accidents, detours, severe storms all happen. Then there's weird stuff, like rolling into a city that's all blocked off because the president has an appearance, or it's daylight savings, and you forget about the hour change, or the club lets you know they double booked the night, so you're playing at a different address, or a million other quirky things that all happen. We haven't even gotten into flat tires and other van breakdowns. There's no margin for error.

You play in Dubuque, IA and have a gig the next night in Colorado Springs, CO. That's a thirteen-hour drive under perfect conditions and without ever needing to stop to pee or eat or to fill up the tank with gas.

So, you're late. The promoter is already worried. The sound guy is miffed. The club owner hasn't arrived yet, but he's calling to see what the hold up is. You stretch out your sore body by hauling gear. You set it up on stage quickly and feel the ramifications of making the sound guy wait for a few minutes as he barks orders. You can clearly see his mic placement around your kit is amateur hour, not to mention the equipment itself is held together by tape and the gum of the previous night's band. You try making suggestions, but all you get are eyerolls and condescension. Now, don't get me wrong, I'm thrilled when we have the opportunity to soundcheck at all, because it often isn't even an option. You play a few bits of a tune and feel good. The juices start to flow as you shake off the drive and feel the buzz and excitement of playing music with your buddies. It's time to let loose, finally get some aggression out and have a great set.

BUT ...

There's two hours until the doors open. There's three hours before the first band. The bill has two local openers playing thirty minutes each before you play. At least one of the bands will start late due to broken equipment, band drama, one of the guys being too drunk or trying to Facetime his girl. The other band will completely ignore the set time and just keep playing. They brought fifteen friends, and they are damn sure going to entertain them for as long as possible. So, when they end a song at minute thirty-five over their set, they will blast right into their seven-minute epic closer, a half-baked cover of the same song you've heard a dozen other bands do.

In the meantime, since you don't drink and you're getting paid with a few drink tickets, you have given your share to the other guys. You've also set up the merch stand.

You have written bits, posted photos, and done live videos on various social media platforms to raise awareness of the show tonight and other upcoming shows. While at the merch stand or mingling in the crowd, you put out feelers for places to crash that night. This is a very important step in your day. If you find someone gracious enough to give you a floor and a couch, your life improves a thousand-fold. When you know where you'll sleep that night, you can relax and let everything else take care of itself. At least until after the set.

You play and kick ass. Sure, there's a moment or two you wish you could redo, and the mix up during the first song kind of sucked again until the sound person dialed it in, but the crowd still loved it. The hour or so on stage is a blur. It's fucking fun and full of energy, but afterward, it's hazy. Adrenaline is still going. People in the crowd are asking you about guitar solos and stage banter, and even though it was fifteen minutes earlier, you can't recall it all. Some want to hug you while you're all sweaty or slap you on the back to acknowledge a good performance. Others want all your attention and are "close talkers" that get right in your face and unknowingly spit all over you while speaking because usually, they're sloshed.

Why?

On stage, you're focused on performing and communicating and several other factors that all go into making a concert successful. It's a release, and it's awesome, but it can be nerve racking as well. You couldn't hear the bassist almost all night, the drunk asshole upfront has been clapping off time and screaming, "Skynyrd," the whole set, and the monitor next to you hasn't worked since WASP played here on their first tour. The club has changed names six times, it's had four different owners, hell, cellphones and microwaves are now a thing, but this fucking monitor hasn't moved an inch. It has several dents from smashed guitars, stains from several bodily fluids, and it smells like the wiring inside is on fire, but no sound is coming out.

After the set, you find out the place you were going to crash at is no longer available, because the guy and his girl got in a fight when she touched some other girl's boob, but then got all mad at him when she allowed him to touch it too. Apparently, they were the couple screaming at each other throughout the set that got so heated security kicked them both out.

You then stand at the merch booth and sell what you can before haggling with the same three or four people who are inebriated and want to barter for a shirt. This guy has seventeen dollars, but he wants four CDs, a beer koozie, and three dozen stickers. The next person has two dollars and a broken Casio watch, which he'd like to trade for the largest shirt you have and the limited-edition vinyl that costs you $20 per copy to print. The next person is a female who flashes you, hoping that's enough for a CD.

She gets it, along with a couple of the stickers that the first guy dropped as he stumbled away.

You pack up, glancing at the time. You need to book a hotel within the next fifteen minutes before the websites switch to the following night.

Flotsam is well into their set, so you know you're going to miss the entire thing. They sound awesome tonight, by the way. Great energy. You take a few moments to watch and enjoy. You take a calm breath and feel that stirring, that excitement, those nerves. The same feeling you got when you saw these guys twenty years ago and you were just a teenager. You soak up that moment, that energy, that memory of a youth long gone. You're a part of the story now. You're touring and doing what you've wanted to do ever since you heard that first KISS song and thought about buying a guitar.

You book the non-refundable room two minutes before your bassist says he found a place for you to crash. You pack up the merch.

The promoter has disappeared.

You find him in the back, and he's shifty. His eyes are darting all over. He is full of apologies and reasons why the packed house didn't bring in what he expected so he can only give you half of what you were expecting.

You load out, feeling every bit of the drums and amps and effects pedals in your lower back. You drive a half hour to the motel. They inform you that they are having a plumbing issue so there is no hot water. Also, if you want to drink the water, you need to boil it first—that is, if you had a stove to boil it with.

You trudge down the hall only to discover they've given you the wrong room key or that the card hasn't activated properly. You head back to the front desk, but the person has slunk back to their office to do paperwork, grab a call, or to fall back to sleep, so you spend an extra fifteen to twenty minutes standing there, ringing the bell on the desk and saying, "Hello?" like an asshole.

You get into the room, and it's 4:15 a.m. You all get settled and crash, except for the singer, who is still beating himself up over that third song mishap and because he misses home.

You have four and a half hours to sleep before you do it all again.

Groundhog Day. Touring is like Groundhog Day but without Bill Murray there to put a comic spin on it all.

The best time on the road are the all too brief minutes I get to spend on stage. Obviously, I love meeting people and seeing the sights and trying new foods, but I left my house and I put up with all the dumb shit and lack of accommodations on the road so I can perform.

I've met lifelong friends on tour. I have spent nights partying with some of the best people on the planet. People who were strangers to me the day before have taken me to special locations, given me new experiences and knowledge, and that means so much, but for me, I'm telling you nothing beats the thrill of the show.

Recording with a band is also special. I absolutely love the studio and creating. That's probably my favorite place to be. It's a completely different animal than the live show, because you have a different set of focuses and stresses and roadblocks and freedoms. Live, you can't double or triple the guitar tracks, you can't overdub vocal miscues, and you certainly can't mute and readjust missed drum hits ... not that I would know, as I've never missed.

Well, maybe once.

You can practice and plan your studio session down to the minute, but things happen, life happens, and when that clock starts rolling, you get to work making new babies and whatever comes out, comes out. This is where I thrive. Writing and then recording a tune is such a pure, exciting process. If I could spend all my time and energy on that, plus some touring mixed in, I'd be a happy man. Promoting, booking and marketing is a grind. It's part of the business side that makes the band experience a little less fun.

When people say that music is easy, they aren't talking about the music industry or music as a business. Well, if they are saying that success in the music industry is easy, they are either lying or they have no fucking clue what they are talking about.

You can write and record a song in a few hours, sure. Even some albums can flow with minimal effort, but that's the easy part. You get a band together, you jam, you record. Simple. Now, can you promote? Can you book and play shows? Can you sell the product? Can you attract a manager, a label, and the press? Do you have solid pro equipment that can hold up, night after night? Do you have reliable transportation? Does your band have a sound and an image a fanbase can identify with and latch onto? Have you established affordable and eye-catching merchandise channels? Do you have an inner circle you can trust both at home and out on the road? After all that, when you start to face success and failure, can you hold it all together?

We had been through so much as a band up to that point, and we had earned an opening slot with New England metal heavyweights, Shadows Fall. This was for their final farewell tour, which to me, was a big deal. We had history with the band, as we had opened for them previously. Going back even further, I knew their drummer, Jason Bittner, years before he was in Shadows Fall. I had booked some of his other bands, Burning Human, Stigmata, and even Crisis. We also almost came to blows at one point when I signed on to tech for him for one of his long European tour runs. Great drummer, good dude, but can be a tough cookie to work for, but I find myself understanding his daily touring aggravations more and more these days. But this story is about unity, so let's stick to the subject. We all came up in bands around the area and had crossed paths.

Brian Fair, the vocalist for Shadows Fall, said, "Back then, if you were involved in the New England scene, you pretty much knew everyone. There were only like a few hundred of us. People always want to hear about shows from back then. They say, 'Oh my God, I can't even imagine Shadows Fall and Converge together!' and I tell them, 'There was about seventy-five people in the crowd, and the venue didn't even have a stage.'"

Shadows Fall had made some great strides into the mainstream of metal and metalcore by that point, and Brian, who had been in Overcast, had already cut his teeth on the road.

This tour leg represented one of the best opportunities DBW had to showcase our talent outside of our home crowds. Not only did we gain new fans, but the touring gave us a great chance to get closer to our buds. They were cool, respectful, hardworking, and made the tour a blast. Living on the road isn't just about playing the show; in fact, it's typically the easiest part. You need to learn how to stay sharp, stay afloat, and stay sane out there. The guys taught us a lot. They made us comfortable.

Brian Fair said, "Back in the Overcast days, Connecticut was like our second home. Opus always seemed to be around at the shows, and he was always hustling. This was back as Hatebreed was coming together. Opus did some stuff with Jamey, so I got to know him more personally rather than just another dude at a show."

As we played some of the biggest shows of our lives, however, our singer Joe Morbidelli was falling, falling hard off the edge. I knew we as a band were in trouble. Joe had developed a pattern of letting us down, time after time, but I had hoped the road would be exciting enough to keep him in line. In fact, it proved to have the opposite effect. Joe had proven he couldn't be trusted, but we fought for him, tried to help him. We all went out of our way to make it work. He just wasn't reliable or consistent.

We scraped by. And when Joe was invested and present, we could blow the tops off stages. He had talent, presence, and a unique charisma. We had nights when the crowds were eating out of our hands, but ... then there was that night in Michigan ...

Imagine this: sold-out show. Seven hundred and fifty people somewhere in Michigan. Seven hundred and fifty potential new fans, since most likely most of them had never seen us live before, let alone even heard our music. The place is buzzing. We set up. We are ready. Joe is nowhere to be found. We're racing around the club to see if he's just chatting with someone or out back or asleep backstage. We call him. Nothing. He's gone. Vanished. He's not caught in traffic. This isn't a one-off show. I mean, it's a twenty-date run, and we're halfway in. The guy came with us in our van. We've been battling together for over a week to entertain crowds and to push ourselves, to push each other to be better, louder, tighter, and melt faces.

We're standing on stage with our dicks in our hands, about to embarrass ourselves by announcing we cannot play because or singer is MIA. Years of hustle, thousands of handshakes, time, investment, blood, sweat, and tears all combined to get us here, and he didn't care at all. I was mortified. I was fucking pissed.

This isn't a local show. We are not a local bar band. We don't have a friend in the crowd to pull on stage who knows the songs.

We had been down this road with him too many times. I hate to air dirty laundry, so I know we got a lot of shit from people when we split with him, because all they saw was what we and he let them see. They weren't around for moments like this. They weren't at the Roadrunner showcase when Joe showed up with a cast on his arm, clearly wasted on whatever. It seemed to me like he had broken body parts on purpose so he could get prescribed pills. He must've taken several of them before our set that night and drank, which he did all the time. He was slurring his words, clumsy, and literally nodding out in the bathroom before and even a little as we played.

Joe? Has anyone seen Joe?

Joe had apparently taken off on a bender. He just left after sound check and was out on the town, partying. I guess,

I mean, I don't recall ever getting a straight answer or remember believing anything said after that.

What the fuck was I supposed to do? There's nowhere to hide; trust me, I looked. I'm looking at seven hundred and fifty pairs of expecting, confused, and anxious eyes staring right at me.

Brian Fair could've been a prick about everything. He or his other band members could've been pissed and rightfully thrown us off the tour. I mean, we let them down. Sure, just Joe let them down, but I felt responsible as his bandmate and acting manager. I was the guy on the hook, you know? I set this stuff up. I worked for months to secure this opportunity. I asked, begged, prepared, worked, and hoped for this all to come together, and when it did, Dead By Wednesday couldn't come through now because of Joe.

But Brian is such a solid dude who knows the game. Brian Fair said, "I asked them what covers they knew. I tried to find songs we could all play. The whole point of that run of dates was to have fun with friends, so why not try something crazy and turn a bad situation into something special?"

Shadows Fall played "Bark at the Moon" by Ozzy Osborne, and we knew that song. We had jammed out Pantera's "Domination." We threw out a few other covers I don't even remember; it was such a crazy moment.

Brian told us to "Get the fuck back up on the stage." He then came up with us. Brian said, "Look, stuff happens on the road, but you don't miss shows. And these are my friends, so I want to help. It was getting down to crunch time, but even then, I told Opus, if Joe shows up, forget about it, and play the show like nothing happened. Worry about all that shit later. The show comes first. I was standing off stage as the band got ready to play, still looking out for Joe until the lights went down." Brian joined us and gave a politically correct speech to the crowd to explain what was going on without throwing Joe under the bus. He told them Joe was late on a flight and unavailable or whatever. Brian added, "They knew riffs from 'Live Wire' by Mötley Crüe and other random stuff. We were in a smaller town, and the kids were ready to rage. There was a ton of energy in the room that night. Instead of the DBW guys having to cancel after having traveled there and set up the merch booth and go through all the trouble for nothing, we just made it a party. I told the crowd, 'Look, we don't know what's going to happen for the next twenty minutes, but it's a once-in-a-lifetime thing, so enjoy it.'"

Class fucking act. He stepped up in a way that so few people would've done in that situation, especially being the singer from the headlining band. One of the sweetest things anyone has ever done for this band. It humbled me, it taught me, and it has stuck with me ever since.

We played a set of covers. We killed those covers, like, out of control. The crowd had a great time. I mean, what an unexpected thing for all involved. So much energy and positivity came from an ugly and disappointing situation.

Brian Fair added, "The DBW guys are all sick musicians. They were playing songs by memory. I remember we listened to a few things before going on, and that's all the prep they had. The crowd appreciated that the guys found a way to carry on. I knew going into it that I was going to butcher 'Live Wire,' because it had been years since I tried to sing it. I channeled my inner Vince Neil and just went with it."

I'm not overselling it when I say that Brian Fair saved the day!

Brian Fair didn't totally see it that way. For him, it was just what homies do.

He said, "We came up in a scene where bands looked out for each other, especially if you're on a tour package together.

That's always been our vibe. We've been picked up by other bands on the side of the highway when our van broke down. We have played festivals when our guitars didn't show up. Nobody wants to lend someone else a guitar. It's a more personalized set up than other instruments. Amps? Sure. Drums? Maybe. Guitars? No. But sometimes you just gotta do it, and the people we asked were always cool about those things. I'm glad that's the scene I came up in, because they aren't all like that, and once you get into bigger festivals and stuff, there's no fucking around."

After the show, a little past midnight, Joe creeps back in the club and sneaks backstage. His eyes are glazed over. He's all dirty; I mean, his clothes were a wreck. It looked like he had been crawling on the ground through a bunch of mud and garbage for two days.

I was too upset. I thought if I talked to him and heard his voice, I might just choke him, so I stayed away. Avoided eye contact.

We continued on the tour and finished the run in silence, but I was reeling.

Joe never contributed financially. Not even a dime. He had to be picked up and dropped off to practice; he drank and drank and drank throughout the day. From morning until night, and even when he woke up in the middle of the night for some reason, he would sip on his makeshift "water bottle" that was not water at all but usually cheap vodka. He mixed booze with pills at times. Lied about it. I had defended him and helped for as long as I could. I hoped being back home, we could concentrate on our new album and get him on the straight and narrow. I thought maybe all this would give him perspective, and he could prove us all wrong by killing it on the newer songs.

Soon after, he got his face plastered and our band mentioned on the news: Blabbermouth and a whole bunch of places worldwide including the news but for negative reasons. Apparently, Joe had robbed a pharmacy and got caught.

Once again, he had made a mockery of all our hard work, all our effort, all the second, third, fourth, and fifth chances. I had no ammunition to hold back the truth anymore. Dead By Wednesday needed a change. We deserved better. In this business, nothing comes without hustle, dedication, and sacrifice, and we couldn't do what we needed with Joe at the helm any longer.

I had prematurely announced his departure without talking to Joe first. It was impossible to do so being that he was currently in jail. For that, I take responsibility for being wrong. I should've spoken to him man-to-man and told him to his face first that he was out, but I was so disheartened, upset, and embarrassed that I felt like I needed to take immediate action. Afterward, when we finally told him we had decided to split with him, I hoped it would be a wakeup call. Instead, he blamed everyone and everything else but himself for his problems. We even gave him a chance to prove himself after the fact by giving him a few ultimatums, but he failed every time at every one and showed us that it was impossible. He took zero responsibility. He even lashed out at me. I was the problem. I was the bad guy all of a sudden. He just couldn't handle the truth. The truth hurts! Change yourself, and maybe other things will change. I know this firsthand.

I ran into Joe at a concert recently. I got right up into his face. I said, "You've got a lot of shit to talk about online. I'm right here. Why don't you say that shit now?"

The club ended up kicking him out. They didn't want any issues.

No joke, I still have a soft spot for the dude. I respect his talents. I still respect what he did with us, even as rocky and uneven as his time in the band ended up being.

He tried to reach out again recently, but I am done. I don't see the point. Any time I've tried, it has only gone in circles and becomes exhausting. He is a narcissist. I fully believe he is incapable of feeling respect and friendship and the comradery that I feel.

He is always right. I am always wrong. That will never change.

After basically doing everything for him while he was in the band and him turning around and fucking us over, time after time, he is the one guy who I've made peace with the fact I don't care if I never see him again. I don't hate him, but I don't consider him part of the DBW familia.

When I cut him out of my life, I realized how stressed out I allowed myself to get when dealing with him. Every practice, every show, every day, I waited for the other shoe to drop. Would he come to practice? Would he get to the concert on time? Will he show up fucked up? Did I have enough money to cover his share of recording, merch, band room rental, or whatever else he needed me to pay for?

Jessica saw how I'd changed after he was out of my life. Without his cloud of stress, I am much more at peace—meaning I have more time and anxiety and drive to expend on other worries, heh.

What can I say? I'm a worry wart. My next worry was what to do with our incredible album we had written and recorded now that we didn't have a vocalist.

CHAPTER NINE
Darkest of Albums

With songs demoed and some tracks recorded, DBW wasn't in a position to slow down or even consider taking a break. Okay, so maybe we totally could have, but that's just not in my nature. I like taking on challenges like that head on. I like to experiment. I like to push and persevere.

We got together to take stock of what we had and what we needed.

As we pulled all the riffs and grooves and demos together, we realized we were way further than halfway to a full album without even writing a single note more, but obviously, you want to constantly be creating and adding new ideas to the pile. So, Joey C, Michael Modeste, and I started working on an album, again. I thought that perhaps instead of just one singer on the album, we could have a different one for each song. This way we could release the album without stressing out over finding a new singer and, meanwhile, take our time to find the right one. Plus, adding a variety of known voices to the album would definitely help with exposure. We took the songs we had and gave them a fresh update without needing to cater to Joe's vocals. I reached out to various singers I knew or have worked with in the past in some way and started pitching the idea.

Now, I know a ton of people in rock and metal, having been involved with live music for more than twenty years, so I got a lot of quick "yes" answers, but it wasn't that simple. A lot of these guys have busy bands, managers, labels, contract restrictions, tour dates, recordings booked, family obligations, or hell, most of them lived across the country. It wasn't a matter of them saying yes, and then the track is done.

It became a fulltime job for me. I'd spend a few hours each day emailing managers, calling the various singers, uploading demos for them to hear, downloading what they sent back, booking studio time, booking travel, planning around a thousand obstacles. It was tedious, I'm not going to lie. There were days upon days with no forward momentum built. I would go weeks without getting any new tracks or keeper tracks. I got frustrated at times.

The counterpoint to that was when we got major steps done in one day. Maybe I got a clearance from a label for one singer, and another guy sent his tracks, and they blew me away. Then I'm walking around the house like the king of the world. I wasn't curing cancer or putting out fires, but the press inquiries were proof that people had taken notice of what we were cooking up.

I started seeing comments on social media from fans of these other bands about Dead By Wednesday too. We would announce Brian Fair from Shadows Fall was doing guest vocals, and then saw chatter around the internet from Shadows Fall fans. It was a small amount from different fanbases, but when you get a few new people to talk from thirteen to fourteen fanbases, word can really spread around. We realized then if the fans of these other bands dug the song their singer had done, maybe they would buy the whole album and help spread the word. We didn't expect everyone who heard Rob Dukes from Exodus's track to fall in love with it. We get it, you like Exodus maybe for more than just the singer's voice, but some people would give it a chance, which is cool. And some of the people who gave it a chance might realize they dig the tune. They might share it with a friend and start a chain reaction. Just like how mixtapes work in hip-hop. They make the beats and different rappers perform on each song. Same concept but put to metal. Like a compilation of different voices but all written with the same band musically. We were the band writing and performing the tunes, and we just had a different singer on each track. It worked!

As things came together, and tracks started coming in. We noticed a pattern or theme in the music and decided to take things a step further. John Arch, a veteran progressive vocalist of Fates Warning also from CT., got involved with what would become the title track of the album, "Darkest of Angels." His lyrics and our music became a rallying cry to shine the light on addiction and the massive effect it has on all of us directly or indirectly.

We then decided to make this a loosely constructed concept album. When word spread about what we were doing, we heard whispers of dissent from some fans and friends of our old singer, because they didn't understand what we were doing. This wasn't a middle finger pointed at him at all. It wasn't a dig at our former singer; in fact, it was the opposite. It was our version of an intervention, you know? We wanted to tell him, "Hey, you need to get cleaned up. You need to make some changes. You need to talk to someone and make better choices and better yourself."

We didn't mean for him to do that stuff for us. We didn't dangle the idea of bringing him back or anything. We simply, desperately wanted him to seek help on his terms before it was too late. We knew, after all we had been through, we couldn't force him to do anything. We had no power over his actions or his mind. Only the alcohol and drugs did at that point. They were all he would listen to. It was an ugly process to slog through for me to understand that truth. The rock-and-roll lifestyle is intimately tied to partying, booze, drugs, sex, and letting loose, so there isn't a good measure for when things have gone too far. Until they've gone too far. Then it's all too clear and typically too late to change or adjust.

I know for a fact that addicts can change, but only when they want to. I've seen it with my sister, though she has struggled back and forth for years. But one of my closest friends from childhood, Frank, is a clear example of how you can hit rock bottom and still find a way to climb out of it. We spent a lot of our teen years glued at the hip, along with two other friends, Hoz and Eric. While we all had our wild moments, Frank went down a much darker path and found himself extremely strung out on heroin. We didn't talk for years because of it. But he managed to kick his habit eventually and has been clean for over twenty years and managed to carve out a nice quiet life for himself and his wife. So, recovery is possible. You just have to want it for yourself. I give him and anyone who can beat it a lot of credit.

So, while we wanted the album's message to be about recovery, we didn't go to each singer and say, "Hey, you need to make the lyrics about this or that." It just started happening that way. You could read lines and come away with the message if you read them with an open mind. Not every song fit the mold exactly, and we certainly weren't out to preach or beat the listener over the head with it, but it meant a lot for us at that time to have those vibes out there, given our situation.

The message isn't always a pretty one. Not everyone recovers. Not everyone survives. Not everyone gets sober without permanent physical and/or mental damage. This album gave us and the various vocalists a chance to explore those dark possibilities. The truth is that most fulltime or career musicians have had to deal with drugs and alcohol abuse, either personally to face those demons or watch a bandmate, friend, manager, fan, or someone else close go through it, so I think it provided some catharsis to everyone involved.

I've said it before, and I'll repeat it over and over, because it's not an easy thing to comprehend from the outside: being a working, touring musician is a grind. It's … well, it's work and a hustle. You don't get much free time to assess your operation, because there's always something you're supposed to be working on. In fact, there's never just one thing to do that might actually be easy. If I just showed up and played drums, that would rule! But that's never the case; it's a DIY business even when you have a label, agent, or manager. The expression, "You want something done right, you have to do it yourself," rings so true in this biz!

You've got to write the songs, sure, and that's fucking fun. But first you need to have somewhere to practice and work together with your band, which usually costs money. You've got to have decent equipment to hear each other and sound good, which also costs money. You've got to have a way to record your ideas—again, money. You've got to have a band logo to slap on the cover. You've got to design the cover art. You've got to pay for the CDs. You've got to book the shows so you can sell the CDs. You need t-shirts, stickers, guitar picks, drumsticks, backdrop and a van to put your equipment in. Money, money, money… and what you put out throughout the years can usually never be recouped, so you suck it up and just do the best you can. Do you know how expensive banners are? Because you need a few big ones for when you open big shows, or you play out of your local market. What good is playing a show or touring and getting in front of people if you don't have your name up behind you anywhere for people to know who you are? I've seen so many great bands who didn't have a banner, and I left never knowing their name. It's all about branding yourself.

It's not an exaggeration to say that the midlevel touring bands who have gotten you through the toughest times in your life have invested tens of thousands of dollars over the course of several years, sometimes decades, for the chance to come play a thirty-minute set in your city for 2, 3 or maybe 400 bucks (if that, sometimes) after haggling with the club, just to split with everyone after our expenses were covered and then a couple of drink tickets each too if you're lucky. Think about that!?

I won't break that down for you here, because we were talking about *Darkest of Angels*, but I'll get back to that later.

One of the first people I reached out to was Kris Keyes, my former bandmate and singer in Gargantua Soul. We had been through so much together I thought it would've felt awesome to collaborate and "check in" with each other musically.

There was no pressure on either of us, as he wasn't expected to "save" the band, just create one song, and that made reconnecting with him easy and fun. I have so much respect for that dude, being a pioneer in that style of music, which he used to call rap-n-roll.

The song we collaborated on became "Phoenix Rising." The lyrics and song title clearly reflect the general concept of the album. The song was kind of a throwback in a way, combining the edge of DBW with classic nu-metal type rapping/singing verses from Kris, who even name-dropped our old band name in the chorus lyrics.

Kris Keyes said, "After Gargantua Soul broke up, I gave up all my possessions and flew to India to go live in a cave.

That was my plan. I renounced the world. I was done with it. When I got to India, it was … it was India, man. Dirt streets, extreme poverty, no TV, no American comforts, and I got schooled real fucking fast at how spoiled of an American I am. I was a spoiled kid with spiritual interests. I kept moving and learning and working on music and spirituality. When Opus called me about doing some guest vocals for Dead By Wednesday, I had so much more experience to bring along with me. For a long time, I was asleep. Many factors kept me in what I call the sleep of life. Fame is a very big sleep for me. Living off other people's acknowledgment of what you do is a big sleep for me. When we got together, I jammed and wrote lyrics for several songs with Dead By Wednesday, I think four or five, and I let Opus pick what he used. Being around my soul brother Opus again helped me reawaken."

After we finished the song, I pitched the idea of filming a video for it. You can see the finished product on YouTube, and you'll notice Opus ironically predicted the future by wearing a Bane style mask in the video, ha!

Jessica Spinelli once again got onboard with helping put it all together. Finding a location is always the first step. Luckily my buddy Mark Clapp, a.k.a. Red Beard offered us his land to shoot all the madness on as a favor.

She recalled, "I remember we had to find someone to spend a few hours painting Kris." A friend of ours did it. It was a lot of work. She had to continuously touch him up as well. Other than that, Kris was easy to work with, tons of energy. We just filmed one day. It was my concept. The main girl was actually dressed like a phoenix. Though solid, it didn't really come out the way I had pictured, because I think the film crew was inexperienced. Though I directed it, the crew was hired guns who I didn't know. It was a lesson learned."

At the time, Kris was living in the area, so logistically, it was easy to put together. Now he's out West, doing his thing. He's always moving around, place to place, project to project, like a real musical nomad.

Video was shot of the band playing. Kris had his full makeup on. We ran through the song a few times, and Jessica had us try a few things for additional footage. We gathered a few flame/fire performers on the set and had them each do their thing. The lyrics mention fire and prophecy, and it seemed to fit the theme of the tune.

Jessica said, "I did a Facebook post to find fire dancers and breathers. We did a lot of cool stuff with them that didn't make it in. The phoenix girl never worked with fire before but embraced it."

It was pretty wild on set with all the flames and emotions flying.

Kris, like I said, is a performer, so we got a lot of energy and intensity from him, and it translates to the screen. The "Phoenix Rising" video started with a quote to frame our intentions, as again, we weren't saying our old singer was out and forgotten; we were letting him know that for the phoenix to rise from the ashes and smoke, it first has to burn. Though, the quote by Octavia E. Butler, that the editor, Gary Sandler chose to open the video, said it much more eloquently than I can.

Brian Fair was another vocalist who was a no-brainer. We had to call and ask him to be involved—not to mention, he had seen us and Joe firsthand and what we, as a band, had gone through. I felt like even if no one else understood what I was doing and why I was doing it, Brian would. Especially after witnessing everything.

Fair said, "Dead By Wednesday had a really sick lineup, and they were super tight, fresh off some touring. They were clicking on all cylinders. When Opus asked me about it and told me the concept, I thought, man, it takes a lot of balls to put yourself out there like that, taking a chance on all these different singers. It was a killer idea. They sent me a great thrash song that I thought, while it wasn't tailored to me or written for me, the song allowed me to showcase my style and be a part of the song rather than just an extra layer. Listening to the rest of the album, it seems like that's how it went for the other singers as well."

If you read his lyrics for "Live Again," he nailed it. The whole song is basically saying, "It's time to quit this shit and live again. Stop this bullshit. You're hurting everyone around you, and worst of all, you're hurting yourself."

Brian Fair added, "The lyrics came together super fast, and the chorus got stuck in my head almost right away. The biggest issue was logistics, as I was living in the Midwest. Luckily, I had an Overcast reunion show coming up, and at the same festival, Downpour was playing. That was another project I had going with a guy from Unearth and a couple other guys. I did the two festival sets with the bands, and as soon as I got off stage, Christian was waiting for me. He drove us to Connecticut, and I passed out for a few hours, and then got into the studio to lay down the vocals. There's definitely a rawness to the vocals due to the hectic nature of it all, but it totally fits that tune. It was only later when I realized that, subconsciously, I might've ripped off 'Rio' by Duran Duran for that chorus."

A year after the album came out, I was setting up my annual birthday bash at Toad's Place in New Haven, CT. The show is a well-known event and always packed, so I can usually get some bigger name bands to jump on the bill. People hit me up all year to be a part of that gig. Success breeds success and all that. When you have a built-in crowd, a lot of people want to tap into that. Well, I decided to tap into that for myself and for the band. Obviously, we couldn't tour the *Darkest of Angels* record with all the various singers, but my show provided a good opportunity to gather as many of the guys together as I could in one place.

Brian Fair, Kris Keyes, John Arch, and Rob Roy all made it and performed their songs. I ended up billing the show as, like, a special release show for the album, even though it had been out already for a while, because this was the first genuine time to be able to do a chunk of it.

Rob, Kris, and John were semi local, but we flew in Brian, and I was more than happy to do it.

I thought, why not kill two birds with one stone? (Not that I kill birds or like harming animals.) We were going to have Brian Fair at the club to perform his song anyway; why not film a video for it too?

What you see in the video is a jumblefuck of footage we shot preshow, during soundcheck, during our set, and at some other points, with the help of Jo Shuftan of Horns Up Rocks as well.

Jessica set up a shot down in the bowels of Toad's Place for the bulk of it. It was your basic, old-school hardcore shot with Brian making his way around the alleys down there and singing right in front of the camera. We also got a gang of people to follow over his shoulders and mug for the camera.

Brian Fair said, "We got a bunch of angry dudes in a hallway, Biohazard style. Keep it simple, keep it hard."

It all came together easily. More importantly, it came together quickly, and we had fun doing it. Brian was only here for a day or two, so we had to go full steam ahead and not overthink any part of it.

Brian Fair said, "Just step back and take a look at the Opus Blizzard Bash, and you can see how much the guy means to his scene. He gets a night at one of the top clubs in the state each year to throw a party in his honor. He gets great bands to play, the place is always packed, and it's a huge party. That night, I sang a Shadows Fall song, "Destroyer of Senses," with DBW, which was the first time I had played one of those songs with another band."

It's pretty cool what you can get done under pressure with the crunch of time and a small budget, even without any major plan going in. Brian is a professional. He's super cool and laid back. And once again, we were honored to have him involved.

The middle section of "Live Again" is a bitch to play on drums. I love hearing it. I love how it sounds live. I love how intense the song drives forward, but it stands as the biggest test for me to pull off every time it makes it onto the setlist (besides a newer tune I wrote called "Manimal," which has a lot of fast double bass patterns). The double bass section in "Live Again" is tricky to play only because it's so constant but rewarding when it works.

"Donner's Pass" was a sick tune made much better by Rob Dukes, the former singer of Exodus. He and I had jammed once, years before, when I was playing some shows with Marc Rizzo. Rizzo tours solo, as a trio, and now with a full band when he's not out playing lead guitar with Ill Niño, Soulfly, or whoever else.

We were in NYC at, I think, Trash Bar this one night. The show was a tribute to Dimebag Darrell and Jeff Hanneman from Slayer, who had passed away earlier that year. Marc called up Dukes to the stage, and they exchanged a few pleasantries. It was clear there was mutual respect. Game recognizes game, as they say.

We played "Mandatory Suicide" by Slayer with Rob on vocals, and then jumped into a few other tunes. He sounded awesome. I had never really had the chance to see him live, so I was blown away.

The funny thing is that at times, the music industry feels so small, like you know everyone, because either you've been in a band with a person or on a bill or you share a label; there's almost always some connection. Rob and I didn't have one before that night, and we didn't get much of a chance to talk, so, for all I knew, he had no idea who I was, and, for all I knew, he might be a jerk or uptight or just not want to be bothered about our little record.

At times like those, the industry can feel massive. Musicians come from all over, and there's a certain hierarchy that comes with success, longevity, and, to an extent, ego can play a part as well.

I wasn't sure if he would remember me, but I decided to cold call him and ask him to be a part of our album. I mean, fuck it. It's a longshot, but to work with Dukes, it was worth putting myself out there.

I said, "Hey Rob, you probably don't remember me, but I jammed with you and Rizzo in Brooklyn a ways back."

He immediately told me he remembered. He was super nice and down to Earth. I relaxed and explained what I was doing with the guest vocals album and that I was hoping to get him involved. He loved the concept and jumped onboard right away.

"Let's do it."

It was that simple. He is an established singer who had made his living through music, but he didn't even ask for money or anything. He just wanted to be a part of it, and I'm forever grateful.

His opening screams in the song are blood curdling and powerful. As far as the lyrics go, if you aren't familiar with the Donner party story, you're missing out on one of the most gruesome tales of the American western expanse. You can listen to the story and take it at face value and relate to the horror of the message, but I think this song is a double entendre, hiding a second, deeper meaning underneath. Rob told me to look at it more internally, as if the story is about eating oneself alive from the inside, whether through drug use or whatever. The person is consciously doing it. They are aware of the massive damage they are causing and that it cannot end well, but they are unable to stop.

The song sticks out for me as a solid, throwback metal tune, with some thrash thrown in for good measure. The guitar solo is strong too. I've seen Rob downplay his melodic vocals in interviews, saying he was so nervous when he started singing, he couldn't pull off the stuff he grew up listening to, but he brought it on this tune.

Dead By Wednesday wouldn't be where it is without my cousins, David and Ceschi Ramos. We go back, way before the band, so getting them on the album was great. (See, I told you they would be back in the story!) I'm always rooting for them. Even if we aren't still in a band together, we are literally family. Hell, we get together every Sunday for dinner. They are a huge part of my life and part of my blood.

So, on this album, they contributed vocals to the song, "Power Troopers."

Thematically, it doesn't fit with the concept of addiction and recovery. They told me up front as soon as they heard the tune that they weren't going to explore the concept. I was bummed, but they knew Joe very well; there's a lot of history, and they weren't ready or interested in exploring those wounds at that point. Plus, they had other ideas in mind.

Ceschi and David are both entrenched in an anti-government, anti-police, anti-establishment mentality, so they keep up on current events and reflect their views in their music, which I totally respect.

Ceschi said, "I had recently been released from prison, and it was still fresh in my mind. Twenty fourteen was a particularly brutal time of police brutality. Protests were happening everywhere, but the metal scene can be politically backward at times, although there were bands, such as

Sepultura, RATM and Body Count, who were always very vocal about their stances. Though, on the flipside, this was also in the realm of SOD's 'Speak English or Die' and other insanely ignorant, contrarian douchebaggery. When DBW sent me the song to write, I wanted it to be about the ever-present problem of police violence in this country, but I wanted to write it from a personal perspective. I wrote, 'They put those same guns to the back of my head.' It was directly empathizing with victims of police brutality and also calling out cops. My brother jumped on the song for old times' sake and made the sentiment even more clear. It was fun to get on that album, but I don't miss losing my voice so much after every damn recording session or show."

At the time, the nation was reeling over high-profile police killings of Eric Garner, Tamir Rice, Michael Brown, and Walter Scott, among several others. Here we are, several years later, and it has only gotten worse and worse.

"Power Troopers" is brutal. No punches were pulled. I hate that the song is almost more relevant today than it was back then. It's like we're going backward.

"Darkest of Angels," as a song, had a progressive bent to it. I mean, if you're going to get the singer for Fates Warning on a track, you're going to cater to his style, right? That meant I had to make sure I had my shit together when recording. The song has a more technical element than other DBW songs because of that progressiveness. It stretched me to second guess every cymbal hit, every drum fill, and to examine the role my drums played within the song. Not that I stand back or passively take other songs off, but with most songs, I get a feel. I find my spots, and I go. With "Darkest of Angels," I had to adjust, push through, and put in a little extra work, which paid off in both my playing and the song, I think.

Another big challenge drum-wise for this album was the work I did playing to riffs written by Joey Concepcion. His stuff is fast, man. It's brutal. I had to adjust my style to match his playing a bit. It gave me a chance to work on my speed. I'm a guy who can hit hard, play solid, and even fast, but playing super-fast double bass or progressively has never been my main focus. With Joey's blazing fingers, I had no choice but to step up my game and ball out.

Even still reeling from losing a singer, I started to feel good about what we were doing. It was new, interesting and fresh from the normal grind. Also, hearing these different voices over our music helped give me insights into our sound and what we were capable of as a band.

Basically, I took a total negative situation and flipped it into something positive.

The process of putting the songs together involved loading the tracks online in a grid that these vocalists could access and jam to. We gave them freedom to help with the arrangement. Like, if John Arch requested we double the length of the verse, no problem. It was all there online, so we just had to copy and paste and shift a few things around.

Each singer has their own style and preferences, so we had people extend parts, trim parts, or even cut out some elements all together. We worked with them to help make it feel seamless and natural on their end. I think this also helped the songs vary more in tone and speed and style, giving us a diverse collection that stayed fresh while still sounding cohesive. That might not sound like a lot on paper, but try it, that's a big deal. It's hard enough for some bands to sound cohesive with the same people on each track. Try different singers on each track or, better yet, different singers on each album. Not an easy task, but I think regardless of our singer situation, DBW has that New England metal sound you know right away.

Brian Fair didn't really touch anything. We gave him the song, and he recorded his vocals to it as is, for the most part. Simple as that. John Arch had specific edit notes that we worked with. Neither path was wrong or bad. Both ways served the song, which is all you can ask and strive for when creating an album, right?

Eric AK from Flotz stepped up when we asked him to sing on a song as well.

Eric said, "I remember hoping the song would be cool so I wouldn't have to tell Christian no. Luckily for me, it's a cool song. Unlucky for him, I did not do a very good job writing or performing the song. DBW does a much better job at the song than I did."

Even though the album had a theme, Eric told me about the meaning behind his lyrics. "'I'll Break When I'm Dead' is my little tribute to Christian. He's one of those people you can't put down. He keeps getting back up and going full speed. No rest. He'll take a break when he's dead."

As easy as most of the songs came together, one of them needed a little extra time, love, and editing to get it to where we needed it.

"I Will Define," with vocals by Waylon Reavis from A Killer's Confession and formerly of Mushroomhead, who were our labelmates at EMP (thanks to my introduction), started out as a few separate parts, which resisted melding together without a few not-so-gentle pushes. It was like a random smorgasbord of riffs and beats and parts. We liked it. No doubt about it. We put in a lot of work before all the randomness started to make sense and form into a single, unified idea.

We had two versions of the song with drastically different patterns, lyrics, and vibes. One of the versions had vocals by Antony Hämäläinen. He's a vocalist from Finland who was also in a band with our guitarist Joey at the time called Armageddon. The guy sang in a bunch of bands, and Joey wanted to get him on.

It's always better to have too much rather than not enough, but in this case, it caused confusion and delay. After we had put in so much effort to make it a song, we felt like we took a few steps backward. It totally wasn't true, because Waylon sounded great, but I think we were ready to just coast to the finish line by then on it, you know?

So, since we couldn't figure out the next step, we played it for friends, media contacts, and longtime fans to get feedback to guide us along. The problem was that the people who we played the song for were split right down the middle on which of the two versions they preferred. That's a rarity. Yes, everyone has their own tastes and opinions, but generally, if you've got a song, a crowd will recognize and appreciate it. Only, we had a great song with two different vocal takes on it. It brought progress to a halt. We were ready to finalize the tracks and mix and push forward, but decisions had to be made. There was talk about leaving the track behind for future use, but I wanted Waylon on this CD.

If you look back at Waylon's days in Mushroomhead, or even before that when he was with Three Quarters Dead, he's always had a spark on stage. You just know certain people are career performers. Waylon is one of those guys. He belongs on stage in front of a crowd. Or, if you've seen the two horror movies he's in, you can see he is comfortable in front of a camera as well. So, I wanted him to get the spotlight a bit on our CD. We all went back and forth over it—probably the biggest, most-heated discussions about anything about this CD. In the end, neither side won, and neither side lost. I liked Waylon's version and Joey liked his friend Antony's, so the label decided we should just meet in the middle and mush them both together somehow. What we ended up doing was combining elements from both Waylon's vocal takes and Antony's.

We retitled this new song as, "Defining Fire."

I think it came out amazing and really stands up to the rest of the album. It's funny how that happens sometimes. I have a soft spot for that song, maybe because it was more of a struggle and because I had to get more involved. It could also be because I fought for it and rushed to get it done in time.

After the record came out, I still was thinking about Waylon's version, "I Will Define." I thought it was great, and it stood on its own. At first, he wasn't too happy about the song blending. I talked with him about it, and what we ended up doing was releasing his version, after the fact, as a bonus track. We put together a lyric video for it, so you can watch and listen on YouTube and it's doing great. It's cool to hear both versions, since they each have cool elements, and now that you know the whole story, it might put the song into proper perspective. Now go listen to both and decide which version you like better?

That song was work. It was a struggle, but we got two cool songs out of it and made everyone happy.

Carley from Candiria is my boy. We have been working together on and off with shows and stuff since the early '90s. He and I go back. Way back. I love his voice, his presence, the band, Ken's drumming, all of it. To work with him was on my bucket list. Putting together "Chosen" was a treat.

I've been doing my birthday bash since the early '90s, and it's always been kind of a big deal, because back then, Gargantua Soul was pulling in big crowds, and I always tried to get another big area band or two to really put the show over the top. One year, I signed up Candiria for, get this, $200! Yeah, now this was before they had gotten all the national attention and toured worldwide and whatnot, but there was certainly a growing buzz around them. To put it into perspective, the week of my birthday bash, this band who I paid two hundred bucks to play my show, was featured in *Rolling Stone* magazine as an up-and-coming band to look out for. No joke! No bullshit. I almost felt bad for only paying them that much ... almost.

From that day on, we've kept in touch and built a relationship. It's been great to watch them skyrocket into the industry and get mentioned along with the heavyweights in metal and hardcore.

The song he sings on is actually a remix of an older DBW tune we did on, *The Killing Project*. I fucking loved that song and thought it never got the proper attention it deserved. I called up Carley and told him what we were doing with the guest vocalist album and asked his permission to sort of dig up that old skeleton and give it a makeover. He was cool with it, so we had Nick Bellmore (Charlie Bellmore's brother, who has engineered/produced a majority of DBW's music) take a stab at it with fresh ears. DBW also had new members, and we had years' more experience under our belts, so we were able to approach it as a new track.

While compiling the songs and going through names of people we would want to approach, I wanted to try a few people who some fans might not be aware of or that might not be considered a fit for DBW's sound. We're already taking a weird trajectory to finish our album, why not experiment? Why not have some fun? Why not take a few risks?

For those of you who know Smile Empty Soul, you understand they stretch boundaries within the heavy music genre. Their singer, Sean Danielson, and I came together through coincidence, timing, and similar work ethics. He and I were both doing solo acoustic projects around the same time, so combining for a tour worked well.

Sean's awesome. He's sort of an oddball in the lineup of guest vocals because he's so different from the other guys. Then again, as I go through the list, all these guys have their own styles and identities, and they all stand out in their own ways. Maybe they are all oddballs; I mean, me and the guys in the band are too.

My buddy Nic Bell is not only a member of the band Left4Dead, but he books events through his agency under his Godsize Records umbrella. When I asked about getting shows for my acoustic solo stuff, he mentioned Sean. I got a slot opening the entire tour leg, billed as Opus of Dead by Wednesday. Just me and a guitar doing my thing. Pretty cool. That was a wild and learning experience for me, especially being a drummer for so long, but I also love playing guitar, singing, and writing songs too.

Throughout that tour, Sean and I built a relationship. It's funny looking back on the road sometimes. It's such a weird, vagabond existence, so the relationships you make on the road are different from, say, someone you meet at a grocery store, gym or PTA meeting. You share these bizarre and awesome life experiences that give you a connection. Not to mention, playing live is an intimate experience with a band. You've got four or five people on stage working together to perform a song that communicates your deepest emotions, your darkest secrets, or your political beliefs and philosophies on life. It's heavy.

Then take away the other guys on stage. It's just you and a guitar. No filter, no pretense, nothing but you and the crowd. They are there to really get inside your brain and your heart. You're baring your soul to complete strangers and saying take it or leave it. Being on a tour like that with Sean, you spend a lot of time together. You've got soundcheck, dinner, the show, the after show. Some days, you end up at the club for ten to twelve hours for larger bills. You also eat a lot of the same food, get the same drink tickets, stop at the same rest stops, visit the same sites in the same cities, meet the same bands, and so many other aspects of your life get tied together. You can't help but connect on a level beyond pleasantries and small talk.

By the end of the run, Sean had my respect, and he had made a new fan. I brought up the Dead By Wednesday concept album and explained about the guest vocal idea. He thought it was, as he put it, "rad."

DBW had this groove-based song that had come from a jam that none of us really knew what to do with. We couldn't fit it into the DBW sound, but we all liked the tune. I had no idea if Sean would have any interest in it or if his style would mesh with us, but I knew getting him involved would be a positive for both of us. I sold it to him like, "Look, you're not a metal guy, but this is a way to reach a new audience and vice versa that might help DBW reach new ears as well, and as a creative person, you can experiment with a different sound and voice than you typically use."

As a band, you're constantly promoting events and releases, but you also have to market, and those are two different ideas and processes. Dead By Wednesday is known around the New England and Northeast area, and we've made waves in metal scenes around the States, especially the Midwest but to get exposure to new crowds and younger music fans isn't easy. An opportunity like this felt like a no-brainer. Also, and more importantly, I figured it would be fun.

Sean was totally into it.

He said, "I'd love to try some heavier stuff."

The song became "You Must Like Suffering," and not only did it fit the theme of addictions, battling his own as well, but it's a standout track.

Oddly enough, even as I was neck deep in collaborations with some of the biggest names in metal, hardcore, metalcore, and whatever other labels you throw out, I couldn't help but wonder how our old singer, Joe, would've sounded on some of the material. Again, we had written riffs and songs and demos with him around, so it was only natural to think about it. He had screwed me over, time and time again, but I really try not to be an asshole and have made it a priority to forgive and forget, when possible.

I'm all about unity. I'm all about keeping doors open. I hate burning bridges, although I'm sure I have at some point. I care about all the people I have worked with. Look no further than the album I was working on to confirm how I try to keep everyone from my past in mind. I had two ex-singers of mine already on the album. If Joe could play nice, so could I. He couldn't.

Joe started a hate campaign about the band and targeted me in many of his posts. He exaggerated and shared all kinds of stories told to him in private to make me look bad. He tried to get people to turn on me, to hate me, to withdraw support for our band. Very childish stuff. What was he thinking? He mentioned I had a misunderstanding with pot and stuff back in college, and that made it okay for him to tell the world I was a scumbag drug dealer and whatever else? Fine. Sure, go ahead. No one bought it. I have too much of a track record to get taken down by baseless slander. He had issues, and the actively growing, productive band wasn't the best fit for him. It's that simple.

I understand that music is tough, and it can't always be the top priority for everyone. People in bands often come and go, especially nowadays, not just because they don't get along but for a million other reasons. Jobs can be too restrictive. Relationships and family commitments strain under the pressure of keeping a band going. A desire to go back to school or follow a different path or passion for a while can cause a split. Change in style? Loss of interest? Burned out? Sick of the road? Another band opportunity? Fuck, when you think about all that can and does change or get in the way, any band who can stick around for an extended amount of time is a miracle.

I don't want to be at odds with Joe my entire life. I don't want him or his friends and family to hate DBW. I don't want people needlessly talking shit. I don't want to worry about running into Joe at a show and not knowing where we stand. Fuck that. Life is too important to waste it on petty bullshit. We are all better when we help each other out.

And with Joe, it was none of those things. He had a much bigger demon to face. He was hurting. He was suffering. He needed help. I had tried to be the right person, but I wasn't able to straighten him out. He would look at me as some weird father-figure type who he had to push the boundaries with all the time or purposely go against the grain and butt heads with me for some reason. I tried to understand his pain, and I recognized the journey he was on, hopefully toward recovery. He deserved a nice, long period of sobriety and the peace of mind that comes with it.

The blatant truth is, if Joe wasn't such a cocksucker, I probably would've gotten him on a song. Instead, he was attacking us about large sums of royalties he felt like he had earned and that we owed him that were never there. I handled most of the money directly. I can say with full transparency that Joe was delusional. If we had all kinds of money, would we seriously need to scrape together money to rent rusted-out old vans to tour, and would we spend time organizing a reality TV show to help us make a free practice spot? If anything, we were usually in the red. Working with multiple singers had many positives and some negatives, but the process also came with some unexpected discoveries.

There's an old saying, "You don't know what you don't know until you know it," and that proved so true while working on this record.

Hearing your music and giving it critical listens can help you as a songwriter, as a performer, and it can guide your decisions on future recordings. Now, hearing your music through the experienced ears of peers outside of your band can prove straight up enlightening. We gave some of the singers multiple songs to choose from; in fact, we even demoed several tracks with Kris Keyes, and then picked the one we thought fit best.

Going through that process, you hear how your music sounds with multiple different styles sung or screamed over them. You get to follow their logic and improve your songwriting process. Even cooler and more inspiring was watching several of the tracks getting recorded. I was in the studio with Kris Keyes, Ceschi Ramos, and Carley Coma when they punched in to work with Dead By Wednesday.

My role in the studio was to watch and observe and be there, if needed. I wasn't standing over anyone's shoulders, whispering suggestions—or worse, barking orders and making the whole scene uncomfortable. I wasn't even butting my head in if I heard something I didn't like or that I thought wouldn't fit. If the vocalist had a question or asked for feedback, fine, but these songs became their songs in a way. That couldn't happen if I forced them into the DBW box.

We tried to stick with the mantra of doing whatever served the song above all else. If the song didn't need tinkering, we left it alone.

I might sound overly confident, maybe even egotistical, but the reason I knew things were great without overthinking it was we had our ace in the hole on board with the project. With Nicky Bellmore engineering and producing, DBW was in good hands. He has a knack for adjusting awkward moments, editing out-of-tune notes, and cleaning up whatever mess we throw his way. If a song fell off time or had other issues, Nicky could still make it sound dope or just be blunt enough to at least tell us the truth. That's what good producers do. They make good bands sound great!

Now, I'd be lying if I said that during all of this process, I didn't face any fears or doubts. I mean, I'm out doing acoustic tours, my band doesn't have a singer, Joey Concepcion was growing distant because of it all, and every day you aren't making progress, you're falling behind.

Our search for a singer hadn't netted any results. I knew we would be finished with the new album soon, and we'd have to have a plan in place to keep the momentum rolling. Hell, I had hoped to get our new guy involved to help promote his joining the band as we put out the album. Time was ticking, and things didn't look good. We had an awesome fill-in singer named Leroy, who was cool, but he lived so far away (in upstate NY) and had family obligations that wouldn't allow him to tour extensively like we needed, so the search was on. We reached out to friends, bands, managers, booking agents, and anyone else we could think of who might be someone who could fit the bill.

I also scoured on websites like Craigslist. I felt desperate. I didn't want to release an album without having a new singer in place. We would need to recreate these songs and tour if the band were to take full advantage of this gamble we had taken with the new album. I created an ad and started to spread it around. I listed exactly what I wanted. I laid out what the opportunity meant and what DBW would have coming up in the near future. I was precise. I was particular with every detail.

I got a lot of emails and calls. I got a few videos, links, demos, and whatever. One of those submissions was a guy proactive enough to not only send a passionate note, but to direct me on how to hear him. You'd be amazed at some of the egos and clueless responses that also came in. Some people think they walk on water, and they … well, let's just say they don't, and others who might be great are too clueless to navigate the process. I would get emails without music or demos, without contact info, and all sorts of other situations that leave you scratching your head.

This is your chance to impress. Your demo is your resume. Take it seriously. Have some pride in what you do. Show some respect to those you're trying to work with. Seems like common sense, but I can assure you, it's not.

Anyway, I listened to this guy's old band. The music sounded good. The vocals were clearly the highlight though. They stood out. Any doubt I had about that was quickly tossed aside when Jessica, who was listening nearby, asked who was singing. She liked it too. I told her the guy's name was Rob Roy.

My first impression of Rob's vocals was that he sounded like a combo of Corey Taylor mixed with Phil Anselmo. He can scream like Phil and sing like Corey, which is a rare talent to find. That's about as high praise as you can get in my book.

I called him up and we had a brief conversation. I gave him some background and info on the band. I gave him some links to check out our stuff, and we decided to check back in together when he'd had a chance to get a feel for us.

During the second call, we got off on the wrong foot. I don't even know what it was, but it just didn't feel right from the first few moments of the call. I wasn't expecting that start, so I got off balance and couldn't connect with him at all. He was very up front with me that our style wasn't what he was looking for. Whereas we are a type of band that screams first and mixes in singing at points where it fits, he wanted something where he could sing melodically the majority of the time and use his screams to accent and take songs over the top. He had also heard some of the old material we had recorded with rapping and some hardcore parts, and some of it got pretty nuts. He wasn't into that at all. I appreciated that he was honest, but I also didn't see DBW going in the direction he wanted to take the band. I told him that we had a deal in place and that we were an established band with a successful history, so take it or leave it, basically. He understood and mutually we understood that was that, you know? No harm, no foul, we just weren't the right fit for each other. We would both move on, no big deal, nothing personal.

We ended the call, and I remember thinking, man, that was a mistake. I'm never talking to that guy again.

A few weeks went by, and I heard a bunch more vocalists, but nothing blew me away; in fact, nothing was even moving the needle. I didn't hear anything that had a spark. I got really down. Here I am polishing off a stellar album with these metal heavyweights, yet my band can't even find a singer.

I was talking with Matt Bachand, the guitarist from Shadow's Fall. He tells me that he had just seen a guy doing metal karaoke here in Massachusetts. He said the guy nailed a Pantera song. Yes, I get it, we're talking karaoke, which is a far cry from the real thing, but Matty is saying how this singer had captured everyone's attention. I mean, if you can impress a professional in a setting like that, who am I to say the guy isn't worth looking into?

Turns out, after some investigation, that guy was Rob, the same guy I had spoken to weeks earlier.

We got on the phone, and we both shared a good chuckle at us getting in touch again.

I told him, "Look, we might not be the perfect fit for each other, but something brought us together again. I think we owe it to ourselves to at least meet up, face-to-face, and see what develops."

He agreed.

My pitch to him was that we could find a compromise in our differences in how the vocals should be. I told him I wasn't against clean, melodic vocals as long as he could give the heavier stuff a try to honor the past history of the band.

He agreed, but it wasn't enthusiastic. He wasn't a dick about it but simply said, "Eh, will see."

He came down to a band practice. I don't know what he was expecting, but I still think he was assuming we wouldn't be the right band for his next move. That changed as we started jamming. His whole demeanor changed. His expression lit up. His jaw dropped.

When we finished playing a few songs, he said, "Yeah, I want to sing in this band and didn't expect you guys to be this good."

Meanwhile, the album was done.

After officially joining us, it felt weird to be prepping a release without any sign of Rob's vocals, but we didn't have any more songs finished or even many riffs to splice together. All our material had been used up on the other songs.

We had burned through all our nerves to ride the craziest rollercoaster ever, and we were toast as the car slowed down toward the finish line. We could see the crowds lined up for the next ride, but we were beat. Our creative juices were all spent, and we needed time to process the songs, which always happened best by blasting through them at live shows. There's nothing that beats watching the crowd react to material you've written.

After a few days of considering, I realized it would just be too bizarre to not include him, so we tried to experiment a little. I mean, this whole thing was one giant experiment anyway, right?

I grabbed my acoustic and noodled around. We had a punishing and unique metal album in the bag, so I thought, why not give it some dynamics and dimension by adding a simple rock ballad? Rob has a great voice whether he is singing or screaming.

We got together a couple times, and we wrote "The Surgeon." His lyrics were inspired by his uncle, a surgeon who had passed away. I knew we could get the tune recorded quickly and on the cheap since it was just vocals and me on acoustic guitar. We set up a porta-studio at my spot with Nicky and did the tracks. Rob added a few vocal layers, harmony, doubling, and background stuff, and, just like that, we had the last piece of the puzzle. At that point, I knew we could put out the new Dead By Wednesday album and introduce the world to our new mammoth of a singer.

We had this kickass record recorded. We had star power behind it. We had a socially conscious message in the lyrics. We had a fanbase and the potential to crossover to all these other fan bases.

But ...

When we shopped it around, we couldn't find a champion at a label to lock step with our music. We had a lot of ears listening and saying incredible things, even Metal Blade gave it a spin, but no one knew how to fit it into the market at the time. No one seemed to grasp the importance of the album's theme in the current music industry landscape.

That is, until I spent the weekend with Thom Hazaert at NAMM and broke it down for him. I followed him around the place non-stop and barked at him every free chance I could until he listened. At the time, Thom Haazart was the A&R guy for David Ellefson's label, EMP. He took it to Ellefson as a star-studded concept album. Ellefson is a recovering addict, so he understood and appreciated what we were doing. No matter how gruff Thom's voice is or how intimidating a figure he poses, he has a huge heart too. He took the reins and fought for our record. The merging of EMP and Dead by Wednesday for *Darkest of Angels* made total sense.

The acoustic song I had written with Rob stood out the more I listened. It held its own against these other massive songs. Obviously, I was slightly biased, so I wondered how other people would take the song.

Ironically, Thom called me up immediately after listening to the album and asked, "Who is that guy singing on 'The Surgeon?'"

I said, "That's our new singer, Rob."

He said, "Good."

Just like that.

He heard what I heard. We knew we had our man.

We were all rewarded by the album's success. The band reached new fans, the label had a top seller, and I like to think we furthered the discussion on addiction and recovery in a positive, open, and honest way that both addicts and the people who love them came to use it as a guidepost. I'm not saying we cured addiction or that the album is a miracle. C'mon, don't put words in my mouth. What I'm saying, though, is that if you give the album more than a cursory listen and if you read the lyrics, allowing your mind to examine them a bit, you'll see you're not alone. You'll learn you have options, no matter how bleak life looks. There are people who will talk to you. There are things you can do. You don't have to give up.

The process wasn't quick or easy or always pleasant, but it really solidified Dead By Wednesday's relationship with Ellefson and Thom. It was a period with some doubt, strife, and discomfort, for sure, but looking back at all that was more like growing pains. We were a caterpillar building our cocoon as one thing and emerging as something stronger, smarter, and with a hunger we had never experienced before.

And then Joey Concepcion left.

He wasn't happy with our direction. He liked things heavy and brutal. Rob wanted to mix in more melodic elements.

I'm not going to lie; his leaving hurt. By this point, I was used to people in my band walking out on me—putting their names and faces all over an album, then walking away, leaving the rest of us scrambling to pick up the pieces. But with Joey, it hit differently. I thought we were on our way to creating something really big, really special together. And I still believe that. He just couldn't see the bigger picture. We are still friends, actually having grown closer recently. But in all honesty, his leaving screwed me up a bit. I hit a low point, not only with where DBW was at, but also with my drive to play and tour. I contemplated quitting. I don't think I ever could walk away completely, but I seriously considered a long break from it all or at least DBW.

Thom called with news. He was going to work with Chuck Mosley on a record. Chuck had helped Faith No More get their start. I didn't know much about him or what he had done since, but it seemed like a cool opportunity. The weird part was that Chuck was touring as a solo acoustic thing, and it wouldn't make any sense for him to play with DBW.

Or maybe it actually provided the perfect next step.

We didn't have a guitarist, and our bassist Mike Modeste couldn't make the dates, so we decided to strip down and play acoustic and give Rob a chance to showcase his voice without the rest of the band competing with him. We scrambled to put together a set that would fit the unplugged sound. At that time, I was already experimenting with going out and doing the solo acoustic singer-songwriter thing, so it wasn't too farfetched for me to pull this off. We did covers of songs by Alice in Chains and Black Sabbath and mixed in a couple new tunes we had written with Rob, "The Surgeon" and "You and Die."

For the tour leg, we didn't need a full drumkit, so I played rhythm guitar and brought along some hand percussion to play during a song or two, and I built a tribal style jam session into the set for when the mood struck us. It was a new experience to jump in a single car with our stripped-down gear and go from show to show without the full band.

Marc Rizzo played lead guitar for us on the run. His playing is a punishing blur of speed and technicality mixed with intricate melodic layering and some of the best fingerpicking on the planet. He is also a down to Earth, cool-as-fuck dude.

Marc had been with Ill Niño for a few years but was in a new project called Coretez. They were looking for a drummer. Jamey Jasta got me in contact with those guys. He was managing them. We jammed and wrote songs. The music was brutal, like Ill Niño on steroids. Marc and I hit it off, but then he left the project to join Soulfly. He was the main reason I had gotten excited about joining, but I wanted to see where the band could go. It was a solid group.

The band turned out to be less than a footnote, but meeting and working with Marc Rizzo clearly proved important. I always enjoyed playing with Marc, and he really vibed with the band, sound, and personality-wise. We dabbled with Marc joining Dead By Wednesday as our fulltime guitarist, even going so far as to announce him as a member of the band to the press. In truth, his schedule proved too crazy to make it work on our end. It's a bummer because we work together so well.

I helped book some of the dates with Chuck, which took place in July of 2016. My first impression of Chuck, well, it was impossible to get a first impression on the opening night of the tour leg, because he was a ghost. We played a free show at a record shop in Kutztown, PA—a few streets of shops built around a small college. It was July, so the kids were all at home, thus the turnout was sparse. Not that any of us knew what to expect. Chuck hadn't toured in years. He hadn't had any success in years. In fact, he had only had the briefest glimpse of success when the band that had kicked him out got huge with a new singer. But the FNM stuff with Chuck is cool, and it was ahead of its time. He had joined Bad Brains for a while but got lost in the shuffle of contracts when the band reunited with their original singer HR for a big payday. I knew he had a couple other bands, but I never listened to them.

Anyway, when we got to the club and set up our stuff, Chuck was asleep in his car, and then when he finally came into the club, he said a brief hello and fell asleep in the backstage area. Not the best foot forward, but I know he'd had a long drive and might just be beat.

I have dealt with drug addicts all my life. Family, friends, and musicians have all come in and out of my life, dealing with issues, so I know the signs really well. Chuck couldn't stay awake, he was sweating like he had run a marathon, and what little interaction I had with him, he was distant and spacey.

We played. They played. Chuck went right back into his car and fell asleep.

Marc and I shared our disappointment. We really wanted Chuck to sound awesome. We also realized our acoustic set didn't mesh with his sound at all. Whereas we were tight, polished, and attempting to sound as professional as possible, Chuck came off like he didn't give a fuck. He was an old-school punk, I get that. His fans also apparently got it. You either loved his devil-may-care attitude or you hated it. His playing was sloppy. He had songs where he would just play a single note and sing along. He didn't have a guitar strap, so he sat with the guitar in his lap and had a hard time keeping it from falling.

That weekend, we had a show at the Hard Rock Café in downtown Philadelphia. There was a protest on the streets right outside and around the club. The city was on edge. I don't know how much it affected the turnout, but the club looked empty. There might possibly have been more staff working than people in the crowd. It kind of sucked, but I did get to talk to Chuck a bit. He sat with us for a while and seemed pretty chill. We ate and talked. He was super open and honest. His distance wasn't an ego thing. Sadly, I assumed by his actions and appearance that he had scored drugs to help him function that day. I flashed back to my sister, who battled heroin and acted in much the same way.

Douglas Esper, who was Chuck's percussionist, came off as a super normal dude. I spent the first few nights sizing him up and wondering if he was on drugs like Chuck was. He was funny and friendly, but eventually, I came to believe he was a fish out of water. They were opposites in many ways, though they apparently found a way to make things work.

After the first three shows, Chuck went his way for more shows, and we returned home, because Marc Rizzo had to fly out for a solo gig across the country. Doug called me about possibly playing at a club on Long Island for one of the dates without Marc, but then the club canceled the gig. Doug was calling around, frantically looking to fill the date. They had played two free shows in less than a week, and they couldn't absorb another night of not making any money.

We had more shows with Chuck. One was at a rock-n-roll hair salon in CT., a classy wine bar in MA, and out in the middle of nowhere in RI. for a private party in the woods—not the most traditional of spots. We got to know Chuck and Doug a little more each night, but we never got a proper chance to hang or even to say goodbye, because the party in the woods ended unexpectedly. We started our set but had to stop a couple times when it began to rain. We had to scramble to cover gear and the sound system. Eventually, the skies opened up and dumped on us. We were deep in the woods, and the only way out was a rocky dirt path now slick with mud.

The show was part of a weekend campout, but Chuck didn't have a tent. Chuck and Doug loaded out their equipment to their car and must've left, because we never saw them again.

In a quick amount of time, after Rob joined, and after fiddling around with a bunch of other jokers, we found our new guitarist in Dave Sharpe. I had actually talked to him on and off for a while, but he just couldn't commit to our schedule. He had a solid job and real-life responsibilities, but eventually, he decided that if he didn't give it a chance, he might never get another chance.

We wrote powerful songs, we cultivated a brutal live show, and we established through touring that we weren't going to miss a beat after losing our last singer and guitarist. Look, that's not easy to do. A lot of bands are identified by their singer. The vocalist is front and center, often the star. By nature, vocalists are charismatic and thrive when they get attention. That often means they'll do anything to earn the looks, the whispers, and the benefits of having fans.

It can be addicting.

So, when a singer splits with the band or they get fired or they pass away or whatever, it can destroy the marketability and fanbase of the band. You and I could easily come up with a list of bands who didn't survive the process, while only agreeing on a few who did make a change and stayed relevant.

I had already seen a few guitarists and vocalists come and go in DBW without losing steam.

Rob had the qualities we wanted, and I'll even admit, I liked that he had the backbone to turn us down a couple times rather than beg for the position. He had put in some legwork to establish his own brand and identity, so he wasn't desperate to give that up.

But …

A working band must be flexible. Yes, you need to be one hundred percent dedicated to the cause, but life happens. While touring as the opener on a long Flotsam and Jetsam tour, Mike Modeste told us that his wife was pregnant, and he felt he needed to show his wife support by being present during the birth. Totally agree. We were cool with it. The only issue was that her due date fell smack dab in the middle of our tour.

A buddy of mine, Corey Nash, who manages a bunch of bands, suggested a bassist named Ricky Bonanza. I trusted Corey, but Ricky lived across the country. We needed to be able to practice and get him up to speed. It's hard for anyone to pick up a set without a few jams to work out the kinks. The other hesitation, like I've mentioned before, is you need to assure you can co-exist for the other twenty-three hours in the day. I didn't think Corey would send me someone who was a jerk, but everyone has their own vibe.

There's plenty of people I like and respect and even admire that I wouldn't want to tour with. No disrespect to anyone, I'm just being honest. I like things done a certain way. I'm not saying it's right or wrong, but when it comes to my band, this is how it goes.

My preference was to find someone local. Logistically, it made a lot of sense, and economically, it was the only true way to make it work. I have high standards. I already play with one of the best bassists in Mike Modeste, but I've spent time on stage with David Ellefson and Frank Bello, who aren't too shabby as well. You're not going to come in and knock my socks off. I've seen the best of the best. Mike is a beast, and his playing, energy, and passion fit DBW perfectly. He is a force to be recognized.

Corey, though, was adamant that I at least give his guy a shot. He felt strongly that Ricky and I would hit it off. I told him I'd look Ricky up online. Damn if his videos didn't blow me away. Now, he was an Italian dude, from Italy, and you know any Pasian is going to score bonus points with me. He was in the States on a work visa for music, which shows how dedicated he was to playing. Think about it. He uprooted his life and came to America specifically to play heavy music. God bless him!

I watched the videos and found myself doing a 180. I'm not sure if I can point to a specific thing—his playing, his attitude, or whatever—that made me feel so comfortable about him being so far away and a complete stranger to our music. I just had a feeling. I didn't have any worries, which is so out of character for me. He proved that feeling right by jumping at the opportunity to tour with us.

He wasn't concerned with how much he was going to make and what type of hotel he'd get and how big our van was or anything other than learning the music and kicking ass on stage. He sent me videos of him playing our stuff. He was open to feedback, and he adjusted on the fly. We spoke a lot on the phone and hit it off. As the tour came to a close, Ricky cemented himself as a dear member of the DBW family.

That summer, we played the Metal Hall of Fame show at NAMM, but David Ellefson couldn't make it. Ricky filled in. Here he was, playing bass licks from "Peace Sells" and several other monster songs, and he sounded great doing them.

You learn a lot about your bandmates on the road, especially when they come in as the new guy. When we went out with Ricky, the rest of us already knew each other and were sick of hearing the same stories, so we all pestered Ricky for fresh shit to discuss. Here's what I learned: Ricky needs to know where the Wi-Fi is at all times, he showers three times a day, and though he loves pizza, he is misguided about where the best pizza comes from.

He has an open invite to play with us, collaborate, or anything. If he needs me, I'm there. I wouldn't be surprised to see him on stage with us again during long tours, because Mike has limitations on getting out of work for more than a week, here or there.

Then again, Ricky has since joined the Butcher Babies as their bassist, so his time will be more limited as well. I imagine we'll all see and hear a lot of Ricky as more and more people become aware of him and his extreme talents.

Our first tour with Rob was opening for Raven, who Metallica opened for when they first started. As we were heading to one of our shows in Texas, we got news of a category 4 hurricane, Hurricane Harvey, was heading our way. We had to literally drive through the heart of the hurricane. The water on the side of the roads looked like lakes. Everything was flooding. Most of the road was covered by water, except for the center, so we had to literally drive on the center yellow line. Rob was driving. Water was literally coming up into the back of the vehicle. It was absolutely terrifying. At one point I turned to Rob and said, "I don't want to die." How he remained calm and got us through it was short of a miracle. Especially since there were so many detours and road closings, that we had to drive hours out of the way of the hurricane to be able to navigate to the show.

The show's location was clear of the path of the hurricane. Our bass player was supposed to fly out to meet us there, but his flight got canceled. After everything we went through to get there, we didn't want to cancel the show. So, we played without a bass player, which is detrimental to the sound of a one-guitar band. He wasn't going to be able to meet us for the next few shows either, so we started panicking. The bass player of the opening band was pretty good, so on a whim we asked him if he'd be willing to learn a shortened set ASAP and play the next few shows with us. He actually accepted the offer, and learned the set overnight, and toured a bit with us. His name is Michael Canales, and he killed it. I give him a lot of credit. We are still in contact till this day, and even the Raven guys were shocked how he pulled it off so last minute.

By our third tour both Mike and I saw a slow change in our vocalist's demeanor. Rob is a few years younger than Dave, Mike and me, and even though it's not a huge gap, we approached the business of music in vastly different ways. Part of that is our different experiences, history, and drive, but it also seems to be a generational thing too. I know, I know. I'm pulling the "get off my lawn" card here and showing my age, but I think there's something to this, a legit factor that played a part in how it all turned out. We wanted him to be the end-all and be-all as far as vocalists for DBW were concerned, and I think at the start he wanted that as well, but as we went along, I had my doubts. He did too.

When we jumped on that month-long tour, opening for Flotsam and Jetsam, Rob seemed miserable.

Why?

Several factors were adding up to prevent him from enjoying the ride. You can guess most of it by reading the rest of this book, but it's not underselling it to say Rob was starving on this run. He was broke, and we weren't making any money, day to day.

He had been with us for three years and benefited a lot from what we had built, but this tour was a real eye opener for him. This was more of a typical opening slot metal tour. No money, no frills, and not many signs that we were building into something bigger as fast as he expected. As a singer, you need a bit of an ego. Rob had a healthy one, not an over-the-top one. He wasn't difficult to deal with at all. He wasn't being a dick, but I think he harbored some belief that he was the last missing piece of the puzzle for DBW. I think, in his mind—and maybe I'm wrong—we would record an album and tour with him on vocals and success would follow. Put his voice and face on the radio, YouTube, and in all the metal 'zines, and fans would flock to us. To an extent, they did, and they have, and they continue to, but just not quick enough and with enough unit sales to quit his day job and live the rockstar life, you know?

It's a lot easier to make sacrifices on the road, in your social life, in your checkbook, and in your relationships if you believe there's a big pot of gold waiting around the next corner. It can fuel you forward to say and do and think in a manner that you might not typically do. As you start to turn corner after corner without a payoff, you start asking yourself what the fuck you're doing. All of us musicians do.

That's not a sellout thing. That's not a quitter-mentality thing. That's not an egomaniac thing. In fact, it's the opposite. Think about it.

None of us career musicians say, 'I'm going to stop being creative and go live a normal life.'

That's not in our blood. We just adjust our lives. Maybe we don't tour, or we form cover bands to make money, or we record ourselves, or we build a studio or a million other things that allow us to remain active, exercising those brain muscles.

You have to be a bit mad to face constant rejection and ridicule and unpaid bills and broken promises and shattered dreams every day and maintain the attitude that things are good, and your choice of career is healthy. There's no shame in throwing in the towel or changing directions or choosing a real job over a fantasy or accepting a stable life with a wife and kids, weekend BBQs, watching the game with your boys, and all of that. That's what a sane, smart, well-adjusted person probably *should* decide makes the most sense for themselves.

Not me.

My body aches some nights after shows. I don't have a retirement plan. I might never be a household name.

But I'm sure as shit not stopping. There are no delusions of grandeur.

Success in metal is often tied to how long you can gut it out as you grow your fanbase. Metallica took years to get their first taste of money. Megadeth starved, literally starved, as they toured and recorded and promoted those first couple albums. And those are two of the biggest names. There are hundreds of bands on the circuit still paying dues, day after day, tour after tour, record after record.

Perseverance is key. Consistency is a must.

Rob, though, had to face some big decisions out there on the road with us. I love Rob. He's one of my favorite humans. I could tell how much his involvement with the band weighed on him more every day. Rob had started off all guns-a-blazin' with DBW. He grinded with us. He sacrificed with us, but he quickly realized some hard truths about the business that knocked him back.

As we hummed along and opportunities started to come our way, I noticed he responded a little less enthusiastically than he had in the past. He had conflicts come up, so we had to turn down shows. Or if it wasn't a no, he told us why saying yes would prove difficult for him. Eventually, everything we were doing seemed to conflict with his life and put him in tough spots. He was working until seven or eight at night, and he lived an hour and a half away. We couldn't rehearse with him. He physically couldn't make it, even if he wanted to.

I felt guilty, and I wanted to help, but the grind is part of the game. I didn't demand much. I wanted one day a week to practice. There must be some consistency. I need to stay sharp and push forward.

Before Rob joined Dead By Wednesday, he had a solid job with growth potential. In the time he was with us, Rob had put his career on hold to put the band first to give it an honest shot, and in turn, he racked up bills and debt, and that caused stress. I'm not saying he didn't work. He had waiter jobs and stuff to bring in some money, but just like most of us, he lived paycheck to paycheck.

Again, when you believe that nugget is just out of reach, you can sustain that type of life for a while, but let's be honest, Rob is a big boy, and he needs to eat. The guy is in great shape, and to stay that way, you need to fuel yourself properly and exercise a ton. That's tough to do on the road, sucking down quarter pounders and hotel breakfasts and sitting sedentary for ten hours a day, stuck in a van.

I still think with all that, Rob could've continued, but he had met a gal and things started getting serious. He was on the road. She was at home. That is brutal. She had a career and made money. He was sleeping on the floor with me and a few other guys for days on end. Sometimes we literally slept together in the same bed even to save money. She is active and athletic and smart, and they share a lot of common interests. He was stuck listening to us rehash that time we saw Iron Maiden in '87 for the one-hundredth time. Get it?

Be honest, what would you choose?

I don't want to downplay Rob's passion for music or his talent. He had both, but there is a vast canyon separating musicians who are lifers and those who want to dip their toes in the water and see if it's warm enough. Rob had a life outside of music. He had passions outside of music. He wanted a family and stability and respect and a certain way of life.

Me? I saw KISS when I was twelve, and that was all she wrote. I was in. The music industry had its hooks in me before I became a teenager. I didn't know another way, and I didn't care to learn another way. I wanted to carve out my path and be a part of that energy. I have dedicated my life to that passion and those goals.

Ellefson is a lifer. The guy left his house on the farm at an early age, fourteen or fifteen or whatever, and started a band in LA. That's maybe not the smartest move to make at that age and in that situation. McDonald's is always hiring. Bring in a few bucks. Eat right. Get a roof over your head. That sounds reasonable and logical even, but that's not how it works. I saw how bright those lights were on stage. I heard the crowd. I felt the buzz and drank in the energy of it all. David took up his bass, and decades later, he is still going at it, hard. He grinds and grinds, and he's always looking for ways to branch out and stay relevant and challenge himself with new sounds and new audiences. There's a hunger in him. I'm the same way.

There were signs, clear and obvious, that we no longer had a singer.

Rob gathered DBW in a room and sat us down to break the news like a man.

He said, "Look, I don't want to leave the band. I don't want to quit, but …"

He had gotten a job offer in his old industry—an offer he couldn't refuse. He had real money and opportunity on the table, and he wanted to stay local to give his relationship a chance at normalcy.

He said, "With this job, I cannot give Dead By Wednesday the time or energy it deserves to continue. I won't be able to tour anymore. I need to bank the vacation days they offered to go visit my sick grandfather or to enjoy life with my gal. Maybe travel a bit in a relaxed setting and not on a grueling tour. No offense."

We understood.

Rob also didn't want to leave us hanging, so he fulfilled all the obligations we had set up. He came at us straight and respectful and was a man about the whole thing. In all my years inside the music industry, that hasn't happened many times, so my respect for how he handled the situation is as high as I can feel.

He recognized how serious we all were and that in the end, the music thing was more of a hobby to him than a realistic career, and he didn't lead us on or ask us to bend to his schedule.

He needed to look out for his gal. He needed to get out of debt. We can all relate. We wish him the best, and I hope he knows my door is open if he needs help down the line or maybe he wants to come up and sing a song when we're in his neck of the woods. He is part of the DBW family, always.

As one door shuts …

We started our search for the next singer right away. 2020 was already filling up with tour dates. We didn't want to cancel or postpone anything. We wanted a year to remember. (Little did we know how true that statement would be.) We wanted to focus on new music and new energy and put as much positivity out into the world.

Now that we were established on a label and had some national touring under our belts, we found it easier to get the ball rolling in our member search. Instead of us researching and advertising and trying to reach out to people, they were calling us.

I am not going to name names, but we had some interest from some known guys in the industry. We jammed with a few people, but honestly, nothing caught our ear.

The positive energy quickly deflated. Some of these guys were pros, but we had people showing up drunk or unprepared or uninspired.

Thankfully though, the process didn't last long.

Through a suggestion by my friend and now Mindsnap Music partner, G-Rock, we found Esteban Alvarez (no, not the same Esteban who sold infomercial guitars), who killed it at his tryout and then quickly joined the band. He has the same mindset as us. He is sober. He does martial arts. He has a family, stable relationship with his wife and kids. He's mature, has been around a bit and understands the game.

For those of you reading who are musicians thinking about forming or joining a band, look, drinking and partying and being wild is cool, but put the music first. Show up on time. Show up sober. Show up with ideas or at least a willingness to put yourself out there and try new things.

This guy memorized a setlist of our older catalogue, and we jammed out brand-new ideas together. It was clear he was the next guy. It's always a weird process. It can be uncomfortable. You can stumble, fumble, and face awkward moments, but everyone does. Fight through that and stick out your chest a bit. Give some attitude, bring the aggression, and lay it on the line. This is serious shit ... but make sure to have fun too. If you're not having fun, then forget it!

CHAPTER TEN
Earth and Apps

Earth is my classic Black Sabbath tribute band. We have been playing together for a while. I believe it started around 2001. I mentioned him earlier, but our bassist, Erick Heller, and I have known each other since we both got into music as kids. He was in Screaming Fetus, my first neighborhood cover band.

Like I said before, he stepped away from music for a while to be a good dad. I understand that way more now. He had two kids and wasn't able to tour. Now his kids are older and all grown up, so he has a bit more freedom. I mean, he owns a small hometown bar, so he can't get too crazy, but the itch to make or at least play music is still strong with him after all these years. Our singer Ray, who we call Razzy, (you know Ozzy/Ray=Razzy) looks and sounds like Ozzy. He really knows how to sell it. We even convinced him to get "Ozzy" tattooed on his knuckles while on tour in Europe. Cover bands can make a few bucks playing bars, sure, but we do Earth as a tribute for the love of Sabbath and still make some duckets. On paper, Alchoholica is still a band, but it's been inactive for some time.

I thought about trying a few different bands, but Sabbath has always been such a favorite of mine, and it's sort of universal music, even though considered heavy metal. I mean how many times have you heard "Iron Man," "War Pigs," or "Paranoid." Over the years, my respect for them has grown. It's at the point that when people ask those hypothetical questions about being stranded on an island with only one album, I almost always pick Sabbath. Don't get me wrong, I love a lot of bands with a passion, but Sabbath checks off all the boxes. Part of it is they came first. Without them, there isn't Metallica, Megadeth, hell, maybe there is no KISS. That list goes on and on.

Through the years, as with many tribute bands, members have come and gone. Lineups are fluid in any band, but in a working band/side-project band like this, it's harder to keep people together. You know, some people have a passion for originals, or they get sick of only doing covers, or they have a different vision for what the setlist should consist of or what the stage set up should be, or shit, some people find other tribute bands that pay more. There's all kinds of reasons. You try not to take it personally. I'm the only original Earth member.

Now, I grew up listening and playing fast stuff. Lars Ulrich, Charlie Benante, and Dave Lombardo are some of the guys who I admired early on. I learned to play by emulating what they did, which was to play fast and furious. For a blip in time and at a young age, I had a trio band called The Putrid, which was sort of a punk-style band. My beats kept the pace. I raced forward. A lot of overly eager, sloppy drum rolls. Some might think playing fast makes it harder, but I find it to be quite the opposite. You have less time between notes when your tempo is up, so you have less space to fill and less options to explore. You just keep it simple for the most part and go.

It's harder to play slow. You have to be in the pocket and find ways to fill the space without disrupting the groove. You can't just play whatever white noise you feel like. That will throw off the other players and anyone listening. You need to stay within the song, serve the song. Ghost notes are important when playing slower. Dynamics play a huge part in playing slower. Hitting the correct notes hard, and then pulling back on others. The impact of that can't be overstated. Those little subtle elements can make or break the performance.

I approach playing shows with Earth completely differently than I do with Dead By Wednesday. The experience playing that style helped me out a ton when I filled in on a short run of dates with the Bullet Boys. That was fun until their singer, Marq, literally looked me dead in my eyes and said, "You know you're playing with a legend now, right?" It took me controlling every muscle of my body not to laugh in his face. But I focused on slowing down, hitting hard, and filling the voids. You think "Smooth Up in Ya" is easy until you have to rock it correctly.

A lot of drummers have a harder time playing slow than going super fast. It's an adjustment that you can only make with practice and experience. There's a beauty in slowing things down. It's an art, in that it's less about technique and more about creativity.

I learned a lot of this while studying Bill Ward. Another master of slow rock drumming is John Bonham. Those two are definitely favorites of mine. John lived in the pocket and knew how to groove. Sure, he could speed up and rock, but they both mixed in blues and jazz beats in many songs as well.

My approach to playing someone else's songs, whether Sabbath, Megadeth, or whoever, is to play the song about 90 percent faithful to how it sounds on the album so people can recognize the song they love. And always focus on perfecting the recognizable parts first. The last 10 percent is to add my own style and instincts to it. Now, sometimes the reason I need to adjust the song is because I can't figure out exactly how they played it, whether there's no video out there to examine or due to crappy old recordings (for example, some of the early Megadeth stuff), so I do what makes sense and works for me and my playing. I think doing a completely straight cover misses the spirit of why you're covering the song in the first place. Put yourself into the song and their shoes but maybe put your own little spin on it. I'm a musician, not a robot.

So, if Zakk Wylde is reading and you ever need a drummer for Zakk Sabbath, hit me up! I can literally sit in for that band any time without any rehearsals and pull it off.

My first experience with marijuana also played a part in my love of Sabbath, I think. I was young, not old enough to drive yet, and a greaser dude I knew, Ed Londa picked me up once while I was walking, and we hung out. He was blasting "Sweet Leaf" by Black Sabbath, in his Camaro, and we ended up smoking pot.

I like to joke around about why I love Sabbath so much, but seriously, that day, the music and the lyrics to that song just hit me in a way that nothing else ever did.

A few years later, I was with the band, and we all decided to take mescaline together. We watched this old-school Black Sabbath documentary that ended up getting played over and over on repeat throughout the night. It became like white noise in the background, but every once in a while, we'd focus on a song or a quote and bang our heads or giggle or whatever. Even though we weren't actively watching it, it seeped into our night at various times and definitely our DNA. We were tripping our faces off. I mean, the walls were breathing, the stereo was melting, the TV was sweating—you know the feeling.

The next morning, I'm coming down from the trip. I glanced over at my buddy Frank, who was sitting on a hard wooden chair scrunched up all night, and said, "I think Black Sabbath is my favorite band."

One time when I was in LA, touring with Gargantua Soul, me and another buddy of mine, Hooch, hit up a popular sushi joint. I look across the restaurant, and there is Tony Iommi. No shit. How do I know it's him? Because he looks exactly like he does on stage. He's got the same glasses, the same jacket, the cross necklace on. Now, I was stoned out of my mind, but I was sure it was him. I tell Hooch what I think.

But Hooch didn't think it was Tony.

We look who he is with, and it's one of the women from L7, who he was dating. He might still be with her, I don't know. Anyway, once we recognized her, Hooch got convinced it was Tony Iommi in the same restaurant as us!

I didn't want to bother him, but I had to know for sure.

I yelled from across the room, "Tony!"

Sure enough, he looked in my direction and smiled, like he knew me already.

I started rambling, "Hey man, Black Sabbath rules. I'm a big fan. You're great."

I felt stupid, so eventually I just stopped talking. He smiled politely, and we both went back to eating. On the way out, I had an empty wine bottle from dinner, so I asked him to sign it. He did, and I still have that bottle. I gave him a Gargantua Soul EP that I had with me. He probably never listened to it, but he was gracious and cool about it.

Sabbath has gone strong in several lineups for decades. We decided early on, though to concentrate our set on songs from the Ozzy years, mainly the first four albums. When we headline shows, we'll do two hours of material. That is a marathon, let me tell you.

Last year, I spoke to Lord Bishop, the promoter friend I mentioned earlier who booked some of my first bands. He now lives in Germany, and two years prior, he booked me a solo acoustic tour in Europe, opening for his band Lord Bishop Rocks. He's an amazing guitar player and a soulful singer. And another lifer. He lives for the music, like I do. His live vibe is unlike any other. It was an amazing experience. Jess got to come with me. And people really seemed to dig what I was doing. We discussed booking a tour for Earth out there next, and he followed through. Even though there are a million Sabbath tribute bands, the response was way better than anyone expected, so we planned another second full month tour in September of 2020, which obviously got canceled due to covid. We waited until the last second to drop the shows as the number of infected people rose over there, and then rose over here, and then fell over there and stayed steady here all summer. In the end, it just didn't make sense to risk it for anyone. I'm hoping we can pick up where we left off someday, but the opinions on vaccines has become so divided and political, who knows.

A lot of times, when you see me play in shitty clubs or dealing with half-assed sound guys—no offense to the sound engineers out there who actually care about their job and do it correctly—but a lot of times, the drums don't get the love and attention they deserve. I feel like at over 60 percent of the shows I play, the bass drum gets lost in the shuffle, especially when you have multiple guitars and stuff like that. Some bands have keyboards and percussion and samples getting triggered, all kinds of extra layers making the drums get buried more and more.

I wanted to start triggering my drum set, but at the time, all they had was DM fours and DM fives and these big, bulky rack systems they would use to trigger drums. And some drummers would carry all that around for literally one drum input.

Well, I had an idea!

We have iPhones playing music, keeping our schedule, sharing content, and doing everything in our lives short of feeding us, so why can't I come up with an app that allows a player to trigger at least one drum?

I knew the app didn't have to trigger all the drums. Most drummers would be thrilled to at least have the capacity to trigger their bass drum in a live setting. They, just like myself, would be thrilled to control an effect or certain sound coming from a single pad during a show. The other added benefit of focusing on one drum only was you wouldn't need to lug a bulky D5 unit all over the Earth on tour. No more carrying that thing through an airport or up and down a couple flights of stairs to the stage each night and back down again, along with everything else. With my app, you can set up your drums, grab your phone, and boom, you've got yourself a trigger system in moments.

So, I was asking around, asking around, asking around, thinking I've got to know someone who knows something about building an app. If I didn't know someone who did, I knew that I knew someone who knew someone or maybe even someone who knew someone who knew someone. Are you following all that? My friend Lara always says, I'm blessed because I'm that guy, who always knows a guy that can help.

Turns out, Jessica's brother Alex knew a guy. Ralph Seamen. Yes, before you ask, his real name is Ralph. He is a computer wizard and knows a lot about app creation. I pitched him my idea, and not only did he say he could do it, he loved my idea. Once he understood the 'how' and the 'why' of how the app would prove an important tool for touring and non-touring drummers, he signed on as a 50/50 partner with me.

We went back and forth, forth and back, and maybe forth or back again, along with a bunch of testing, I don't quite remember. In the end, Ralph actually figured out how to make an app born from my idea. We called it the EZTrigger app.

We tested it out. I used it live several times, and it works like a charm. I did notice when heavy rock drummers and heavy-metal guys went beyond a certain BPM (beats per minute), some issues crept up. Like when you start getting into ridiculous, death-metal blast EPMs, the sound starts fizzing out on you especially when the phone battery was dying. If you keep pushing, you'd sometimes hear double hits and extra misfires. He kept revamping and tweaking the app to fix the bugs and help dial it in. My idea and Ralph's knowhow had created an easy-to-use tool to help musicians, and I felt pretty good about it.

How does it work? Listen to how simple this is. When I think about the huge money spent on this stuff, it blows my mind, because we made it so affordable. Your phone acts as the brain of the operation, but first, you need to put it on airplane mode.

When you open the app, there's all these different premade sounds available. For example, you can play through a filter that mimics my bass drum from a couple different albums. Maybe you prefer to sound like Lars did on Metallica's *Black Album*? How about adding the tone of John Bonham? Vinny Paul's snap? Want to trigger the boom from an 808? You can use the app like an eDrum pad with all sorts of crazy sounds. It opens a lot of refreshing, unique possibilities to your live setup.

The other thing you'll need is an adapter. We found that the iRig works perfectly. So, you plug the iRig into your phone. One chord goes to the PA, the sound system, and the other chord goes to the trigger. The trigger attaches to your bass drum. Talk about an affordable, easy-to-use, and ultra-portable option for a trigger, eh?

I even used the EZTrigger on a studio recording with stellar results.

(Yup, this section is definitely a shameless plug.)

The problem is I haven't had a lot of money to dump into advertising and marketing for it. Even still, people find it somehow, so we make a little bit of money every month just for having it available in the iTunes app store. I went to NAMM, and I demonstrated it to a bunch of people DIY style. Since then, we have managed to get some press, and people seem to dig it.

Since EZTrigger hit the market, Roland released this little square box that's super transportable, and it does all the same stuff. It's easy to give up at that point and say the market caught on, but at the same time, their unit costs $100, whereas my app costs $9.99.

CHAPTER ELEVEN
Countdown to Ellefson

Fast forward to around five years ago, Dead By Wednesday is gearing up to release *Darkest of Angels*. I heard through the grapevine that David Ellefson was starting a record label. We saw Doll Skin getting a lot of hype, and they were signed with him. Seemed like he had invested time and experience into his operation. Our sound fit his style way better than Gargantua Soul ever did. The more I looked into what he was building, the more I wanted to reach out. I still had his email, so I hit him up.

Wait. Let me rewind a little bit first.

Before that went down, I had started doing my acoustic stuff. I saw he was doing a bunch of spoken word events. He'd be talking, almost like a clinic style, and answering questions, but at the end, he would jam a bit. So, I hit him up out of the blue.

I said, "Hey, you know, it would be cool if you want to go do some dates in the New England area. I'll book it, and I would love to open up."

It was hard to match up my solo project with anything, because I didn't want to play dive bars, doing three hours of covers. I'd basically be a jukebox. I wanted to do more of a showcase-type set, so I pitched it as an opening act to his spoken word set. He had just gotten back from a few dates in the UK, so I know he was tired and busy, but he took the time to write back. He's a personable guy. Not only did he remember me from the Gargantua Soul days, but he also loved the idea.

David Ellefson explained, "I was aware of Christian back in my Peavy days in 2002-2010. I was in artist relations, and we had some interactions, but my first real engagement with him professionally was when he booked a little clinic/spoken word tour for me."

I booked a spoken word show for David at the Angry Chair, a rock-n-roll salon in Newington, Connecticut. The owner of the place, Dave, cleared out all the haircutting stuff and made a venue out of his shop.

David added, "Hair salon by day, quasi concert venue by night. It was a bass guitar masterclass that ended with a jam session."

You want to talk about a special night? How about gathering fifty friends for a hangout with one of the best-known bassists on the planet.

But ...

I showed up extra early to the gig with a PA sound system I had borrowed from my friend Gerald and his musician son Adam Pawlik. The system was on the small side, but for what we were doing, it should've worked fine. We set it up, and I start to do soundcheck. No issues. I'm just about to open the doors, and out of nowhere, the whole thing blows. Marc Rizzo plugs in and almost gets electrocuted.

The PA system is fried. I mean, there was smoke billowing out of the PA head. You could smell it burning.

I almost shit my pants. It was an hour until showtime, and I had no idea what to do. No joke. I was starting to plan how to break the news to the crowd, the club, and shit. I've got to cancel on David too. The first chance I have to make an impression, and this is how it's gonna go?

This dude we all knew, Tommy, who happened to be there, said, "I have a PA about fifteen minutes from here that you can use."

He grabbed the PA from his spot and got back a few minutes before showtime. People were lined up and waiting, but we had to hold off from letting people in. I was "sweating bullets." I had to tear down the broken PA and load in the new one as fast as I could.

Tommy saved the day. No doubt.

So, as soon as I get things set up, I've got to play, right? I was the opener. I'm still frazzled. I'm still sweating, but we're already running late. I do my set. It's just me and a guitar, no safety net. It goes well, all things considered.

David could've been annoyed or pissed. Heck, I've seen bands cancel for less drama. And those were bands with way less clout than a member of Megadeth. He stayed polite and patient and rolled with the punches.

Now that I know David better, having toured and recorded with him, I know what a genuinely good person he is, day in and day out. At the time, though, he could've blown up, and I wouldn't have known how rare that is for him.

David Ellefson said, "Look, every musician starts at the same place. There are some musicians who, once they reach a certain level, aren't willing to go back down into the trenches. I am. I want to make music my livelihood—not just my livelihood in terms of income, but my living as far as who I am, what I think, what I breathe, what I do, and what I talk about. My real life is that of a musician, a songwriter, and an entertainer. If you want to do that full time and make it your life, you can't sit back and expect everything to stay at the same level, no matter how much you want it to be. Sure, you aim for the big leagues, but some people, when they reach that pinnacle, decide they won't ever go back down to the minor leagues. The reality is that the record industry, which is almost now nonexistent compared to what it used to be, is going through major changes. There is a Clint Eastwood line in *Heartbreak Ridge*, 'We overcome, adapt, and improvise.' I figure if that's good enough for the marines, it's good enough for a musician like me."

We set up David, and he starts to do his thing. He tells stories. He answers questions.

I can finally relax and enjoy the night, right?

David is wrapping up his set, and he says, "Hey, Opus, let's jam something together."

Now remember, I am a drummer by trade. I can play guitar, which I do on my solo acoustic stuff, but I wouldn't call myself a guitarist. I don't have a catalogue of cover songs memorized. I don't play the flashy stuff.

Knowing he felt comfortable enough with me as a person and a musician to take a chance in front of a crowd is a testament to not only how much work I put into things, but also to him for noticing and appreciating what had been done.

He has his bass set up ready. "You know 'Symphony of Destruction,' right?"

I felt my jaw hit the ground. "Uhhhh … Well, I know the main riff."

He shrugs and nods.

I sit down with my acoustic guitar and jam with David Ellefson at a hair salon in Connecticut, playing a song I've been listening to my whole life. You want to talk about surreal moments?

I spent the entire song trying to keep up and figure things out. I'm thinking, Man, this guy is never going to want to play with me again, but he had a great time.

David had fun. The crowd had fun. There were coolers of beer on the roof; man, it was a total party.

From there, David and I were cool.

Well, I'll let David explain. "When doing a tour like this, you're literally putting your day-to-day life into someone else's hands. They control if you have a place to stay, if you're going to eat, what you're going to eat, all your accommodations. I mean, there's your basics: food and shelter, you know? Am I going to eat food that I like and have a roof over my head similar in line to what I'm accustomed to when I do this kind of work? Christian was accommodating on all sides. He made sure I was comfortable. He made sure I was well taken care of, and when you can relax and have confidence, playing the music is the easy part."

Around the same time, I heard David was starting a record label. I saw it all over Loudmouth and other music websites. The band Doll Skin was working with his label, and they were everywhere as well.

Now at that point, I was like, okay, well I already have a relationship with him somewhat, so I'm going to email him and ask him what the fucking deal is with that, because Dead By Wednesday seemed like a perfect fit.

So, I hit him up.

He responded quickly. "Oh yeah, it sounds pretty cool, you know? I'm definitely interested, but I don't do any of that stuff personally. I have an A&R guy, Thom Hazaert. You've got to hit him up. Tell him I sent you."

I reached out to Thom, but he didn't let me get a word in edgewise.

He just talked at me.

Having a conversation with Thom gives me perspective on how people feel when I'm talking with them but on a smaller scale. I can be the same way at times. I talk fast, and it can be hard to get a word in.

Though he was talking fast and furious, with his deep, gravelly voice, I heard, "If you want to talk about this in person, come to NAMM. You could hang out with us a little bit here and there. We'll find time to chat."

I booked my first NAMM ever. I had never been involved with it before, which was exciting by itself, let alone traveling across the country to talk with label executives about my band. I was a fucking hungry dog by Thom's side the entire weekend. Breaking his balls and trying to get the right moments in to talk to him about everything, which was pretty tough.

And I'm sure I came across as slightly annoying.

But you know, that's what you got to do with guys like Thom. You need to be vigilant, aggressive. So, I kept on, I kept on it, kept on it.

At the end of the weekend, we still hadn't discussed my band or any chance of a deal. I thought my whole pitch might've been in vain. Maybe he didn't dig our stuff? Maybe I had annoyed him too much?

As we parted, Thom said, "Yeah, kid. Yeah, yeah, yeah, whatever. Just call me on Monday when we get home, or Tuesday, whatever, and we'll figure it all out."

I was buzzing. The whole trip seemed like a victory. I had made new contacts, broadened my horizon, and came home with great news … or so I had thought.

A few days go by, and I hear nothing, no word. So, I call and email again. Wait a few more days and I hear nothing from him. Thom seems like he couldn't care less.

I start to feel deflated and keep telling myself, well, at least I found a bunch of endorsement possibilities out there. I met a bunch of new contacts out there. I got the word out for my EZTrigger app. And I realized just how important

NAMM is for working musicians. I told myself that even if Thom and David didn't have interest, NAMM hadn't been a total waste.

I went to NAMM hoping to get a deal. I came home thinking I had a deal, but all I heard was crickets. It sucked. As much as I justified things, I was still pissed. It seemed like a no-brainer for us to team up. I decided to hit him up again and break his balls one last time. No response. Nothing.

Tried again.

Nothing.

Finally, he gets back to me. It was a relief, at first, but he basically said he needed time but that he wanted to assure me that he would respond.

So, that was good news, right? We're back in the saddle and moving toward a possible home to release the next Dead By Wednesday disc.

Then a few weeks go by.

A month.

And I was like, you know what? Fuck this guy. I'm going to look elsewhere. I'm just going to make a random post to ask if there's anyone out there who has relationships with any labels or A&R people who might be interested in listening to the new DBW. As soon as I hit post, I got an inbox from Thom.

His message boils down to, "What the fuck, dude? I thought I was putting this out?!"

I asked, "What are you talking about? I haven't heard from you in, like, a month, dude. You don't respond to me. I don't know if anything's going on. Why would I think you're wanting to put it out?"

He responds, "Hang on. Give me a minute."

He then listens to the album.

Within ten minutes of Thom listening to the *Darkest of Angels*, he calls me back.

He said, "Oh shit, dude. This fucking album is incredible. You've got all these guests on here, and they all sound great."

He starts asking who sang on certain songs and guessing a few as well. He asked me about our vision for the album.

I told him it had a theme. Each song had focused on addiction because our old singer had battled against it. It was why we had finished it and why it had to be marketed the way we wanted.

I mean, it did get shopped to Metal Blade and Nuclear Blast and a few others. We had contacts at places, and we knew it was a killer record, but we wanted the right place and the right conditions for it to come out.

Thom said, "We're definitely doing it."

After that, things got fast-tracked.

Within a month, the record was packaged and released. EMP Label Group did a great job. With the album out and with our new singer secured, we had a full head of steam. Doors started opening with cool opportunities.

Since that album, Dead By Wednesday has flourished. David and Thom even pushed our band up to their top-tier label, Combat Records (which is now defunct, but that's another story).

As with our old manager, Ford, who got into the acting thing, Thom started to prioritize being a singer. As far as I saw it, he and Ellefson began touring together, leaving less time to run the label as Thom strove to achieve his goals in the rock/metal world.

I don't mean that as a dis. I just mean that as reality. Things that needed to be taken care of have fell to the wayside. Luckily, we didn't have anything in writing with them. We weren't tied to a lengthy contract that would hold us back or keep us in limbo if Thom decided Dead By Wednesday was not a priority moving forward.

DBW has built a reputation and a respect for our actions and our music. All we can do is keep pushing forward and decide what next step makes the most sense. And that's what we were doing.

When young musicians are told to keep pushing, to help the other bands and people in their scene and to avoid burning bridges, this is why. My whole relationship with Ellefson and Hazaert started way before it ever blossomed into anything. Our paths started way back when I was with a completely different band, doing different things and with a different sound; hell, our relationship started before the industry became a different animal.

That brief encounter turned into a relationship that got rekindled when I helped him by booking him in Connecticut. The connection built slowly as we bonded, gained trust, and when things were at the right level of comfort, we found an opportunity to team up.

Another thing you need to learn quickly is the balance of persistence. You're going to hear "no" a ton in this business, even from friends. You need to learn when to ignore the "no" and push until you get what you want. I broke Thom's balls until he responded, like I always do, and still do to this day. That's what it takes. You've got to hit him up ten times to get an answer. And then finally, you know, you might get the answer you want. On the flipside, sometimes you need to walk away and look at the "no" from a distance to see if maybe that's the wrong tree to bark up at that time.

Thom was a busy guy. He was always juggling a lot of balls. Too many. But he also got a lot of things done. He's a great 'idea man.' He has a lot of awesome marketing ideas. The problem is that when you go from one thing to the other so quickly, some things fall through the cracks. That's when communication breakdowns happen, and opportunities get missed. If you discuss six ideas and form a plan, but then only one or two of the steps get followed up on, it can hurt.

He might've been better off allowing people he trusted to help instead of doing everything himself. He has a fiery drive and a passion, but also had a hard time letting go of control.

I recognize this in him because I'm like that too. I'm guilty of that same thing. You know the old expression, 'You want to get something done right, do it yourself?' I say that often because this statement rings true a lot in this business. Often the bands and musicians and label execs and managers and whomever that makes it can find a balance of drive, passion, control, cooperation, skill, teamwork, market awareness, and a bit of luck never hurts.

Thom and David saw enough potential and talent and marketability in Dead By Wednesday to take a chance on our album. When *Darkest of Angels* got released, they also saw the demand. People responded to our record. They dug what we were doing.

Shortly after that, David expanded on his spoken word appearances to create his BASStory tour. While still spinning stories and discussing his history, David was now actually playing some Megadeth songs live. He would book these shows around the country and pick one of his EMP bands from different areas, who he appreciated and who he thought was talented enough to learn a few songs. The band would open, then he would play, but he would do his solo thing. Then at the end, he would bring different musicians up to jam with him, which included me.

We did more stuff close to my neck of the woods, under the BASStory name, in Waterbury, CT and Manchester, NH. Then we added stops in Massachusetts, New Jersey, New York. In Buffalo, we played the Evening Star. On Long Island, we played in Amityville. It grew and helped solidify my relationship with David as a drummer, as well as a standup guy who understood the hustle.

I booked shows. I promoted. I played. I loaded gear. I road managed. I handled money. I made myself as useful as I could. David follows his 'yes man' mentality, so I tried too as well.

David Ellefson added, "'To whom much is given, much is expected.' Right? It's a biblical quote that applies, because if you're given a lot and you sit back and do nothing, you squander the blessing, you know? If you're given a gift, don't waste it. You need to use those talents. You have an obligation to live life following those words. Sometimes that means you gotta roll up your sleeves and get your hands dirty. Christian has his sights set on higher things, better things, a better life. He is not opposed to work.

"I grew up on a farm, and no matter how long you had been in the farming business, every year, you broke open the equipment, and you started tilling the soil. It doesn't matter how rich of a farmer you are; you tilled the soil and got your hands dirty in the process. The soil gives you your crop, and your crop is your livelihood. It's the same as a musician in the entertainment industry. You have to go back to the beginning of the cycle. Each song, each album, each tour has a beginning. We set the same gear up for each show, you know? In the music business, no one is above humping gear. You get out your tools and get your hands dirty. If you're too cool to load in or load out your gear, you don't belong there."

I took it really seriously. Wouldn't you? Think about it, this is my chance to play Megadeth tunes with the bass player of fucking Megadeth. These opportunities don't happen often. Shit, a lot of musicians never get a chance like this, so there was no way I was going to blow it. I decided I'd show David what I'm all about.

I planted myself in front of my kit, and I learned all these crazy songs to a tee. I was not going to show up looking like a slacker, because this could represent my one and only chance with David. If I failed, I'd harbor that regret for the rest of my life. If I kicked ass, it could lead to all sorts of cool stuff. Maybe David records a solo record or starts a new band, or maybe when I build enough trust with him, he might refer me to another band or label or solo artist to tour and record with them as well. Maybe it leads to him helping DBW get opening slots with national and international bands. For all I know, if I blew him away, I might one day get tapped as the fucking drummer for Megadeth.

But only if I nailed my parts and showed I could handle myself on the road.

Gar Samuelson, the drummer in the early days of the band, came from a jazz background. He incorporated a lot of weird stuff into his beats that most metal guys aren't used to playing. He's probably one of the best metal drummers, which is funny, because he wasn't even a metalhead himself. I really enjoy a lot of songs from the Nick Menza era too. Some of the beats require a very different approach and techniques, and I won't sugarcoat it; I had a hard time transcribing some of it.

Why?

Go back and listen to those early Megadeth records, and you'll hear they aren't the most well-produced songs. They worked with a limited budget back in those days. The songs are great, and I love the albums, but there I was, sitting at my kit, trying to pick parts out and dissect each tune, and I had a hard time with some of it. Is that double bass right there or not? What did he just do with that fill? It was a tedious process. I'd play a section and listen via headphones. I'd map it out. I'd play it a few times. I wasn't sure if I had it, so I'd listen again. Maybe watch some old YouTube videos. Repeat. Repeat. Repeat.

Growing up, I was a big Metallica fan. Because of the whole animosity between Dave Mustaine and Metallica, I felt like I had to pick sides, so I didn't listen to Megadeth as much as I probably would have if things were cool. So, I was familiar with the back catalogue, but I didn't have a deep knowledge of them. As I delved deeper and deeper into the bones of the music, I gained a new perspective beyond the lo-fi production value on stuff like, "Black Friday," "The Conjuring," and "Devil's Island."

What they wrote, their musicianship, how they wrote, and the technicality of the songs raise Megadeth's catalogue up so much higher than almost any other band, including Metallica, whom I love. The music is aggressive and busy. There's less open space than you find in the songs of their peers.

And, in hindsight, you look at the trajectory Megadeth took, then you can't help but respect it. They went through so much to get where they are. They never compromised. They never sold out. They never altered their sound to please the masses. They stayed true to themselves, and all these years later, they are still part of the "big four."

I'm not saying that as a guy who has played drums for David Ellefson, though I can see how it would look that way. I'm saying it as a musician who enjoyed them but never truly appreciated their talent until I took the extra time to understand just how fucking great they are as a band. They don't have many simple, catchy hooks, and the production is rough around the edges, so I can see how a lot of people don't give that early stuff enough of a chance.

It wasn't easy or quick to learn, but it made me a better drummer.

There's always preshow nerves, no matter how much you practice. There's also pre-tour nerves. Those are more intense because you've got more risk and reward riding on the line. If you bomb on stage at a local gig, you just tuck your tail and go home to fix the issues. When you're going on the road, there's no time to adjust or revamp the tour. You can either stick your chest out, kill it on stage, and show your pride, or you take the abuse from unhappy customers every night.

Add in the fact this was a tour with a well-established musician taking a chance on us, and that pressure builds and builds and builds. We wanted everything to go perfectly, so only having one soundcheck to mess with was less than ideal.

We were pros though, and so was David.

The only practice we had before the first show was at the soundcheck. I've heard that approach referred to as a "throw and go." David had told us to learn "Go to Hell," "Symphony of Destruction," and a couple others. We ran through stuff, and David offered feedback. He told us what he liked and what he didn't. He reminded us to watch for a certain change. General stuff. Now, on this first of BASStory dates, the jam part at the end was almost an afterthought. It was like the encore. To me though, it was a job I was expected to nail.

After soundcheck, the general feeling was very positive. David knew we could play.

David Ellefson said, "It normally only takes me until the first chorus of a song to know if the drummer can hang. Can he find the groove? You're not going to impress me with flashy fills and overplaying if you can't keep the basic groove. If you have that, the rest will fall into place. At a concert, the music is almost the least important thing. It has to be a given that the music is going to shine, but there are so many other elements to the day of a concert. The music is an hour to an hour and a half out of that day."

Ron "Bumblefoot" Thal is a guitarist with a stellar resume, who was now going to have the honor of touring with me. Ha! He opened the shows, playing guitar and doing his solo thing too, and then he joined for the jam at the end as well.

Most of you reading know the name and need no explanation, but some of you are searching your memory banks. He might best be known for his work on "Chinese Democracy" in Guns N' Roses, though that is ignoring his strong output of solo stuff as well as Sons of Apollo, Asia, and a bunch more. He has solo records, he's toured as a hired gun, and he's been the main songwriter in projects. Bumblefoot has done it all, but I still don't think he gets enough credit for his vocals. Actually, he could record a record of him reading cereal labels and I'd buy it, since the tone and timbre of his speaking voice is relaxing and welcoming.

We hit it off right away.

Why? Bumblefoot is a walking, talking jukebox. He can play anything. He is a chameleon on the guitar, and he can sing too. Very few people come close to the talent that dude possesses. Yet, with all his skill and experience, Bumblefoot comes across as a genuine person. He is real. He doesn't have an ego. He doesn't have hang-ups.

When asked about clicking with drummers, Bumblefoot said, "First thing, before we even play, is that they've got to be a cool person, a good person. Is this someone I'll want to share the stage with, have in my life, and hang out with? Then, of course, they've got to be able to play. Can they groove? They don't have to be fancy. They don't need to do a million fills. They just need to be steady. The drummer lays the foundation, and you need a solid foundation. If they want to get fancy with fills, it's all good, as long as they get in and out without breaking the groove. Christian is all of that. Cool on and off stage, solid, and can play fancy without breaking the groove."

I knew it could work.

Bumblefoot said, "Christian is his own dude, from the hair to the way he talks. I can relate to his strong, East Coast accent and vibe. He's focused and organized. He can beat the shit out of a drumkit with Dead By Wednesday, and then shift into a fucking solo acoustic song, where he's singing and playing guitar and hitting his cajon box. He's very versatile. Christian is more of a musician. Some people are just drummers, which is great too. They sit behind the kit, and they play, but Christian can do a lot of other things as well."

Dave Sharpe had joined DBW about a month before my relationship with Ellefson started to bear fruit. You want to talk about being in the right place at the right time? He joined the band, and then almost as quickly, Ellefson needed a guitarist for his tour. Now, it could've been any of another thousand guitarists who were available, but Dave is also a 'Yes, and ...?' guy. He is smart. He is professional. We just work really well together. He always has my back, and I his. I would also be a dick if I didn't spend a few seconds to say my bandmate, Dave Sharpe, is a kickass guitarist.

Now, whereas I am animated, and I wear my heart on my sleeve, Dave is reserved. He doesn't get excited. He doesn't get caught up in the moment like I do. He is a metal guitarist who just landed a gig playing with an established metal act which is led by arguably the best-known metal bassist, and he took it all in stride. He remained stone-faced, holding it all in for himself. Dave can be hard to read sometimes. That's part of being professional, sure, but come on, I was jumping out of my shoes with excitement. Would it kill you to crack a smile, Dave?

So, soundcheck was great. David gave us feedback. Everyone knew what they needed to do to make the first show a success. On my end, the only other worry was to make sure DBW had a great set as well. Double duty once again. No pressure, right?

David came out on stage alone with just a laptop and did his spoken word thing. He told stories, he got into philosophy, and then he pivoted into teaching bass playing.

He would play along to some things he had programmed on his computer for a bit, and then about halfway through his set, he started to call us up, one by one. Dead By Wednesday was the opening band, so we were there and already set up. He'd call me up first to do a drum and bass thing. He and I did parts from "Peace Sells" and "Dawn Patrol." He would talk about the riffs and the style and get into tidbits about writing songs. He would answer questions throughout the whole set too.

Then Dave Sharpe came out, and the DBW vocalist would come out, and we played a few full songs.

By the third show on the run, we were tight.

Bumblefoot was comfortable. "When you get on stage with Christian, you can count on him to play the song without worrying about anything train-wrecking … at least from the drummer's side."

The shows drew well, and we all saw the potential to keep the BASStory tour rolling.

David had several dates booked in Florida a few weeks after our shows with him. The tour leg was booked before our run, so we weren't involved. I wanted to keep my name and face in front of David. I wanted the ride to continue.

I told Thom, "I know Dave and I are the new guys in your operation, and you haven't budgeted us for those Florida shows. We will fly down on our own dime, get ourselves from show to show, and bring it every night."

I started making phone calls, intent on making both myself and Dave available to perform at the Florida shows. The first number on my list was my buddy Greg DiErrico. He was a Connecticut musician buddy of mine who I've played on and off with, that relocated to Florida. He told me he could put me and Dave up for a few nights, but being the good soul that he is, he took it further. Being a bassist himself, Greg said that if we came, we could even borrow his car as long as we would introduce him to David, being one of his favorite bass players. After a quick search online, I secured two plane tickets for ninety-nine dollars apiece.

Boom. Without putting us too much out of pocket, we had a way down, a place to stay, and a car to follow David's tour van. Without my old buddy Greg DiErrico offering to help me with a ride and a place to crash in Florida, I probably couldn't have afforded or done the trip. If I hadn't gone on that second run, who knows what could've happened? David might've found another drummer capable of taking my place. He might've decided he didn't need a drummer for BASStory. Those first dates might've been my last.

Was it easy? No.

Did my family need to sacrifice on my behalf? They sure did.

Would I do it again? Hell yes.

Author's note: Shortly after writing the previous section, Greg DiErrico was found dead at his Florida home. Apparently, he had committed suicide. Our hearts and thoughts are with his family. Thanks for the memories, Greg. We love and miss you "Uncle Sausage." Rest in peace and power.

Dave and I traveled to all the shows that David was playing. It was fun keeping our own schedule, and since we were using the house band equipment, we didn't have to lug all our gear around. We didn't need any rehearsal, as we were still fresh from the other shows. We just got up with him and kicked ass. No egos, no expectations, no looking for handouts. We handled ourselves professionally, had fun and David saw that. More importantly, he recognized and appreciated it.

David Ellefson talked a bit about getting to know me and my style of playing. "Christian is solid. He shows up prepared. He's got a good feel. I like that he's always willing to jump in on background vocals, because anyone who can sing, automatically adds value to their place in the ensemble. People at the show are listening to the vocals.

So, I don't really view Christian as just a drummer. When I call on him, I get the whole package. He can advance shows, he can drive the truck, he can handle the money, he can work the merch booth. In the tech world, they call it a solutions provider. That's what Christian is to me."

In the music industry, relationships matter. Sure, you have to be a professional, and you have to have talent, but if you're a dick on the road, no one will want you around. Touring is close quarters. You ride in a van full of people; hell, even if you have a tour bus, it's not like you ever have any privacy. You have rows of bunks. When one of you snores, you all hear it. When one of them talks in their sleep, everyone knows what they're dreaming about. You can't hold your booze? People get sick of stumbling to the bathroom and stepping in your throw up. Get it?

And word travels fast. You have no idea how small the community of touring musicians is until you mess up on the road. You want to stunt your growth and trim your opportunities to tour? Well, that's easy. Pack your ego. Treat the roadcrew like dirt. Complain that the soundman is clueless. Berate the crowd on and off the stage. Disrespect the fans, the club, the promoter, or just about anyone else helping your band succeed and you'll find yourself back in mom-and-pop's basement doing Skynyrd covers.

So, we punched in on time. And we brought our hard hats. We worked. We played. We set up. We tore down. We watched the merch booth. We kept the equipment safe. We treated the fans like old friends. We held our openers in high regard and our fellow bandmates with due respect. In return, we became a true part of the band. We were as tied in with Ellefson and crew (Thom and Melody Myers) as we could do on our own. Now it was up to them.

Why?

You can't force respect. You can't bully your way onto the team. David and Thom had seen our talent. They had witnessed our desire. They had benefited from our sacrifice and our hard work, but if they weren't comfortable enough to trust us, none of that would matter.

I mean, maybe for a time. We might play more shows. We might keep in touch and grab dinner occasionally. We already had a handful of stories to share, lifelong memories, so there would always be common ground. A certain amount of respect, but to me, that wasn't enough.

I didn't work this hard for a nod and a handshake. I didn't practice and push myself for a couple watercooler stories. I came to find a place on stage with a legend. I desired to see a sea of heads banging to my beat. City after city, country after country, album after album, I wanted to experience it all.

At one point, during an off day on the tour, Dave Sharpe and I got asked to join David at a studio in Tampa, Florida to work on some new material. He had set up a late-night session to get some stuff on tape. I think it was midnight or later as we recorded.

Thom and Melody were there as well. Thom sang on the song, and Melody helped with all the graphic design and media.

I don't think they had initially planned on creating and recording a complete song that night, because when we showed up, the drum set wasn't studio ready. The drumheads were pretty beat up, and they only had a couple drum mics available. I spent about an hour tuning and performing surgery on the kit to improve it as much as I could with what I had brought with me on the road. Always be overprepared.

David had some guitar riffs that we jammed out and expanded. Within a few short hours, we had the song, "Vultures," which ended up as the opening track on the *Sleeping Giants* album, which would get released under his Ellefson band moniker in July of 2019.

"With the other stuff we had done up to that point, Christian was playing beats that were already established," David Ellefson said. "'Vultures' was the first time Christian and I really were able to create together. The song basically wrote itself from riffs I put together in about an hour. Christian understood that I needed him to fit the song. I needed him available. I didn't want 'busy' playing that would get in the way. He is supportive in that role. I really appreciated that. His drum fills and beats were very complimentary to my guitar riffs. To be honest, I didn't have to think about what he was doing or make any suggestions or changes.

As a composer in the studio, where time is money, and being in the midst of a tour, where time is super limited, to be able to get a complete thought out in one night is satisfying. I mean, we got a solid song committed to tape, and Christian added an electrifying drum take to the mix."

Looking back, it was such a fun night, flying by the seat of our pants. I hear things I'd change if I'd had more time with the song and time in the studio, but the song itself is killer, and I'm proud to be a part of it.

David is always on the move, so he works with whoever he has close by. A lot of that album got recorded with his "European Ellefson" lineup, but Dave Sharpe and I are a part of the opener, and that'll always be a career highlight.

Also in Florida, around this time, was the Playback Independent Music Expo, which took place over the course of a couple warm and wonderful days in October of 2018. David had teamed his record labels (EMP and Combat), his coffee brand (Ellefson Coffee), and his merch arm (MerchLive) with the Recording Academy and a local music equipment store (Replay Guitar Exchange) to create an event at a storied venue called Brass Mug.

The two-day conference had seminars, meet and greets, panels, workshops, and masterclasses taught by some of the best heavy musicians, engineers, and producers working in the industry, including ... hold on, I need to take a deep breath to get through all of these ... Troy Sanders of Mastodon, Brian "Head" Welch of Korn, Bumblefoot of Bumblefoot, Grammy-winning producer Max Norman, freakin' Mike Clink was there, Toby Wright, Dirk Verbeuren of Megadeth, Kyle Sanders of HELLYEAH!, and, shit, like another twenty names you've been listening to your whole lives either playing on an album or helping produce it.

Kyle and Troy are brothers, and they both play bass in kickass bands. I got to jam with both of them, which was a trip. We did a couple of KISS songs. I remember doing "God of Thunder" for sure and having the dudes from Mastodon turning to me afterward, saying, "Hey, good fuckin' job dude!" I was glowing.

After jamming with more and more people, you build the confidence that you belong on stage with them. Each guitarist and bassist and vocalist brings their unique character and background and preferences, so part of the job as a drummer is to listen and observe and find ways to serve that particular performer's style.

Looking at it from the opposite side, Bumblefoot explained how he sees it from the guitarist's perspective. "When you play, you need to know that you can lose yourself in something without getting sucker-punched by people who don't know what the fuck they are doing."

I was having a blast on the BASStory tour, but the end of the run was closer than I'd admit to myself. I needed one last moment to prove myself. I had to guarantee a spot on a roster hitting the road. What could I do?

I laid in my hotel room, plotting, planning, hoping, committing to not rest until I figured it out. Nothing was going to distract me, nothing would stop me, nothing—dammit! My phone wouldn't stop beeping. I couldn't let that bother me now. I …

I needed to check my fucking messages.

David texted me from his hotel room, *Hey, what are your plans for June?*

CHAPTER TWELVE

The Conjuring of More Tours

I reread the text from David about June.

I'm at a hotel, fresh out of the shower, post gig. I'm still running on adrenaline and thinking of the things through my head about how I played, who I met, and trying to shut things down for the night. I was drained.

I replied, As far as I know, not much planned. Why? What's up?

I'm thinking he's got a BBQ to invite us to or something.

His response almost knocked me out of my hotel bed. How would you like to play drums for me and Frank Bello for a couple shows?

Of course, you know Frank plays bass in Anthrax, but he and David also have a project together called Altitudes and Attitude (A&A).

My first thought was 'Holy shit,' before my cynical side forced me to question whether the whole thing could be a joke.

Hmmm, play drums in a project with two of the biggest metal bass players ever? I showed the text to Dave Sharpe, who was in the hotel room with me. We were geeking out at the thought, even if it was only to play for a couple shows.

We started talking about how cool it would be and sharing stories about Anthrax and Megadeth memories from when we were younger. We got so wrapped up that I had forgotten to text David back. He had sent a few more texts: *We have a CD release show in Brooklyn. ... We might have more dates. ... There's a free in-store appearance. ...* And *There's a few other possibilities.*

I was too excited to read or comprehend what he was telling me. I joked with Dave Sharpe about messaging that I wasn't interested, but in the end, I couldn't even take a chance like that.

I texted back that I was game for whatever. Bring me along for the ride, and I'll prove myself.

On the recording, Altitudes and Attitude had used a hired gun, Jeff Friedl. Jeff has a great track record. He can bring it. He's laid down stuff for A Perfect Circle, Filter, Devo, and others. He wasn't available for the release show in NYC, however, so here I was in the right spot at the right time.

This band was a departure for Ellefson from his Megadeth and solo efforts. I mean, the songs have an edge, and at points, the album gets heavy, but I consider the band more hard rock than metal. Both Frank and David were able to try new sounds and stretch into fresh territory than they get to explore with their main bands. I think that's why they enjoy doing this material as much as they do.

So, the logical assumption to make about how I got the gig is to say I was on tour with David and because I'm reliable, proven talent, sober, and cheaper labor than most. I live near NYC, so transporting me would be easy too. That's what I assumed anyway, but it turns out I was wrong. See if you can keep up with this:

The bassist of Anthrax needs a drummer for a side project. He talks to the bassist of Megadeth, who is also in the band, and they discuss some names. I am in the mix, though I don't know that yet. From what I gather, David didn't push for me at first, because everything was so fresh, and they were probably looking for someone with more of a known name. So, he just wasn't sure yet, but since I was on the road with them, he asked Ron "Bumblefoot" Thal.

Bumblefoot has a passion for music, and it comes through. He loves sharing that joy with fellow musicians and fans alike. He's not an egomaniac. He's not a phony rock star.

I promise I'm not just saying that because of what happens next …

So, David asks Bumblefoot who he thinks Altitudes and Attitude should work with as a live drummer for the band's upcoming CD release show. Bumblefoot was going to be the lead guitarist for the band's live lineup.

When Bumblefoot was asked about suggesting me for the tour, he grinned and said, "I really tried to talk Bello and Ellefson out of using Christian. I tried my hardest. I told them, 'Look, there's a million drummers out there. Why would you pick Christian?' But they were stuck on it. They seemed hellbent on using him."

He was joking. At least, I hope so.

He continued, chuckling, "No, no. It was an obvious choice. Christian was already on the road and had proven he could be counted on. You know he's going to nail the shit down. He's consistent too. He's not one of those guys where one night he's drunk and sloppy, the next night he has drama with his girlfriend, he's not showing up late, and all that bullshit. So, when they asked for my vote, I said, 'Why not Christian?'"

"Oh," David said. "Great idea."

It's funny, not even my mother calls me Christian anymore. David does though. I'm not sure if David prefers to call me that due to the religious ties to my name or what, but it cracks me up.

David Ellefson said, "He got on my radar as Christian. I didn't know him as Opus, the local legend from his band, because I'm not from that area. All respect to Dead By Wednesday, but they haven't reached the level of, like, KISS. You know, I call Ace Frehley, Ace, because that's his professional name. He earned it on an international stage. Now, if Christian wants me to call him Opus, I will, but I think he has a great name. Christian Lawrence is a name that exudes professional acumen. Opus has a local hero connotation to me, but I don't view him as just a local guy. I view Christian Lawrence as a global superstar, and I'd rather help raise him up to that level."

In the end, David told me he actually did have me in mind but wanted to get input from the other bandmembers first. As soon as Bumblefoot gave me his stamp of approval though, David felt like it was an 'automatic yes.'

Bumblefoot recognized the dynamics between David and me, and he understood the situation. "Christian wanted to do it, but he didn't want to have to ask to do it. He didn't want to put a blemish on the relationship by pushing or begging. I was glad to talk to David on Christian's behalf. Not that I think it would have tarnished anything, as those guys both respect and appreciate each other, but asking can be tough, and this helped avoid any awkwardness."

I dug into the songs to prepare for the A&A album release happening at the famous Saint Vitus Bar in Brooklyn, NY. I realized quickly how good the songs were. Right off the bat, "Leviathan" and "Here Again" stuck out to me.

The band was started by David and Frank as they wrote music to accompany their playing during a promotional tour for Hartke Amps. They were doing clinics and masterclasses as part of their sponsorships. I guess as they put the songs together, they realized they had something cool happening.

The more they wrote, the more they enjoyed working together. From hearsay, Frank had a bunch of riffs, and he took on the main vocal duties. David slays on rhythm guitar. Frankie is an amazing songwriter and guitarist as well. And obviously they both play bass on the record too. Ace Frehley from KISS also plays on the record. Nita Strauss is on a song. 'Nuff said!

Rehearsals for the A&A shows went well. Even with positive vibes and with egos in check, there is always a learning curve to playing with new musicians. Each of your coworkers, bosses, and subordinates have their own personality and quirks and preferences on how things should go, and it's the same with musicians. It's not about right and wrong; it's a comfort thing, a habit thing, an instinct or feel thing.

As the drummer, backing an all-star lineup, I try to go with the flow and to create an atmosphere conducive to what works for the guys.

I learned quickly that Frank is a business-first guy. To put it another way, Frank doesn't fuck around. He doesn't want a bunch of joking around getting in the way of practice. He is funny, and he likes to cut loose, but not until he has gotten his work done and he gives his obvious permission to relax.

We did the CD release shows and that led to another Northeast and East Coast run.

They gave me a microphone to do some backup vocals. You know me. Even if you don't know me personally, face-to-face, you've read this far and have a sense of my larger-than-life personality. If someone puts me on stage in front of a crowd and gives me a microphone, I'm gonna say something. You know, I learned from watching Lars. I spoke to the crowd between songs at a show one night unannounced, and afterward, I got sat down for a talk.

Frank said, "I'm the singer."

Frank wants all the stage banter to go through him. It's very understandable.

He was cool about it. "It's not an ego thing. I'm the director up there. When was the last time you heard a drummer talk on stage, aside from doing backing vocals or Phil Collins, lol?"

I got the message. I kept my mouth shut and did my job. My feelings weren't hurt, you know? I knew my role. I wouldn't have talked at all if I had been told up front, so I also felt bad, because I tend to take things to heart and need to leave emotions out of business more.

There was a point where he did encourage me to speak up on stage though for a specific purpose. The guys in the band are all huge KISS fans. "Detroit Rock City" was part of our set, but they would fuck around with other KISS songs live from time to time as well. We even sometimes play "Rip It Out," one of Ace's solo tunes. If they weren't playing KISS songs, they were talking about KISS on stage or off stage. Like I said, Ace Frehley played on the album, okay? They were very serious about KISS. So was I.

One night, as they were messing around between songs, someone in the crowd shouted, "Beth!"

Most of you know that's a KISS song. Some of you immediately had the piano and strings of the ballad playing in your head. For the two or three of you reading who didn't catch it, "Beth" was written and sung by the band's dickhead drummer, Peter Criss, who you'll recall I "met" earlier in the book.

Momentarily forgetting my vow of silence, something took over, and I automatically started singing the song, "Beth." Heck, I was the drummer here, so it was my song to sing as much as anyone, right? I didn't want to piss anyone off, but the crowd wanted the best, so I gave them the best. Ha!

I'm doing a good job. The crowd is into it.

Frank turns around, and he is laughing and encouraging me to continue. I sang my heart out until I couldn't remember any more of the lyrics around the third verse, I believe.

I stayed in my lane but still found a moment to cut loose and shine on that tour. There's even video proof of that somewhere online I believe. The guys understood. We're all showmen up there. We love the attention. We love playing to a crowd. Otherwise, we wouldn't put up with most of the rest of the business and bullshit.

Even if I wasn't the front man and wasn't expected to talk and sing and be the focus, Frank is a seasoned pro, and even he knew to go with the flow. The crowd enjoyed the unexpected turn of events. What a cool, unscripted moment. One I'll never forget.

The A&A tour expanded from the East Coast leg to a Midwest run. The clubs we played were full or close to packed. Sure, Frank and David might be accustomed to playing large theaters and festivals, but the crowds were energetic and into it. You had Anthrax fans, Megadeth fans, A&A fans, a few DBW fans even, and everyone was cool. Sometimes metal fans get a bad rap for being impatient or unwilling to give new stuff a chance, but all the shows I played, the vibe stayed so positive, even if it wasn't the certain old-school metal style they expected at first coming from them with this project. I think that has a lot to do with the guys in the band and how positive they stay and how welcoming they are to their fans. It's genuine. It's heartfelt.

I remember playing "Leviathan" in Flint, Michigan at the Machine Shop. It's an instrumental from their album, *Get*

It Out, out on Megaforce Records. I had a front row—or maybe you could say back row—seat, and I got to groove along with three of the top players on the rock touring circuit for the past couple decades. The song sounds great on the record, but live, we did an extended version to let the guys feel the song out a bit and jam. At one point in the song, David cuts loose on the bass and shows his speed and accuracy and his ability to create a cool atmosphere with a little improv solo. His tone is solid, and his playing blew me away. I've seen and heard him play up close countless times, but he still surprises me. The guy is getting better and better with age. He loves playing. He loves learning. It's refreshing to witness. That's what I also try to do. Always strive for getting better. Never stay stagnant or stale. Push yourself.

The BASStory, Altitudes and Attitude, and Ellefson shows blurred together as one mega tour in my mind somehow. I learned a lot of songs. In fact, it was an ongoing joke that my guitarist, Dave Sharpe, and myself would laugh about while traveling. "What songs will David call us with to learn last minute today and throw at us next?" We almost thought he did it on purpose to challenge us and see how we would do under pressure or something, because, for a while there, he would literally hit me up the morning of a show and say, "Hey do you know 'Green Manalishi' by Priest or 'Mr. Brownstone' by Guns N' Roses," or some other crazy cover tune they wanted to jam on that night, and honestly, you can't say no. We were listening to the songs in the van on the way to the gigs, trying to remember the structure for our quick practice, hopefully at soundcheck if we were lucky, before playing it live later at the show. So, Sharpe would be in the back seat with his guitar out, literally learning the notes and solos as we drove, and I'm beating on the steering wheel. All the hard work was worth it for sure though. I made a ton of contacts. I kept Dead By Wednesday going. I kept Dave

Sharpe locked into our team spirit by helping him land the tour manager job for Altitudes and Attitude, as well as playing with Ellefson when needed for most of the shows too.

Each project has different needs. Each tour leg has its own obstacles. Hell, each show has its own personality, quirks, and atmosphere. Part of my job is to be flexible. Part of it is to read the room and know what is needed. Aside from that, I bring personality, aggressive and powerful playing, focus, good vibes, and energy to the table. So far, my traits have helped me earn some great opportunities.

We had a lot of fun supporting his spoken word events, but then Thom took it a step further and asked me and Dave Sharpe to do a full string of dates as David's backing band. This wasn't the same half-a-set format. No talk. No laptop. The shows were billed as an hour-long set of heavy rock and metal, including some rare Mega-songs that they usually didn't ever play live.

We added more dates and more songs, and we were able to carve out time to practice. David and Thom came to my place, and we practiced at the remodeled space in the garage. I told them the whole story about how the studio got made on a reality TV show, and they loved it.

After practice, the room was buzzing. David was smiling and offering great feedback. He told us we "threw down" and we "knew our shit." It felt great to get a positive response.

David Ellefson said, "You know, I never have to worry about what Christian will bring from behind the kit. He's got a deep bag of tricks and an impressive repertoire of songs in his pocket. That's huge to me."

He did offer a mixed compliment and a criticism as well, which helped. He said, in some ways, my playing reminded him of Nick Menza. Apparently, Nick liked to play fast, driving the songs forward, and I do too. It was an efficient way to communicate that David recognized I could play fast and hard but that maybe I didn't have to push the envelope so much.

Getting mentioned in the same league as Menza by one of his former bandmates was a super compliment to me, even if coupled with a lighthearted dig. I grew up along with Megadeth. I read about their tours and recording and drama in magazines, saw them on MTV. Those guys had songs on soundtracks to movies I watched in the theater. They got nominated for Grammys almost every year in the early to mid-'90s. You can sit here reading and stay unimpressed, but Megadeth was headlining festivals around the world, playing to over 100k people on some nights. They are metal royalty. And it seemed I had made my way into their extended family.

I don't want this to turn into a gush fest, but if there was a proper moment to take a breath and allow myself to reflect on what's going on, this is it.

David Ellefson is hanging out in my garage-turned-practice studio room to jam before we head out on a national tour, playing solo stuff, Megadeth material, and some covers. Fuck yes.

We hit the road in 2019, the Sleeping Giants album was due in July via Combat Records, and it seemed like every night brought a different guest appearance on stage.

A few days before the release party, we played on Long Island, and Darryl "DMC" McDaniels from Run-DMC joined us! Not only had he done some guest vocals on the Sleeping Giants record, but they were filming a video for the song that day. Any time you can pick the brain of someone who has carved out a long career in entertainment, you come away better for it. DMC came across as humble, funny, and the man knows his heavy music. Before our set, we were all hanging out backstage, and we jammed out "It's Tricky" by Run-DMC with DMC on vocals and Ellefson on bass. I clapped and beatboxed. There were seven to ten people in the room, no amps and no egos, just excited goodwill. That was a special moment. Not that I need to tell you. You get it. I sometimes have to remind myself to enjoy the genuine cool stuff and to let some of the irritations of the road roll off my back.

DMC said, "You're a beast!" after soundcheck.

You've read about my background, so I don't have to reset the narrative for you to comprehend how huge that was to hear from a legend like him.

On the way to the Token Lounge in Michigan for a mid-August scorcher, David asked me, "Would you mind if Charlie Behler used your kit and joined me for a couple songs tonight?"

Charlie, or Chuck, Behler started with Megadeth as a drum tech back in the '80s, but he became the band's drummer after Gar and Chris Poland were ousted. He wasn't with Megadeth long, but apparently, he and Ellefson had remained on good terms.

Charlie had big shoes to fill with playing Gar's stuff. Again, Gar was a jazz guy playing metal, and thrash was still developing. Today, every metal drummer knows the speed and power and clichés that come with the territory. Back then, they were inventing all that, so Charlie had to retrain himself on the fly.

Charlie walked in, hunched over, using a cane. He appeared unsteady, fragile. I mean, he struggled to walk up to us. I don't want to speak out of school, but that's how it appeared to me. The rest of the band and crew expressed some of the same worries. Would he even get through a couple of songs?

I'm thinking, how is this guy going to play "Hook in Mouth," which we had added to the set, along with "Liar" and some other Megadeth tunes? David was also working on more solo material, giving us a chance to play original stuff.

He and I got a chance to talk. Charlie was humble, polite, and I could tell he still had a passion for the music. Did he have the ability to play it, though? Right before soundcheck, he dropped another bombshell. Charlie hadn't played drums in over ten years.

He hobbled up onto the stage and sat behind my kit. I wanted to stay close by in case he fell off the throne; I mean, that's how unsure of things I felt. I didn't want him getting hurt.

The band started, and Charlie came right in not missing a beat. Double bass, no issue. Hitting the skins hard, no issue. He sounded great.

The whole thing played out like a scene from *Willy Wonka and the Chocolate Factory*. Remember when Willy Wonka first comes out of his factory with his cane? The crowd goes silent, and you can see concern on people's faces. He slowly makes his way toward the gate, and then does the somersault. That's how it felt to watch.

He is up on the stage, having a total blast.

I asked him if he just used the cane to fake people out, and he started laughing. We had dinner that night, and he thanked me for letting him use my drums and complimented my playing as I picked his brain. He offered encouragement to keep going and talked to me like an equal.

There's a lot of drummers vying for a very limited amount of paying gigs, so competition can turn good people ugly. I've experienced it firsthand. Instead of supporting each other, some people try to tear others down to make way for themselves or to feed their own egos and needs. That's why it's so refreshing to chill with a guy who has played in front of huge crowds and been a part of major label dealings, yet he can still remain a decent human being.

The negatives of independent touring can be a hassle, but sometimes happy accidents prove to make things positive. Low budgets mean limiting who you can hire to fill out a band. Smaller vans can cause logistics issues on the merch end. Tough decisions need to be made, with cost as the deciding factor almost one hundred percent of the time. We had a batch of dates on the West Coast, but we needed a guitarist to complete the lineup. For most bands, this can be crippling, especially in a time crunch. Ellefson knows everyone though, which helps. He can make calls and get stuff done. On our suggestion, David called Steve Conley, who was his bandmate in F5 and who was currently playing guitar for Flotsam and Jetsam.

Flotsam isn't a household name, but many remember that, at one point, a young Jason Newstead played bass and wrote lyrics for the band before joining Metallica. Back when I was, like, fifteen, my band opened for them here in Connecticut. The concert happened during a crazy snowstorm, so dragging people out felt like pulling teeth. Our band, being the local kids, convinced twenty or thirty people to check us out and risk driving, which made for almost the entire crowd.

Even back then, the guys in Flotsam and Jetsam couldn't have treated us better. You don't hear many stories about headliners acting cool to the younger openers, especially on crappy snowstorm days when the band plays in front of an almost empty room. I had an idea back then how cool it was for them to treat us as equals, but now with years of experience on the road, I've got to tell you, Flotsam and Jetsam went legend that night.

Eric AK from Flotsam remembered it this way. "The first time I heard Christian, I remember thinking, it's too bad he kinda sucks, 'cause he's a super nice dude. Christian is a musician who wants to get better every time he plays, and so he gives his all every performance. The last time I heard him play I thought, Holy shit! Opus is the dopest!"

The guys hung out after the gig and imparted us with wisdom and tomfoolery from the road. Eric even drove our van one night and helped us load our gear! Success in music is near impossible to achieve and ten times as hard to sustain, but being genuine and respectful human beings goes a long way toward that. I firmly believe the stereotypes of huge egos and flighty creatives does a disservice to the majority of working-class entertainers in the music industry. A small, tight-knitted group of people living and sharing a wild, vagabond lifestyle in small to medium clubs all over the globe makes for an impressive amount of kickass music and experiences. Can you tell me how these people are not essential workers?

So, they made a big impression on me at a young age.

Eric AK said, "For me, it's not really about being humble. Sometimes I can be an egomaniac. But I remember what it was like to be an opening band for a national act, and the national is unfriendly or acts like they are better than you. So, when I have the chance or I'm not in a bad mood from a less-than-acceptable performance, I will always hang with the opening bands."

I remember the concert I played with Ellefson on September 5, 2019, in Fullerton, CA at a club called the Slidebar. All the lights were out except a few small red dots on our equipment. We would start the set with "Dawn Patrol." Well, to be completely accurate, David started the show. You see, as I'm on stage in darkness, the others are still backstage. David has his bass set up with a wireless rig. He starts playing his menacing, slow riff. I come in with some cymbals. David and Thom make their way to the stage in darkness, and just as they climb up, we all join in the groove. The lights come on, the crowd is bobbing their heads, cheering us on, and the vibe is so positive. Steve Conley and Dave Sharpe rush on stage, and we launch forward into the set.

Typically, during the first few minutes of a set, there's a lot to focus on—sound, lighting, stage presence. Once I can hear everything and the adrenaline hits, I can coast through the rest. Sitting behind Steve and David, two of the most polished professionals in metal, certainly makes the early set jitters way more manageable. By the time we blast into "Go to Hell," I'm just hitting hard and taking it all in. Steve's solo is a piece of art. It looks effortless, but we all know the work it takes to get to that level.

Ellefson is friends with everyone, so the insanity didn't end there that night. He brought up his friend and vocalist John Bush to sing "Room for One More" (Anthrax) and a song they collaborated on entitled "If You Were a God." John has logged years on stage with Armored Saint and a stint or two in Anthrax. He has a solid and versatile voice that can handle anything from the melodic to the chaotic. He's a showman too. I mean, to an extent, you have to be.

Ellefson said, "To entertain, you need to be entertaining, right?"

Entertaining? We were blowing the roof off clubs on that run, and then we added guys from Flotsam and Jetsam and Armored Saint. Insane.

You can't top that.

But we did.

With guitars ringing out from a previous song, Chris Poland took the stage. You read that right. Chris Poland.

He was a huge part of Megadeth's success in the '80s, playing on two of the most influential metal albums of the era. He, along with many others, didn't part on great terms with the band, so Poland and Ellefson hadn't shared a stage in decades.

The crowd starts chanting, "Poland! Poland!"

After a bit of fanfare, Chris grinned and started into "The Conjuring," which is not only a fan favorite, but it wasn't played by Megadeth for years due to Mustaine's discomfort with some of the dark-magic-inspired lyrics—a gem that still sounds as fresh as when it came out due to its rarity in setlists.

A measure in and I start hitting the kick pedal, making a simple four count. I see Chris nodding along as he plays, grinning. I can't put myself in his shoes, but I have to imagine this moment feels special for him.

Chris glances over at Ellefson while they both play. Ellefson grins right back, singing along, as Thom starts the vocals. You know that opening groove, man. It's a creepy, powerful slow burn of a build. The music cuts out, and then returns just as suddenly, but this time, the guitars thrash and gnash over the chugging stop-then-start rhythm.

Ellefson crosses the stage to stand right next to Poland. The crowd's eyes are wide with excitement. The duo watches each other play for a few moments, all smiles. I imagine the flashbacks they must be drawing on as we drive forward. The spirit of friendship was reborn, as if they hadn't missed a day, let alone decades ... well, their hair is a bit shorter now than it was back then.

Ellefson stuck right by Chris as we chugged, thrashed, grooved, and melted faces.

After the song ended, Ellefson told the crowd that he and Chris hadn't played that together "Since, I don't know, Hawaii '87."

I helped book some of the shows and took on a lot of the legwork. I morphed into more of the tour manager during the runs. I helped organize all the itineraries. I even handled the nightly pay out.

David Ellefson said, "I would trust Christian with my entire life savings. He has earned that level of trust with me. I've played with a lot of great musicians who I have high respect for but who I wouldn't even trust to watch my wallet for five minutes."

David wanted to have one person running the ship while on the road, so I got tapped for that duty. Think about this for a second; I'm a hired gun, handling everyone's payouts. The band members have to come to me, the crew has to go through me, heck, I have to go through myself. Even Thom, who was David's personal manager, business partner, and the singer for Ellefson who had signed me, had to come to me with his receipts. It's probably the weirdest fucking thing I've ever done in my life. It was so awkward. I'm like, here's my boss coming to me to get paid for his stuff.

Thom did a lot of stuff when home, you know; all the big work happened when he wasn't touring. When he was on the road, it was sort of like he worked in chaos. So, he's like an organized chaos kind of guy. I'm neater and more organized. I've got OCD, so I'm very much all about having things in order and stuff like that, which is a good and bad thing.

All the touring in 2019 got us super tight as we geared up for the biggest metal event of the year. The MegaCruise took place October 13-18.

The cruise, hosted on a Norwegian cruise line's boat called The Jewel, was a metal fan's dream come true. The lineup was insane: Lamb of God, Anthrax, Queensryche, DevilDriver, Testament, Suicidal Tendencies, DragonForce, Overkill, Corrosion of Conformity, Metal Church, Johnny 5, and another dozen bands all packaged onto one ship for a multi-day party. And when the bands weren't playing, the various musicians were jamming together in small areas and interacting directly with everyone. They had coffee jams in the morning, photo booth events all day, autograph signings, charity auctions with all kinds of cool items, a massage parlor, a basketball court, and that's not even getting into the off the ship opportunities for fun in Mexico at the port of call. I played with idols. I played with strangers. I made a lot of contacts.

Now, you might be looking at that lineup and wondering why the biggest band didn't headline. Where was Megadeth? Well, Dave Mustaine had announced his battle with throat cancer shortly before, so he couldn't make it. No MegaCruise could be complete without an appearance by Megadeth members, so Ellefson and his band stepped in.

We were basically Megadeth that night. Insane.

At first, I had some reservations about playing in front of Dirk Verbeuren, Megadeth's current drummer, but he was super cool, supportive, and a really good dude. I turned to him before the set to discuss.

I admitted, "I feel weird playing these songs in front of you."

"Why?" He chuckled. "They're not my songs. To me, they're all cover songs too."

That truth helped me relax.

As I'm playing, I look over and see Dirk side stage, rocking out. It was a total trip. Kiko Loureiro, Megadeth's lead guitarist, was there too, so three-fourths of the band was in the room.

I'm not sure why those three hadn't done the set together. Maybe they did it out of respect for Mustaine? Maybe Mustaine didn't want them to play a Megadeth set without him? During the cruise, I saw David, Kiko, and Dirk jam with other people, and they did end up jamming out a couple songs during our set.

No matter the reason, I was having a blast. Ellefson was in top form too. We really connected. All the hours on the road had gotten us on the same page, and the adrenaline in the room elevated us that much further. We did a full set of their tunes. The crowd was satisfied, and remember, this was a crowd full of the most dedicated, hardcore Megadeth fans and it was packed. They know their stuff, and they expected the highest level of play. Obviously, they would've preferred the genuine thing, but the energy was crazy, and the mood felt so positive. Dirk gave me a high five after the set. "Dude, you kicked ass. Great job."

Getting that praise was amazing. Maybe the highest praise I had ever received on my playing ... until the following morning.

I decided to wake up early; well, to be honest, I was too excited to sleep anymore. I wanted to walk around the boat and soak it all in, mingle with the other metal fans milling about. Metal music blasted from various rooms, metal discussions took place at breakfast tables, and musicians were already planning jam sessions and sets in every nook and cranny on the ship. I wanted to relive the previous night. I hit the gym and started to fuel my workout with the excitement still buzzing through me.

David comes into the gym and sees me. He comes over and leans in close. "You know, a couple of my drummers that I play with were at our show last night, but between you and me, last night you were my drummer. You were my drummer last night bud."

I got chills.

I'm not above admitting how awesome that felt. I was overwhelmed. What a cool, classy move. He didn't have to say anything. My workout rocked. Exercising felt painless because I was floating on air.

David Ellefson said, "I have a theory on drummers; sometimes the best drummers are the ones you don't notice. I would throw Bill Barry out there. He drummed for REM for a long time. You didn't turn on one of their albums to hear Bill Barry playing; you wanted to hear Michael Stipe. Stipe is very charismatic, and the whole band is talented, but Barry was a solid drummer who kept them all together, until he retired after his brain aneurysm. They were never the same after that. What about John Bonham? Page and Plant and Jones are amazing, their songs were great, but once John died, it was over. There are exemplary guys, like Neil Peart and Stuart Copeland, with chops. The music I play and perform is better left to a guy willing to roll up their sleeves and get the job done. When you're creating, the last thing you need or want is someone stepping in ahead of you and redirecting you through life."

Before we get too far past the MegaCruise, I need to share one last surreal experience connected to it. Dave and I had a tour starting before the cruise was ending. So, we needed to disembark at the port in Encino, Mexico. We had no idea what we were getting ourselves into. First, we had to pay a fee to the government of Mexico to get off the boat there, and then had to go through extensive searches. I had no idea that CBD was illegal there … oops. So, letting that slide cost a little more money. Then try getting an Uber in Mexico without knowing Spanish. Good luck! We finally managed to snag one, and got driven through very unsavory areas, ones in which several Americans were shot to death the weeks prior, to get to the border. We had to literally walk over the border, which was overflowing with Mexicans of all walks of life trying to get over themselves. Many were obviously very poor and homeless, lined up against Trump's wall, waiting for their opportunity. It was pretty depressing to witness. After several more checks from border patrol, my feet touched down in California, and I literally kissed the ground. We then had to race to beat the clock to make our flight at LAX.

Circling back to David, I definitely think he and I clicked quickly. I think our connection is due, at least in part, to us coming from similar progressive music backgrounds. We share a lot of musical experiences, life philosophies, and we both have a desire to be entertainers.

We've logged a lot of hours together, and he's helped me learn a lot. You know how they say you don't know what you don't know until you know? Well, I'm not sure if anyone has said that, but that's how I feel.

I can point to jealousy from bandmates from my first-ever band as a driving force to keep me going. The revenge I sought for them kicking me out of a band I started proved to be a powerful motivator. Some members disliked that I got attention when they did not. Yet, those same members wouldn't lift a finger to help do the things I did to get that attention. I used that setback to fuel me. I wanted to show them how to succeed, and damn it if we didn't get close to breaking into the mainstream with Gargantua Soul.

In G-Soul, the beats I played were easy grooves. I stayed in the pocket as my bandmembers rocked over the top. It was far from flashy. I didn't get the limelight from my playing back then. I got it from my hustle.

Ellefson said, "Christian keeps his hustle muscle in great shape."

On stage and off stage, your actions and the work you put in are what matters. I have tried to learn as much as I can and to put that knowledge into action.

Eric AK said, "Christian is a very friendly guy to everyone. And as much of a high-strung pain in the ass he is sometimes, he is very respectful. He's one of those people you want in your corner. He is great at pushing himself onto people. He is great at promoting himself. Maybe he could learn when to back off from people. Sometimes, off stage, he can be too much. Like I said, super nice guy who would give you the shirt off his back, but always going full speed, always loud, always the center of attention. Not bad things, just too much at times."

With Ellefson, DBW, Poland, and these other projects, I've been able to get creative and show off what I can do, flex my musical muscles a bit. I've gotten calls from people sniffing around. It feels good to be wanted.

As stated, Ellefson prefers to call me Christian rather than Opus, and I'm starting to see why. People are taking notice of my work, taking me seriously, rather than looking at me as the local drummer Opus. I'm earning respect from my peers, while understanding I have so much more to prove to them and to myself. I'm not the young guy out there with potential. I am a road dog with experience. Playing isn't as easy as it was ten years ago. I feel it every night. After the buzz of post-show adrenaline wears off, reality is always waiting. The pain doesn't matter though because I know I can't let up. There are dozens of people who would kill for my spot. There will always be, and they are younger, hungry, and full of energy.

Since the last Ellefson tour, I played with Chris Poland as he got inducted into the Heavy Metal Hall of Fame during NAMM along with Phil Demel and more. I lined up a solid year of touring, arguably my biggest slate of touring since my Gargantua Soul days. I finished the year at home with my family, doing some legwork on my label/booking company Mindsnap Music and heading into 2020 with a full head of steam. The future was bright. It seemed like a logical ending to my book ...

CHAPTER THIRTEEN
Drumming Through the Apocalypse

Coauthor's Note: The following chapter is from interviews with Christian that took place from February to April of 2020 as the nation first learned about the new coronavirus, and the world closed down. Emotions were high, and information was scarce. Some of the things discussed might seem outdated or even a bit silly now. Just remember how weird of a time it was. Christian just happened to be in front of a microphone when it all happened in real time. We could've edited this after the fact, but I'm glad we've kept it authentic and unsettling.

By the fall of 2019, I had tours and shows booked until November of the following year. Having been in the game so long, grinding away, 2020 was going to represent the biggest and one of the most successful years in my drumming career. You could argue that some of the early days I had spent with Gargantua Soul, from 1999-2001, would rival this, but I had concerts booked in several countries around the world for multiple musical projects. I had records coming out, I was doing online playthroughs, I was jumping on board with a booking agency, my trivia nights were booming, and I still carved out time for my little man.

Rob sadly left DBW. A step sideways, yes but now we could all move on and do what was best for us both and ourselves. We found our new singer but had yet to play a live show with him.

We jammed several times, and it sounded good. Finding the correct fit is a multi-level process. Sure, he can bring it while singing our old stuff at practice, and sure, he seems to have a knack for coming up with ideas while we play, but can he replicate that live? Can he get on stage and own the crowd? Can he sustain the same energy for forty-five minutes? An hour? Will his voice hold up throughout a headlining slot at my birthday bash?

The only way we could determine that was to get on stage and do it.

I drove, full steam ahead, into 2020 … and then crashed hard into the pandemic.

And just like that, everything I had sacrificed, planned, and strived for went up in smoke. All the tours were up in the air. All the record releases were put on hold. My Tuesday trivia night came to a halt. Almost every source of income had gotten swiped away in the tidal wave known as COVID-19.

Work from home? I'm a touring drummer. I perform in front of crowds around the world. I eat when tickets get sold, when the beer flows at the clubs, and when t-shirts clothe new fans. I can't impress a metal fan in Germany while sitting on my couch in Connecticut. That's not how the system is set up. Sure, people can find my music on the internet, but how many times have you bought an album or discovered a brand-new band out of thin air? It happens, but let's face it; the best way to win fans and attention is to melt faces from the stage in that person's hometown. I have so many lifelong friends and fans I've met after shows, shaking hands at the merch booth, hearing stories about how my songs have affected their lives, or even through simply listening to someone who came to the show and was having a rough night.

Those connections made are a strong bond. They are hard to come by, and a lot of effort goes into forging each one. As much as a song is a product, they don't roll off the assembly line. They aren't uniform. They don't get the same reaction from each listener. It's not an exact science, so you need to be open minded, flexible, and willing to chase down potential fans who also become potential customers. Yes, you're selling them music, but you are also selling them yourself in a way. My bandmates and I are open minded, but how the hell do you do that during a multi-month quarantine?

So, I've built and built and built up to that point only to have it all snatched away. I'll be honest; part of putting together these indie tours with small clubs and low guarantees and few, if any, perks is ignoring the very credible voice in your head telling you to walk away. It tells you that you're not making enough, that you can't support your family, that you're just going to fail again … and again … and again. You can ask, how is completing a tour a failure? Well, it's not that every show has positives and every tour leg you gain new fans, but is it enough to come home with enough money in your pockets to pay bills? 2020 was set up as my coming out party, my big success, but even still the expected returns weren't going to put my son into college or even help him buy his first car. The money would be funneled into the next batch of CDs or t-shirts or gas money for the van, and on and on and on. Get it yet?

Touring as an indie metal musician can't even be described as living paycheck to paycheck, because, for one, there's no paycheck, only the constant hustle, and two, the money earned in the next hustle gets invested to support the hustle after that.

I had no idea when I'd be back on the road. I was supposed to go to Japan in April with Ellefson. Dead By Wednesday was booked to open for Twiztid around the USA that May. We couldn't even get our new singer up to speed because we couldn't get together. I had dates set playing drums at some larger events with both David Ellefson and for Chris Poland, who also spent time in Megadeth. Dead By Wednesday had some bigger fests, like Rock on the River in Indiana with rock bands like Saliva and Trapt. We had Metal in the Mountains coming up with Mushroomhead and Atilla, and it was all up in the air, most of which was eventually canceled. Earth, my Black Sabbath tribute band, had a European tour on the horizon. For once, there was literally no rest or empty space.

You might've read the last paragraph and thought I mistyped when I said Twiztid, but it's the truth. Sure, they come from the Juggalo family, but there is a history of that community and metal bands coming together to party. Mushroomhead, Dog Fashion Disco, and even Biohazard have gone on the road with Juggalo artists as the token metal band on the bill.

I can understand why some people rip on the whole scene, as it can be a little left of center, a little weird, or maybe seen as goofy, but I'll tell you what, those bands bring it every night. They are professional, and they have created a community of fans who are close knit and supremely loyal. They are more family than a crowd of strangers.

In fact, one of the best tours I was ever involved with was when Dead By Wednesday went out to support Insane

Clown Posse. We were just starting out as a band, and it turned into a great opportunity. Again, those fans are loyal. Once they decide they like you, they stick with you and give you their full support. You become part of the family.

So, when you open for those bands, the crowd will let you know where you stand. You certainly aren't unsure if they like you or not.

If they enjoy your show, they chant, "Fa-mi-ly! Fa-mi-ly!"

If they don't ... you had better keep an eye out, because they will throw water bottles, cigarettes, pocket change, or whatever else they can spare until they've successfully made your time on stage as uncomfortable as possible.

I'm proud and honored to say we had a lot of family chants on that tour. We never had full-on boos, but we did have a few mixed crowds. On those nights, you just put your head down, go to work, and win the respect of as many people as you can. We still have fans to this day who we played for and met on that tour over ten years ago. We even played the wedding of one of those fans, who became a good friend, Pete Chaney. Pete worked our street team in the Ohio area, and we formed a close relationship through the years. I never pictured Dead By Wednesday playing a wedding reception, but it turned outto be an incredibly awesome and fun experience for all of us. We all wore tuxedo shirts, and the groom even got up and played drums to "Pawns."

The smallest show on the tour was a Monday night in the middle of a blizzard, but three hundred and fifty crazy fans braved it to see the show, and we sold over $500 worth of merch. An average night on that tour would bring in $500-1500 as an opener!

You can see why we were excited to jump on a full month of dates this May with Twiztid now, right? Those dates will eventually get rescheduled, but it doesn't guarantee that when it happens, we can still do it. We all have other bands and families and jobs to work around.

Life was just one giant question mark. We had no idea how long the quarantine would drag out. How long can indie musicians sit still without earning anything? How will crowds respond when the quarantines get lifted? Will they be too scared to gather at shows? Will small, dirty rock clubs struggle to fill space amid the fear of germs? Will promoters and booking agencies survive long enough to reopen?

All I could do was sit and wait to see where the chips fell. How many dates get double booked? How many can be salvaged? There were so many questions and problems and hurdles to jump before any clarity on the future of touring could be attained. My busy year has been flipped upside down and looked to make for a massive headache and heartache instead.

The fear and doubt and anxious moments grew with each passing day. How could I not feel a bit resentful, angry? Honestly, I was pissed. I wanted to play. I wanted to earn. I wanted to help support my bandmates and my family. Then the depression set in, with so many unanswered questions.

What were the first things to go? COVID-19 was stomping all over the entertainment industry. I'm not just talking about music here. Music, art, movies, theater, TV are all on hold. Jessica and I know tons of people involved in reality TV. Those crews were shut down. Almost no one was producing new content. That would quickly affect the stations. What were they going to do, broadcast reruns all day and night? How would that affect commercial sales? If commercials weren't bringing in as much, what staff would become expendable. If there wasn't a demand for new commercials, what happens to those crews? On and on. You see how these simple things can ripple out and cause mass problems if this thing lingers on? That's one industry. Use that logic to whatever job you work at, your spouse, parents, siblings. It was affecting all of us, as I am sure you know.

From the beginning, I always felt there was more to it than meets the eye here, for sure. I never doubted how serious or real the virus is. I always felt we should be protecting the elderly and the sick and our kids, for sure. Those groups should have been, maybe still be, hibernating. Those people should be in a cocoon, but to shut down the entire world felt a bit extreme.

I'm not a doctor. I'm not even much of a conspiracy theorist, but doesn't there always seem to be nuggets of truth in people's theories? I can't help but think there was/is more going on than we have seen or than we are being told. Just like with most stereotypes or one-liner sayings, like "less is more" or the "grass is always greener," etc., there is always some truth in lies and some lies in truths.

If I've learned anything at this point in my life, it's I'm not going to accept everything the government tells me without question. I can't take it all at face value without at least asking if there's a different truth underneath it all. I can see a world in which we're all walking around like robots or zombies, kind of like the people in *The Wall* by Pink Floyd.

We need free thinking. We need to be more openminded and creative. We need more compassion. We should always question authority. Tolerance should be key along with more love and the use of simple common sense. And, of course, better education.

My gut tells me there was an agenda with this lockdown. Maybe they wanted to eliminate small businesses, squash the independent worker, and cut out the middleman. Maybe it's just about control and power.

It's like the goal revolves around molding our society into a Hunger Games model with two sides, the ultra-rich and the super poor. The have and the have-nots. The rich 1 percent control everything. The poor 99 percent beg for scraps. America, the new third-world country.

You look at the Rockefellers, Rothchild's, Jeff Bezos, Bill Gates, and the family who runs Walmart. Some tied in with our politicians. Greedy people running huge corporations. All they want is more money to stay in power and more power to make more money. Like an addiction, once they have it, they can't stop. They'll never give it up. Not a penny, not an inch.

They only care about the almighty dollar.

I see these people at the top talking about going cashless. They only have one reason to want a cashless society. They want to monitor and control every last penny, which they pretty much already do now anyway. They want to know exactly what gets bought, and where and at what price, by whom, from whom. I mean, everyone knows if you even talk about a product or problem, you may have out loud even remotely near your iPhone or smart TV an hour later (if that), an advertisement will pop up trying to sell, sell, sell. This is no coincidence. You're just a consumer to them. A number.

Why does this worry me?

As an independent musician, a large chunk of my income is under the table. I play a show, and the promoter passes the band a bunch of wrinkled, ripped, dirty dollars. I sell t-shirts after the concert, and our profit is a couple bucks. Typically, those transactions are cash. We get a few drink tickets to enjoy after we play. If I host an event at a bar, same thing. What happens if the few dollars we make to play, the three dollars we get extra per shirt, the drinks we earn, and my side-hustle money all needs to be on the books and gets taxed? It upsets the cart. The bar can no longer afford to give free meals, drinks, or even afford to bring indie bands in at all. At that point, I can no longer afford to tour.

What if an artist needs to pay taxes on every painting they sell? How are buskers and street performers going to entertain you for spare change when there isn't any anymore? What if a band needs to pay taxes on every download or stream? We get less than a penny per stream as it is on most digital platforms. It's pathetic. And it sucks that Lars Ulrich of Metallica was right!

Think about how often you go out to karaoke, trivia, live music, see a DJ, a movie, a play, an art showing, a wine tasting, or enjoy celebrity bartender nights each month. Now imagine how many times you'd go out if all of those were taken away. So, the bars suffer. Restaurants suffer. Their staff suffers. And it trickles down to the artists—all so corporations can assure they leach every last cent into their coffers. Movies and music and art and all that stuff gets virtually eliminated, because no one can afford to produce it. What kind of world is that like to experience? Sounds boring as shit to me. We need art, music, comedy, and entertainment in general.

Watch, I can tell you this already in March of 2020 just as the lockdowns are starting to happen; when they roll things back out, it won't be the same. They'll have made changes to what is considered "normal," taking this time while everyone's distracted to put new rules, regulations, and restrictions into place.

I know some of this will sound crazy, but I've done some research. And not just on YouTube or Facebook. The changes coming aren't a reaction to the virus; these have been planned for years, maybe decades. The virus only represents a clean excuse to start the process now. Scared people are easier to maneuver into situations they might otherwise avoid or fight against. Get them paranoid enough and they'll even thank the powers that be for fucking them over in the end.

My views on government are anarchistic.

I look around at both parties in power, and all I see are the same faces. They're all out to suppress us. They just have a slightly different view on how that should happen. They are all scum. Trump is no different to me than Obama. Obama is no different from Bush. Bush is no different to me than Clinton. Keep going back and back. Different faces, same results.

They purposefully divide us. If they can keep us arguing with each other, it's the perfect distraction to let them work on their own agendas. Our system has failed us. It already has. Think about it. The system put in place by us has gotten us into this mess. We're at each other's throats, arguing. We're fighting with ourselves. We're the 99 percent. They are the 1 percent. Yet, they hold all the cards. They have all the money, so, of course, they hold all the power. They set the policy. They make all the rules we have to follow, and they aren't always in our best interest, at all. We don't need them, and yet, we keep electing them and going along with their agendas. Most of us act like sheep. We follow blindly. Or sometimes out of necessity, like me. If I could not use a cellphone, gas, oil, pay taxes or use banks, I wouldn't, but in a modern world, we are all slaves to these things, especially in the business I am in. How do you tour without a vehicle? How do you book things without a phone or computer? The only way around it would be to literally live off the land and run to the wilderness. Trust, it's crossed my mind, but a reality? No.

In the Dead By Wednesday song, "Pawns," we sing, "They need us more than we need them." This is absolutely the truth. Without us, there is no them!

It's an older song, but it resonates with our fans old and new. It has long been a staple of our sets, so much so that we are going to do a rerecording of it. We want to update it. The original came out back during the GW Bush administration, so we need "Pawns 2.0" (which ended up being "Pawns 2022").

What happens when a business fails? It usually declares bankruptcy. Then it either goes away or the people regroup and try again, right? The people in power right now are bankrupting America. They are declaring us bankrupt and pushing a massive reset button. They are using this virus as a ploy, as an excuse to do it, but it was coming.

I can point out things happening worldwide. Look at how the air is clearing up after just a couple weeks of us locked away. But when there is a yin, there must be a yang, so, of course, there will also now be a rise in pollution due to so much extra wasted plastic and latex gloves, wipes, and disposable masks, which we are already seeing thrown on the ground in parking lots and in our oceans.

Corporations want a robot society. They don't want you to wake up. They want you to get up. Get ready for work. Work your ass off. Don't question politics. Don't question the leadership. Only partake in the entertainment they approve. Only listen to news they control. Strictly listen to music they prescreen. Support movies that don't pose questions. It's propaganda. The only value in it is to make you more subservient, to make you need them more—keep the public quiet.

I feel the same about religion as I do politics.

It's set up like a sport. "My side is right. Your side is wrong. These are my beliefs, and you can't change my mind." My God is better than your God. Of course, common sense tells me that if there's even a God, there is more than likely only one, but we fight and kill over the same story told differently around the globe since the beginning of time.

It's a hamster in a wheel. It goes round and around and never gets anywhere. There is no possibility of progress, no chance for a resolution. Just go and go and go—which is also the definition of insanity. Doing the same thing over and over again but expecting different results which never happen.

We need one party. The party of the people. That's it. Unite the red and the blue and everyone in between for once and for all. If that's even possible, which sadly, I believe isn't.

I'm not saying to not take this virus seriously. I'm not saying don't quarantine, because it's always better to be safe than sorry. I'm just saying they are using this pandemic to put things into motion, so you should also stay vigilant. You should question what they say and do. You should apply common sense and be open to alternate views and ideas.

Will it take a revolution to reclaim our country? I wish. Most of the people in our country are too complacent in comfort for that to ever happen, unfortunately.

There's a lyric from my former singer, Kris Keyes, of Gargantua Soul, "If you don't stand for something, you'll fall for anything."

That line rings true to me today more than ever before.

I ask people this hypothetical all the time. "What if we all just refused to vote?" I don't care, Democrat or Republican or Green Party or Tea Party or liberal or independent or whoever else. We all just say, "No more." We don't vote. We don't give them any power. I know this can never happen because of the lame responses I always get.

People will say, "If you don't vote, you don't have a voice." "If you don't vote, you can't complain."

Listen, I can complain. I'm going to complain, because I still have a fucking voice, whether anyone likes it or not. Our system is broken. I'm not going to vote and support a system that doesn't support me. Our voting system doesn't work. Well, it works, but not for us. It benefits the 1 percent. It benefits the people who can't risk change, the people who have the control. So, Dead By Wednesday's debut album's title still holds water ... *Democracy is Dead*!

If no one voted, the powers that be would have nothing. They'd have no control. You take the power back by standing together and saying, "Enough."

We essentially all would be going on a nationwide organized political strike. We hit our own reset button. No democrats, no republicans. We would be the 99 percent, united in our goal of sweeping changes to make life better for everyone, united in doing what we want to do for us, not them. Take the power back.

I get it, that's a weird theory. Most people can't grasp it, and others don't want to understand what I mean. We have been programmed through years of manipulation and don't even realize it. Freethinkers are not welcome here.

John Lennon ... gone. Bob Marley ... gone. Etc., Etc. Anyone making a mark with massive influence. Gone.

And yes, yes, I know that both men named above have been accused of abusing women and have other flaws, like every human who taints their legacy, but their ideas and philosophies made them dangerous to the powers that be. Their growing amounts of fans made them a target. Their progress in changing, or at least adjusting, the worldview made them a liability. What they preached stands true to this day, but they were silenced. You don't hear those messages on the radio much anymore, do you? Especially from new artists.

People need to question authority. We need more Sid Viciouses in this world (minus the hardcore drugs). Though when they do, they get silenced, so it's understandable why some are afraid to stick their own necks out. That's how they control us. You've got a mass of people. Most of them blindly trudge forward, eating and believing and enjoying whatever is spoon fed to them. Then you have the outliers, the people on the edge. These fringe folk are brave enough to sniff the food before eating it. They look up and around at the surroundings rather than only watching what's directly in front of them. They see and hear and smell the inconsistencies being shoveled by the elite.

So, the freethinkers, the people at the edges, start pushing back and making noise and trying to alert the rest of the herd. If they start to succeed or know something, they go missing or mysteriously commit suicide. Then it's up to the next one to pick up the megaphone and spread the message. All the 1 percent needs to break the chain is one person to stay silent. They need that one person to fear the consequences and to fall back in line. They win. Again.

If I ran for office and somehow won (which would obviously never happen), the first thing I would do is eliminate the multiple party system. Unify everyone. One party of the people, by the people, and for the people, for real. That's it. Make the government work for us, not against us. We would eat the 1 percent, skin and bone, and that's coming from me who is virtually a VAGatarian at this point. I would finally make it all about "we" and "us."

Anyway, where was I? COVID-19, of course. Right now, everything is COVID-19 and coronavirus all day, all night.

The news and the government and the scientists all contradict one another each day. I am hearing the coronavirus has mutated, and there are multiple strains around the world. If the people I heard can be trusted, the strains in Italy and Iran are more deadly than the others. So, if we have the easier-to-fight version, how bad will things get if that Italian version reaches our shores? And it's really not a matter of if rather than when.

Is it manmade?

That theory has been floated by several groups, but I'm not getting fully into conspiracy theories here. I want to deal with the facts on the table. Could it be? Sure. I've read enough studies to know people need to open their minds and look at what's happening. Look back at history and see how things are repeating themselves. It's so obvious.

I need to work. I need to drum. I need to perform. I need my life back!

I still have dates with Chris Poland and Ellefson in August, and then a full European tour in September. Those things, as of now, are in place, but who knows how things will look in the coming months? In fact, there's already talks of it all being canceled as well.

No one knows the future, and that's a tough truth. I'm on hold. I am not good in situations like this where I don't have answers and have to sit on my hands. I can't plan or prepare. I can't build toward anything. I want to feel safe and secure and that my government is looking out for my best interests.

This is no way to live.

Then to cap it off, Earth (my Black Sabbath tribute) was going to play the N.Y. Harvest Festival. A pro-weed festival I've been playing annually with my friend Rob Robinson of Damn Sam Productions since its creation.

This year was all about great gigs, great festivals, reconnecting with fans on the road, building new audiences for these various bands, and sharing new music. Here I am, no gigs, no money, no social life. What else can they take away? My balls? Are they going to come and castrate me in the near future?

No matter what, we can't stop the virus in its tracks. I am at peace with that. It's coming, no matter how nervous or afraid I feel. And I'll say it; I am afraid. I've got a family to worry about. My son could get sick. I don't want that, obviously.

I'll take precautions, but I won't do it blindly. Is the government telling us everything? Is the media being upfront and honest? It seems like instead of being responsible journalists who share legitimate truths and facts in a calm way, they created a massive frenzy by throwing this all in our faces. Negativity sells and gains more views. Positivity does not, unfortunately, which sucks in my eyes. People are scared to leave their homes. They are scared to shop for food or go to work; hell, people are scared to look at one another out in public.

I'm sort of a hypochondriac. Every itch in my throat, I think, okay, this is it. I've got the coronavirus. I'm getting a fever. Oh, now my kid has a stuffed-up nose and isn't feeling good. We're going to be super sick.

Trust me, I understand the trepidation, but I walk outside, and people are wearing masks and coats, and some have protective glasses and bandannas, and they don't want to talk or get close or make eye contact. It's too much. Humanity is being tested.

Scientists are saying that a large percent of the people who get it might be asymptomatic or only get mild symptoms. Most people won't ever know they were exposed to it or that they ever had it. By the time a majority of the population gets tested, they will either already be getting better or have beaten it completely anyway. If you have a strong immune system, you should do fine. Should.

If you're not fine, you might be in trouble, but again, when I hear those stories, typically the patient went in, and then they found out the hard way about an underlying cause. They might have MS or cancer, and their body might've been battling that without them even knowing. It took the coronavirus to get their attention to get themselves looked at.

It seems they're also labeling a lot of extra deaths as COVID-19 now, but then, after doing research, you find out the real truth. For example, there was an incident locally where an infant fell into a closed pool and passed away but already had the virus in his system, so, of course, when they did the autopsy, they put the death down as part of the covid-death counts.

There are exceptions, and sure, all this information is out there, but how much of it is accurate? Who knows right now? Every day, you can hear multiple conflicting reports depending on where you look.

They are letting the economy crash.

They are delaying the inevitable instead of looking for real-world solutions.

Why?

Because they have an agenda.

Look into who is pushing for a cashless society, and then look at why they are saying it. They have financial reasons. They have control reasons. Look at who is involved in the pharmaceutical companies. They aren't acting in good faith.

The government is run by a bunch of hypocrites. For example, they are anti-drug and have no problem locking up dealers and addicts and throwing away the key. But they are the biggest pushers of them all. First, they get you hooked with the big pharma pills. (Never mind booze, which is basically legal poison which everything is promoted around, especially in the music biz and whatever else.) Then suddenly, you are cut off and find yourself a fiend for opiates. You start using street drugs to fulfill the need. But they would never claim responsibility for that. And who knows, maybe in the near future, they'll release a "get high app" where all you need to do is push a button, and the technology will send drugs or whatever into your system. The app is tied to your brain or some shit. It gets you high with a simple press of a button. Watch this. Watch that.

Sound ridiculous? Sure. Sound unrealistic? Not really. Who knows, but a lot of what we used to think was unrealistic or not a possibility we are now seeing come to fruition today right before our very eyes. I wake up every day and feel like I'm in a bad Twilight Zone episode. I pray it's all a nightmare, but it's not.

After all this virus stuff clears up and people get a tiny bit of their freedom restored, even just a few little crumbs of what they had, the masses will rush back to their lives without ever questioning or pushing for more, because they'll be so relieved to have these little bits of normalcy again. Until the next time a little more freedom is taken away.

And then it's just a matter of time before the next pandemic, the next 9/11, the next threat, school shooting or the next emergency comes along or is created to push the agenda further toward what the 1 percent wants. They won't need to ask you to surrender your freedoms, because the masses will gladly give them up for you to feel safe.

The government sold us on fear with weapons of mass destruction already. Remember that? One rumor of impending doom and our whole country changed. We sat back as the powers that be spied on us, as we spied on each other, as we murdered innocent people in savage ways. "If you see something, say something!" No different from the very people we were supposedly fighting against. People were content. Our lives didn't seem to be affected. Of course, the WMD thing turned out to not be true at all, but now that's ancient history. No one cares anymore, and that president's face is gone too.

The whole thing plays out like a script from a reality show. Why, then, are people surprised we had a reality star as our president? We've been down this road before when they voted Ronald Reagan, the actor, into office. Can it be any more obvious what's going on? They're all puppets anyway, all pawns to a higher authority. Money.

As I talk about all this, remember where I'm at—sitting at home waiting to hear when I can work again. I need to know when I can restart the year that was supposed to be the tops in my career, going back over twenty years. Even the Twiztid tour leg was over two years in the making. It was a pain-in-the-ass process. I had to prove myself to their management and make a deal.

That's a lot of phone calls, handshaking (apparently not anymore), emails, favors, relationship building all geared toward this one opportunity for my band, and now it might be up in smoke. The whole thing is derailed. As it stands now, they were trying to rebook the dates for June, and Dead By Wednesday already had several conflicts with the new dates, and now, of course, I just got the call that all of it is off.

Cancelations, conflicts, re-bookings happen, no doubt. I have used deals as opportunities in the past and will continue to seek out ways to get exposure for my bands. All the stuff we did to build our relationship with Ellefson is the same way. We sacrificed a lot to get to this point with him. I mean, these Japan dates came at me out of the blue. David emailed me, asking if I was interested and if Dave Sharpe was available. Hell yes, we were interested and available! But David isn't emailing random strangers to play with him on tour around the globe, right? We worked our way up to that point. I have practiced my ass off, and I'm ready to play those shows, but now we can't. But now, this all seems in jeopardy because ... blah, blah, blah ...

My September tour with Earth was also tons of hard work and building on years of relationships. Lord Bishop, who booked a lot of those shows, and I go way back to my earliest playing days. You'll recall from earlier that he was there the night I almost fought Peter Criss.

Lord Bishop moved to Germany, but we stayed in touch. Last year, he put together a tour for Earth to test the waters. By the time the tour was done, he was already getting requests, and buyers wanted to bring us back again. He put in the effort to get a month of dates done, and I made sure my guys were all available, but now who knows how travel will look by then or if my bandmates will be comfortable going overseas if this virus is still raging. Will they even let us in?

No one knows how this will affect ticket sales. If people are too scared to be in public and tickets sales are low, will certain shows cancel last minute or offer to pay us less? We can't do a proper budget anymore. We can't plan on ordering merch yet. We can't assume it will be business as usual. Hell, how much will plane tickets fluctuate between now and then? That's a huge expense. Transportation costs can make or break the tour. If tickets spike or rental vehicles rise in price, we have to decide whether it's worth it before going. Gas is ok now, but by September, will it skyrocket us out of the ability to get from city to city? (Well, it certainly has!) It's all these unknowns that make this all scary.

Safety is important, sure, but I'd be lying if I said this didn't hurt. Blood, sweat, tears, and money have gone into the concert dates I have this year. I wake up on certain days and think about the lockdown, and I wonder if I'd be better off just exposing myself to the virus and getting it over with. If I have immunity, I can trudge forward.

Now, don't freak out. I understand the ramifications go beyond just me. Right now, Italy is getting hammered. I am one hundred percent Italian, and I have family over there. They are very touchy-feely. That's part of the reason it spread so fast, I think. It's a very different culture than ours. From what I understand, they wash their hands less than many other countries. I'm not proud of that, but that's the way it is over there, I guess. Hold on, let me rephrase that. According to studies, supposedly they don't wash their hands as much as they should, okay? I don't want to piss off a bunch of Italians. I love my people, and I feel for them. They also have a large percentage of young adults who still live at home with their parents, and grandparents even. Smoking, in general, is way more popular in Europe as well. Italy also has a much older population. Most are healthy people though. They eat a Mediterranean diet and live forever. My grandfather was 102 before he died of natural causes.

With Italy's hospitals overwhelmed, they had to pick and choose who they would treat first. That's an awful spot to be in. They've been hit so hard. I've seen a video of the prime minister crying over it all. Real people had to make real life or death decisions. This isn't a movie. These are real people. And some got left behind. Some had to die alone at home or in a car waiting for a hospital bed. Now, that's something you'd actually expect to see in a movie. Not real life.

We haven't even mentioned that Italy has so many tourists each year from all over the world. Chinese people come to northern Italy in large numbers to shop and sightsee, so for all we know, that's what helped the virus spread so quickly there, being that it started there, right? I'm not blaming the Chinese people, and although they pretty much admitted to having it leak from a lab, I do question those wet markets and how they operate all day. I'll say that openly. In my personal opinion, those wet markets are absolutely disgusting! You can use the 'different culture' excuse, but it won't ever change my mind, and this is why. All manners of creatures are stuck in tiny cages and stacked on top of each other in small spaces. Some are dead, and some are still alive, but all stored together. Some, if not most, of these animals are meant to be in the wild, running free. They have homes, territories, diets, and routines, and also affect other wildlife cycles. You don't know what these things are being fed or what conditions they are forced to live in or if they have a family. They are shitting on each other, and they spend their entire lives watching the other animals get slaughtered right in front of them until it's their turn. You don't think they understand or can see this before their very eyes? You don't think they can hear another creature's agony? Whether you want to believe it or not, *all* animals have feelings and can feel pain. Thousands of animals were stolen from their life and packed together. Of course, diseases will spread and mutate and get passed around. Those markets aren't natural.

You want to eat regulated pork, chicken, beef, fish, or whatever? Fine. I guess, though, it's not really my thing, but leave the wildlife in the wild.

I've stated already that I am almost vegetarian at this point. More of a pescatarian. Oh, and definitely a vegetarian as well. Wocka-wocka! I used to eat a lot of meat, but I got grossed out once along with Jessica preparing a meal. I stopped eating pork or turkey or red meats. My buddy had a pet turkey. One day, it fell asleep on my shoulder. I can tell it has a brain with thoughts and ideas and that these animals have feelings. Yet, we slaughter them without a care.

Native Americans honored and cherished the animals they ate. They only killed out of necessity. They needed to feed their families. They took great care to use as much of the parts of it as they could: the skin, the hair, the horns, the meat, the bones. They fed the whole village. We slaughter and slaughter thousands at a time on assembly lines and most of it gets wasted. They chop out the prime cuts. Package it up and throw it on the shelves.

I can understand the Native American way, and to take it further, look, I can even see why desperation led Chinese people to eat whatever they could kill or afford to buy at a market. You can't sit back and watch your children starve. At some point though, they need to rethink the way their food chain is set up. Supposedly, they are even eating bats, rats, zebras, sloths, snakes, squirrels, and, of course, dogs, which really hits me hard and all these things that should get left alone. Shit, I wish all animals could be left alone, but the reality is there is a food chain, and humans are way up on top of it; plus, from research, there are some benefits from organic animal fats and proteins.

Dogs to me are sacred. Dog backward spells God. There's a reason. They have more feelings and more unconditional love than any human being. I'd hang out with a dog over a human any day.

The world is on lockdown, and I can't tour, but that doesn't mean there isn't work to do.

I start the day with a lot of coffee. I'll kickstart the day with a workout. Some days it's yoga; somedays I run, or I might do both.

Then I get behind the kit and practice for about an hour or more. Right now, I have a few different playlists I'm running through. I have the Japan setlist. It's a mix of David Ellefson, Chris Poland and Megadeth songs. I have a Dead By Wednesday set I play through with our songs, and then a few random covers and things I play for fun. There are Black Sabbath songs I go over for Earth. I also have some songs and exercises, like double bass patterns, which are strictly to challenge me and to keep me improving my techniques. In fact, I'm currently in the middle of a nine-week online drum course on improving my double bass speed, stamina, and overall skill. Always strive to be better. Never settle. Practice makes you "better, not perfect." A saying I learned from my favorite sushi chef in West Haven, CT., Jerry San, was "Whoever said you can't teach old dogs new tricks was sorely mistaken."

I have to push myself. I have a lot of songs that I need to be sharp on, but you can't just play those songs. You need to expand and test and revise and learn and better yourself. Recently, I've been posting drum playthrough videos of me playing along to different songs. I am trying to adapt to the current lockdown and take advantage of this forced downtime. People can watch those and be entertained. I can use the clips to look and listen for ways to up my game.

After that, I shift gears into promotion and marketing efforts. Between all my bands and clients, like Marc Rizzo, now Puya (the amazing Latin-fused metal band from Puerto Rico), there's an endless pile of emails and calls and plans and proposals that need to be nurtured each day. The music industry never stops, so you've got to keep your name out there consistently to stay relevant. There are house chores that need to be done, like making the bed, washing dishes, home improvement stuff, which are things I typically do anyway, even if the world isn't fighting the apocalypse.

Jessica is a teacher, so she is adapting to the new way of learning, and she is spearheading the homeschooling for Orion, as well as myself, which is quite funny, being that half the time I feel like Orion is schooling me! She also handles dinner, for the most part. I help where I can. The rest of the time is spent protecting and coddling our child. He is literally the purest soul I know and truly love.

Keeping him in a positive frame of mind where he doesn't need to worry about all the chaos is no easy task. Jessica and I are worried enough. This is not the world we wanted him to grow up in. What if this becomes a yearly thing? It's possible. If the virus mutates and keeps spreading, it could come in wave after wave until there's a cure. Creating a vaccine and herd immunity isn't going to happen quickly. What if another virus hits on top of this one? There are so many scary possibilities. Mother Nature seems pissed.

Take away all that. My son is young and impressionable. If this social distancing lasts for months or stretches into next year, this will leave a scar, no doubt. And not just on him but on all children. He is growing up needing to be afraid of other people. He needs to keep away from people, needs to wear a mask, needs to stay away from friends, some of his family. What kind of childhood is that?

What kind of life is that for anybody? Luckily, he said he is loving all the extra one-on-one daily attention, being the only child, as well as our dog Rocko, who also seems to be in La-La Land since he's used to missing me for weeks on end while being on the road.

A couple weeks ago, as this all started to hit the US, Orion turned to me and said, "I don't want to die."

He's an innocent, six-year-old kid. That's not a thought that should ever need to cross his mind.

I wondered then if I had made a mistake by not sheltering him from all the news of the corona sooner. I don't want him dreading each day. I don't want him worried about anyone getting sick—his family, his friends, his teachers. Since then, we've made an effort to not talk about the virus around him. Jessica and I want to keep things positive. Leave the worrying to us. His childhood innocence is being taken from him. He is learning too early some of the hard truths of life and of our calloused world. I consider that my fault. I want to pull him back away from all of it and just let him be a kid.

A couple years ago, this might not have been such a big deal to him or to me, because he wouldn't remember it, but now this will be some of his earliest memories. This is his first year of school. It's a huge period of development. So, he went to school for six months, got into a rhythm, and then bam, his whole world got upended. How can this not affect kids his age? Will they be resistant to getting close to one another? Will they be afraid to touch another person?

And we're the lucky ones. I have Jessica, Orion, and my faithful Boston terrier Rocko here. I have great neighbors close by. We have some outside space to move around, a firepit, a lawn, a grill, trampoline, I have a studio on my property, etc. Imagine all those people on their own. Imagine being stuck in a tiny apartment in NYC. Put yourself in the shoes of the homeless. Where are they going? How are they going to cope? Are we really surprised to see suicide numbers jumping? Can we be that caught off guard that depression is on the rise or that mental health issues are boiling to the surface? Or drug and alcohol use on the rise.

You think the United States is a superpower? We might have been, but now we are failing. Plain and simple. We are failing as a country. The greedy people who control policy are failing us. The 1 percent is looking out for themselves, as usual. Here we are, talking about real problems, real sickness, real death, real mental issues, and it easily circles right back to those at the top failing us. Don't get me wrong, I love my country. I actually mourn for it. I have nothing but respect for the soldiers and people who have fought and died for mine and all our freedoms, but those are slowly slipping away before our very eyes, and as time marches on, we are realizing more and more that they were all being lied to most of the time. So, fighting, dying, and innocent lives being lost over lies and hidden agendas that "we the people" will never know.

Apparently, our system isn't set up for huge issues like this. Look at how Norway is able to care for their own. They have great schools, great healthcare, a modern prison system, drug care for addicted people, and a government that is open and honest with its people. It seems to be working. I'm not saying we need to copy them or that they are perfect, but if they can get that stuff done, why can't we? Because of capitalism and the "American dream."

But on the positive side of all this, I think people will be forced to reflect on what is most important in life: family. We need to take care of ourselves first inside and out and then the world. Cut out the bullshit. I saw a meme the other day where the Earth was using the corona to send us to our room as punishment for coming so close to ruining this planet. I saw another one where the Earth was thanking the corona for forcing humans to step back so it could have a break, a breather. Those are powerful messages. We're seeing the immediate changes after only a couple weeks of lockdown. Imagine if this stretches on for a year or more. The world itself could be a much healthier place. The one thing this virus proves for a fact is we are all definitely connected. If one person gets it and goes down, we all go down! No one is exempt. Not the old, the young, if you're Black, White, Chinese, whatever. This simple concept being such an issue has always baffled me, because it's literally just common sense. We all bleed the same color, have to eat and drink water to survive, we all poop out of our dirty buttholes, breathe the same air, and the one thing that is inevitable is, eventually, one day, we will all die.

Getting back to music. I'm already seeing a huge uptick in bands doing live-streamed concerts and practices and interviews because of the corona. After things calm down, I don't see this trend going away. I mean, even if this gets one hundred percent taken care of, the fear is now a legit part of our new world. No doubt.

Dead By Wednesday has a song, "Death of the Rockstar," from a previous album that talks about how we felt about the industry at the time, but it's only gotten more important in the current times. The music business squeezes and squeezes you, making it harder and harder to sustain as a career. Right now, while not touring, a band is earning through downloads and streams and, if you're lucky, some online merchandise sales. If DBW gets streamed on Spotify, TouchTunes, or a comparable service, we get less than half a cent. Even a download is a few cents after all the fees and cuts get split.

Think about that.

To create that song, we had to buy gear, find a place to practice, put time in to write and arrange, pay a studio and an engineer and a producer, get the song mastered, we had to design a cover, and then after all that, we pay to get songs hosted and released. That's a lot of money and time and effort for such a small return. I'm not saying the love and feedback we get means nothing—obviously, that's what keeps us doing it—but you have to find ways to pay for the process to go on.

We haven't even talked about the pirating, bootlegging, and stealing that goes on. And again, Lars Ulrich was right for the third time! You can search and find DBW music being offered on websites all over that we don't see anything from. People are making money off our work. Imagine investing a year or two or decades of your life, along with tens of thousands of dollars, to create something, and then someone else rips it away and leaves you with next to nothing. Stings at times.

Actually, it does a lot more than sting. It fucking sucks! It's crippling to bands like DBW, who need every penny we can get to survive—meaning midlevel touring bands like many I work with or play in who are in the "grey area" of being too big for certain things and not big enough for other stuff. These pirate sites and bootleg sites, and even places like YouTube, aren't looking out for people who profit off the backs of others. That shit has to stop. There needs to be regulation and accountability so the money goes to the right people who are trying to create original content and brighten the world a bit with a song or a movie or a music video or a painting or whatever.

Nowadays, the market is so diluted with content that it's taken away from the mystique of rock and metal of past years. Sure, you have viral "stars" getting their fifteen minutes of fame, but what about bands who build a story and a character over decades? Watching these people develop and grow is a great part about finding bands, but it's so hard when musicians are given only one or two releases before they get written off and thrown onto the pile of forgotten things.

So, they turn to whatever methods they can to stay relevant and to make touring possible—especially nowadays, when attention spans are shorter, and ADD is on the rise. People hear one song, and then immediately want what's next. I used to sit down and hold the albums and stare at the cover, the pictures inside, and all the art, read the lyrics and daydream over it all. Now it's all mostly digital. A digital world.

Bands offer meet and greets to help pay for tours and get to know their fans better; well, how can that continue? Those extra events have made it possible for bands of any size to stay on the road. Megadeth and Metallica and those higher-tiered bands don't need it, sure. They can afford to stay distant from everyone backstage. But Dead By Wednesday, not a chance.

Our tours are built around shaking babies and kissing hands ... (Strike that! Reverse it.) Oh, and of course, occasionally slapping asses and hanging out with the people who come to see us. We can't just jump off stage and quarantine away from the crowd. It wouldn't fly with them, and personally, it sounds boring to me. I love meeting new people and hearing about music or what they enjoyed during our set. I spend an hour signing drumsticks and t-shirts, drawing on old drumheads and whatever else they want. How will this be done now?

Even if we are all somehow able to stay six feet away, you can't eliminate sweat and breath and the occasional bit of blood. Do you know how many times at a show I get grabbed and pulled and hugged, and this might not paint the prettiest picture, but people tell me stories and "close talkers" spit when they talk right in your face, you know? Say it, don't spray it, man! It's loud at these clubs, so people lean in close or whisper in my ear, and I can feel their spittle. I'm gracious about it, but now in this new world, which becomes a whole big thing. What if they are sick? How do we blow out the birthday candles now? It's going to cross our minds quicker and in more situations. It has to after all this, right?

I'm looking forward, trying to project what the music industry and touring industry might look like in the near future, and I don't like what I'm seeing. How do you go back to the way it was before corona? So, I'm reassessing my career and my music. I need to make digital sales a priority. Restock and build our online merch store. Learn video editing and more audio recording to do it more myself and save some money. I need to go to my back catalogue and drum up interest in these older bands of mine. I've been posting songs and live videos from my past, partially to kill time, but also to remind people what's available. How will it all shake out? All I can do is guess where it's going and set myself and my bands up for upcoming changes. Adapt or die.

It's easy to get angry. It's easy to feel overwhelmed with it all, but I'm trying to stay focused on the light at the end of the tunnel. Otherwise, how can you have or feel any hope? Without it, this reality could eat you alive.

What's that saying? 'This too shall pass?'

The virus is scary, and the world feels weird, and the uncertainty is terrible, but there's nothing more I can do. This is now forever a part of our world's history. This isn't a manmade terror or problem. This is nature. It's bigger than all of us. Look at the power and importance of water, fire, and air. They get taken for granted every day.

If this thing drags on for two, three, fuck, for five more years, I'll have to find a new career. I would still make music, still record and try to play concerts online or whatever. I'm sure the whole music industry would have to go through major shifts to stick around. It wouldn't look, feel, smell, taste, or sound the same as the industry we have now, that I can tell you for sure.

I'd say to put your trust in the Great Spirit, the Creator, God, your higher power, Allah, Satan, or whatever the fuck you believe in, and let that trust guide you through.

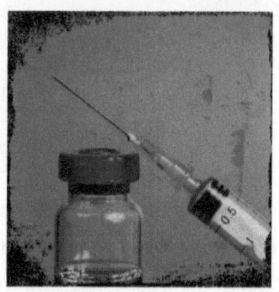

CHAPTER FOURTEEN
Soft Reopening

Flash forward, and we're over six months into the pandemic. All my plans were scuttled. My big year. My comeback. I entered 2020 ready to seize the day and grow my brand and career. Instead, I bought a house and a new car with no solid means to pay for them and began to slowly head into a mild depression.

We moved in and are adjusting to the new digs. DBW has managed to practice at our old spot as me and some friends work on our new studio space here at my new place. In fact, today is Labor Day, and I hired an electrician to install wiring as I chip away on this book.

Our new vocalist, Esteban (a.k.a. Steve), has had a chance to learn and adapt to our way of doing things. We managed to write, record, and release our first single with him, "SOS," along with a video, which ended up receiving rave reviews and views on the web.

I am rehearsing for two short runs with Ellefson this fall. We'll play in Texas, Louisiana, Illinois, Indiana, Wisconsin, and we have a cool live streaming event planned out to celebrate the release of Ellefson's covers disc, *NO COVER*.

I'm apprehensive yet excited. I mean, getting on a plane feels so foreign of a concept right now. Playing shows in a pandemic?

Deaths are down, but cases are up, as are hospitalizations. We have been told that vaccines from a few companies are close, but I'm not holding my breath.

There are protocols in place for me and Dave Sharpe to quarantine before the shows and afterward, which will present problems at home. The shows themselves, at least on the first run, are all outdoors. That helps ease my mind a little. Still a lot of stress involved.

Earlier this year, I really thought I was getting pushed further and further away from the Ellefson camp as they brought in new members from overseas, so to be completely honest, even being asked to play surprised me a bit, even though we all always had a solid relationship. Now, I get that we are in the midst of a pandemic, so bringing the new guys over from Europe is near impossible, but even still, it feels great to have Ellefson still tap Dave and I for this. We were certain by the end of 2020 we would find ourselves on the outside looking in.

The practice space is turning out dope. I needed this. I needed this new space, more than I even realized. It's a restart. A fresh start. We're close. I have sheetrock that needs to go up, soundproofing panels to install, and a paint job, but when it is all said and done, the room will be video-ready. That's how stellar this project is turning out. We can stream practice if we want, which might be the wave of the future anyway.

I'm staying in shape, mentally and physically. I get in my 10k steps a day. I ride my bike to and from practice, and I'm still watching what I eat. The news is still bleak, but I am finding a new normal for my family and for myself.

As I get back from my first string of dates with David and Thom, my head is spinning. The emotions and confusion and anxiety and pride and all that stuff is not strictly due to covid. During these concert dates, I had a serious conversation with Thom.

I asked jokingly, "Why do you treat me like a second-class citizen?"

I don't do anything wrong. I'm pleasant. I follow orders. I promote. I bring it on stage. Why does it seem like I am not as good as the rest of the band and crew?

Now, I knew that bringing this up could possibly end my involvement right then and there, but I had to know, since at the time, things seemed to be going well again while we were out on the road.

Thom handled things professionally as we aired a lot of things out and actually even hugged it out. I don't want to bore you with the details or betray a confidence, but I'll say the conversation was productive and educational. A lot of the thoughts I had were literally just in my own head and based on some paranoia, I guess. You should never lead business with feelings or emotions. When you step back, away from the fact that Ellefson is the big name on the marquee, you can see that when it's all said and done, at that time, Thom really was the boss of the operation. So, from his perspective, all the stuff I was doing—the hustle, the promo, the load in/load out, handling payments, helping manage the merch table, all per David's request at the time—was all of this stuff that sort of stepped on Thom's toes. He should've been the guy making many of the decisions that I had made. From that POV, I can understand some of his frustrations better. So basically, I thought I was doing the right thing, because Ellefson, who in my eyes was the boss, was telling me what to do. There is always a chain of command and a hierarchy that should always be respected in business.

I needed to listen to Thom and work with him more rather than going around or behind him. More than anything, I just wanted to be a friend too. Above and beyond the business, we had space for friendship as well, which, man, let me tell you, is a great thing on the road. Touring is hard enough, but add in confusion and animosity, mistrust and doubt, and you have a lethal mix. If that can be flipped to friendship, teamwork, and mutual respect, then get out of the way, because we're about to take it to another level.

We bonded over the insane working conditions we faced. Both of us were risking our lives and our families lives by going out and touring during the pandemic, all in the name of music. We weren't getting rich. We weren't getting a lot of mainstream attention. We were simply doing what we loved and were meant to do—play loud and in the pocket and help out as much as I can when asked.

Now, Ellefson and Thom still have an album coming out with the European guys, so those two are still technically the "bandmembers" on paper, but it seems like Sharpe and I unknowingly became the American touring band, at least for now, thus the title, ELLEFSON Band-USA (formerly known as the Sleeping Giants).

We want to avoid the "out of sight, out of mind" saying from coming true, so these shows helped refresh our relations and keep us in the forefront of their plans and minds.

David has messaged me since the run ended to thank me and to talk about his birthday, along with Thom's, which are about a week apart. We're planning on celebrating them both during the second run.

These guys could get any number of people to stand in and play a song on camera for a live show, so the fact they chose us, being that we played on the track with them, was very cool. We are workhorses, ready for whatever they need us to do. Speaking of which, David just sent me four new cover songs to learn in less than a week before our second run! He knows I'll work on them until I can not only pull them off live, but rock them hard.

Just getting down to the practice spot was a big deal. I'm kind of a germaphobe whether there is a pandemic or not. Going to the airport and getting crammed into a plane had me losing sleep leading up to my trip.

I'm paranoid.

Picture this: I wore an m95 mask, with a surgical mask over that, then a bandanna on top, gloves, constant hand sanitizer, wiped down everything and any other layer of protection I could manage. Turns out, the airlines are taking so many precautions now that I actually felt a little bit better as I walked onto the plane. That being said, they have us packed in like sardines, sitting next to strangers. People are coughing and sneezing. Mask or not, that is still nerve racking to deal with right now.

As I'm working on the book, the news is reporting that cloth masks might be totally ineffective. I've also seen reports that they could do more damage than help. Does bacteria get trapped and cause the wearer to re-inhale it over and over? Do droplets still escape and spread? I don't know the answers, I am not a scientist, but obviously, some people have serious doubts, and others have valid concerns. What's confusing to me is why they would insist everyone must stand six feet apart in line at the airport but then feel it's ok to cram us all in the actual plane together with no separation? Also, and I know I'm getting a bit off track here, but why aren't we hearing health officials urging people to eat healthy and to exercise? Why aren't we, at least as a nation, taking steps to boost our immune systems and to get healthier? That will go way further in curbing deaths and hospitalizations and the spread of covid than a cloth mask ever will accomplish. Why? Because people are making money off our suffering and our ignorance. Why make people responsible for their actions and face the consequences of their own choices when they can just proceed as if nothing is going on and wait for a pill or a shot to magically save us like we do for everything else. We constantly, as a nation, never find the cure or fix anything; we just put a Band-Aid on and always just try to help relieve the symptoms. Hey, here's an idea. Skip the drive-thru line at McDonald's today and grab an avocado instead. Don't hit Next Episode to extend your binge and take a walk outside during that time.

Shit, while I'm at it, can I express how frustrating it is that for the whole year I've been asked not to work or make money and to sacrifice playing gigs with actual people in the crowd and I've been asked, really forced, to give up my trivia gig at the local bar, and yet, there is a haunted house attraction down the road that has three-thousand-plus people each night lined up with no distancing, and half the people don't wear masks and that is fine with everyone?

Does anyone else see an issue here? I'm not an antivirus conspiracy guy by any means, because I know it's real; I just have a real issue with all the hypocritical mandates that are being forced and put in place that do not make much sense to me.

Tens of thousands gather for political rallies ... no big deal.

Go to restaurants and take off your mask to eat.

The whole nation will wait in line for an election ... nothing to see here.

Two thousand allowed at Walmart to shop.

Sporting events, twelve thousand in a stadium is perfectly safe.

Five hundred gathering at church for a Christmas mass? You have our blessing.

One hundred people outside for a concert ... shut that shit down! Why?

One hundred people indoors at a thousand-capacity venue with their temps taken before they enter, sign an Enter at Your Own Risk release form even, make people wear masks (if you don't like it, don't come) or whatever will make people feel comfortable, but that's so wrong in everyone who has control eyes, so we fine, shut down and throw the promoters in jail instead! So wrong.

We have to work. We make money by playing. We are a part of your economic system whether you choose to acknowledge us or not. We are forced to take the lead here. We will press on, as safe and as smart as possible, and make shows happen.

People have been asking me why and how I'm doing these shows. Well, I've got to work. This is my job. I am a drummer. My way of life was stripped away earlier this year. If I sit back and let another drummer fill my throne, I may never get another crack at it.

I don't have a job in a factory. I don't want to work at a fast-food joint. I can't live off unemployment or a nest egg. I need to work and do what I do best: beat on things with sticks.

I have to give up a few days to quarantine before I go and a few days afterward. All I can do is hope for negative tests when I get back. I don't have other options. And don't think this is just about me. I'm not the only person sacrificing to make this work. Jessica gets left with all the housework and homeschooling and whatever else I can't help with when I'm gone.

Everyone on stage brought their A-games. I mean, bro, we've all been cooped up for nine months. The shadow of the presidential election hovers over everyday life. People we know are sick and dying. We just want a release. Someone flip the pressure valve.

Getting behind the kit in front of an audience after so long came with a wave of nerves, but performing is like riding a bike for me. As we kicked into the opener, it all came flooding back. It felt familiar, comfortable.

The vibe felt incredible up there, and from what the crowds said post show, the audiences felt the energy out there as well. We all had a lot of pent-up angst and anxiety fueling us. Who knows when or if this will ever happen again? The shows had an immediacy and intensity.

These weren't packed concert clubs, mind you. We still took precautions and made it clear that people needed to keep socially distant. We had solid crowds, while still giving people space. It didn't matter how many people came, really, because everyone was so excited to hear live music again that fifty people sounded like five hundred.

A couple shows were in Texas as numbers spiked. We had to go to the areas that were all open and didn't care much about restrictions, like Florida and Texas to play shows. Some people didn't want to wear masks. Some people didn't want to keep distant. That can be frustrating, but in 2020, what isn't? People gave me shit for wearing a mask into one of the shows in Texas. They openly laughed at me. They got mad. No joke.

I'd hear, "Get that tampon off your face!"

After the show, they want a high five or a hug or to shake your hand, and I didn't want to. Not because I don't like or appreciate the fans, but come the fuck on, it's a pandemic.

They would reach out their hands, and I'd offer my elbow, and it would piss them off.

So weird and silly. I'm just trying to be safe and support my family. I want to be a personable drummer too, but I need to stay healthy, and they should understand, as well as try to avoid covid themselves.

Every note, every drum hit, every measure, every song, every set counts more than ever these days. No one knows if or when the next time will be. I left it all up on the stage, just in case.

As we got home from the run, David asked us about playing a streaming event he had signed on to do. They had set it up as an acoustic set to play the songs from the new record, but with us involved, they'll have the ability to play them at full volume. Sharpe and I said yes, of course. We need to learn new songs. I'm sure it's bittersweet for our European counterparts that the songs they wrote and recorded for David will be debuted by other musicians, but it's the same for us when watching them play huge festival crowds in Europe as they've done before playing our tune, "Vultures." So, I've been in their shoes, and it definitely sucks.

This makes for some much-needed promotion for Dead By Wednesday as we introduce our new singer with a new song and video. We've also booked a half-dozen shows at the clubs I'm playing with Ellefson that will happen in a couple months. Well, they'll happen as long as covid doesn't get worse, the USA doesn't implode due to the election, or any number of a dozen things going on right now.

I'm an emotional guy. No one who knows me will debate that. I'm also passionate and driven. I'm serious about my career. I always have been. I am adjusting to being just the drummer. In Ellefson, I don't call any shots, really. I get asked my opinion once in a while, but I don't make any decisions. I show up only when I'm needed. I play only when called upon. I need to leave the rest up to them. It's not easy, but I'm learning. Not only am I learning, but I'm actively practicing that. I am not oblivious to how the business works. At any point and time in this line of work, anyone, including Thom and David, could make a decision to move to another drummer or guitarist and leave us behind. Nothing personal. Business.

After Thom and I cleared the air, I at least knew that it wouldn't be personal, because we are good. We are cool with each other once again, for sure. We're friends whether in a band together or not. Mutual respect on the stage and off, becoming a band of brothers.

It's funny; as a kid, when you dream of being a drummer, you envision playing in front of a sea of people as flames shoot from the stage, and the ground shakes, and people lose their minds along to the beat you play. You don't picture hocking shirts at a merch booth or chasing down promoters for drink tickets or icing your back after loading gear up three flights of stairs just to get through a full set, and yet, that's what I was getting hung up on sometimes. I am not in Ellefson to worry about those types of things. I am paid to play drums and to get asses moving and jumping. I bring energy. (And crap thunder!)

It's freeing to look at it that way. Boiling down my job to what I love best about the whole process is awesome. Why spend so much time worrying about details that shouldn't affect me at all? I've always done that. It feels nice to not always have to know, but it also makes me feel a bit lost at times too, not knowing what to do with myself.

Would I love to be *the* only drummer for Ellefson? One hundred percent. I would love it. I would fight for it, but that's not what they wanted. They might never want that "traditional" set up. Ellefson is the name. He is the draw, so he is the focal point and must do what makes the most sense for him and his band with Thom. Does he want three drummers and a rotation of six guitarists at all times? Sure.

Great. If one guy can't make a show, then it's the next man up, especially since it's really only their two faces you ever see on any of the posters or promo stuff, and I'm okay with that. We are pretty much hired guns who have all become friends, and I'm okay with that too. There's a band and gear on both sides of the continent. Makes sense I guess since you spend less on travel and it's just easier. But I like being in a band. Like Dirk (Megadeth's drummer) said earlier in the book, these are all covers to us (aside from "Vultures"). We, as a backing band, are interchangeable—memorable but interchangeable. You hope not to be, and that's one of the reasons why I worked so damn hard to prove myself and my worth (which almost backfired on me), but, in the end, in this uncertain business, unfortunately, everyone is. Earlier this year, that thought scared me, but my attitude has shifted. Instead of anxiety about my station, I'm finding confidence in my role. There is a comfort level now instead of the constant inner voice screaming to do more. DO MORE! To earn the spot. I can't earn the spot. It doesn't even really exist right now anyway. So, I'll stay in my lane, play my part and happily enjoy the ride when needed.

I came home from our last run satisfied by how the Ellefson live stream turned out. We sounded like a real band. I noticed it, and I know they noticed it as well. They must have. We were tight, and we had natural chemistry and pocket going. Maybe it came from playing together a bunch already and in the past too, but that vibe goes a long way.

Also, I want to be very clear; the guys from Europe are great musicians and cool cats from what I can tell. Dave and I are more like an extended part of the fucked-up, heavy-metal Brady Bunch "musically incestual" #TeamEllefson family, you know? The redheaded stepchildren, if you will. We are all tight and have mad love for each other. David knows we are there for him if needed. Thom has included

Sharpe and I in some of the recent press releases, which feels good. We are back on track.

The Ellefson-Euro Band are dedicated, talented, and have found multiple ways to make an impact in music like Sharpe and I have. Those guys took the time to write and record an album on their own to collaborate with Ellefson. Mad props to them. Younger musicians reading this who feel like they never got a break can just look to those guys and realize that sometimes you need to make your own break.

The guys from Ellefson in Europe are technically sound and can play a million notes per minute, but, as I learned, the songs they wrote, I've found ways to adapt them to suit a live setting more. On record, playing fast and furious and heavy is awesome and comes through audibly, but I find that sometimes pulling things back slightly and simplifying them when you play live can go a long way. Keeping some open space. I'm slowing the song by a few BPM for groove and pocket, reducing some drum fills, and making them ... audience friendlier. I don't know if that's the correct phrase, but at a concert, you want the crowd to be able to groove along with the band and have everyone connect.

Sometimes less is more. We've all heard that saying, but until recently, I didn't appreciate how much that applies to live concerts and songwriting.

Ellefson actually requested some of the changes at practice. He wanted a clean, solid audible sound and groove. When we first started playing, I was sticking exactly to how it was done on the record. After his suggestions, we all seemed to gel more as a band. It clicked.

Sharpe and I have to be chameleons in that way and adapt to various styles of play from the various musicians who wrote and recorded all of these songs that we do.

Now, some of you reading are pissed, maybe even furious or worse, disappointed in me for going on these runs to play shows during a pandemic. I get it. I do. Before you protest my bands and talk shit online, or try to cancel me, please give me a moment to state my case, okay? I think if I have your attention for a few more moments to hear things from my POV, you might find it in your soul to come down off your soapbox to see me eye-to-eye.

Hmmm, there might be some mixed metaphors there, but no time for that now.

Let's say I told Thom and David, "No, I refuse to play those shows or to travel with you guys right now."

The best-case scenario is that I lose my gig, and I never play with them again—best case. What if the word got out that I wasn't willing to tour? How many other shows will I get passed over for? What if there's a band that I try out for down the road who could bring in more than I've ever made, but they pick someone else who they know will never, ever say no? As we spoke about previously, saying yes, and then figuring it out after the fact, even if you're not sure, is always best.

Sure, my family would be safer, in theory, but I could also just as easily pick up covid at the gas station down the street. I could get it from someone at the gym. I could touch a parking meter or a loaf of bread at the grocery store and bring home this thing. There's always risks in life. We take risks every day just getting up in the morning. You can slip in the shower or on ice and bang your head. We take risks driving, going on a plane, swimming in the ocean, etc. So why not be able to work smartly and as safe as possible, all while putting the proper precautions in place?

Throw away my career over the possibility of getting sick? I'm sorry, but I can't do that.

Wear a mask? Sure. Whatever…

Dead By Wednesday left for our short Midwest run, and you could tell we were all nervous. I mean, forget the pandemic, we hadn't played live in almost a year, and we had a new singer. We were performing new material, and … well, yeah, it was a pandemic too and our new singer's debut. All of it.

Our buddy Talon Blaque, from the sleaze-rock band Bomber Alley, wanted to come as our tech to help out, but we were hesitant since the budget was already slashed due to the regulations of touring in the time of covid. We agreed to pay him x-amount to drive and haul our trailer. He is also a top-notch drum tech and plays himself, so he knows how to set my shit up just how I like it.

To be fair, the way it had to work was that two guys had to fly in to the first show, and then two guys had to fly home. So, Mike and our new vocalist, Steve, flew in, and we drove with the equipment to meet them. Then Dave and I were set to fly home as they brought the stuff back. The shows went well for what they were, meaning all the clubs were at a fraction of their capacity, again due to regulations. Technically, we can say that every night we played was a sellout, but it didn't look like it from the stage. Yeah, it's easy to sell out when all the venues are at half or quarter capacity. Obviously, we are still super grateful to everyone who came to any of the shows as a fan or who worked for the club, promoted, or whatever. It was a blessing to be able to do what we love again after all that time and to finally showcase our new singer. He will never forget his debut, which happened during a pandemic, that's for sure. It was his first time out on the road, his first show with us, and he seemed to have a blast.

As excited as I was to debut the new material, I was also pretty nervous, having never played out with him and not knowing how it would go live. I was pleasantly blown away by how good some of the older songs sounded. Like, "Pawns" or "You and Die," a song written by our previous singer, Rob, which is not an easy one to pull off, but our new singer and I nailed the harmonies together. I'm proud of that.

"SOS" is a beast to play live. This is our first release since Rob Roy left and wrote with our new singer, Steve "Esteban" Alvarez. It's so fun to play! The song starts off with the bass pounding, then gets fast and furious but still has a sick groove. We had only recently released the song and video, but we already saw and heard people singing along who had clearly given it a few listens. That felt great. Today's market provides opportunities for instant connection with an audience, even while locked away, miles and miles apart. Can't come see us in concert? Type in a few words, and you've got dozens of live videos to choose from. Pretty incredible.

In fact, I just saw a video from one of the shows, and while I typically hate any live video of us that I watch, this one seemed to genuinely capture us and our energy. You know live music will sound different than in the studio or even from the practice space. There's a lot of factors that go into it, but to hear us live and raw like that and sounding so good and tight, really makes me happy. Those vocals are straight from the mic. We aren't using backing tracks. We aren't using autotune. We don't have a second guitarist to fill in layers of sound, even. Just the four of us playing live. Old-school style, like the real bands I looked up to back in the day did before us, like Van Halen, Pantera, Led Zeppelin, Black Sabbath, Mötley Crüe, etc. One guitar, one bassist, a drummer, and a vocalist. That's it. And you do as much as you can with what you have. Again, less is sometimes more.

That's just us up there killing it. No frills or gimmicks. Straight up!

We were humbled by the amount of merch we sold each night. We sold DBW masks, hoodies, and records at a clip that really helped us offset the cost of playing to a half-full room.

Dave and I jumped on a plane to come home.

Then I got a phone call.

The vehicle that DBW took on the road, which was my buddy Talon's, just broke down at 4 a.m. somewhere in Indiana, stranding half the band and all our equipment. The tour was already over, they were on their way home, and now this. Of course, typical usual tour crap.

Shit.

They had to get a room for the night on the side of the road, leaving our gear there, and then the next day, they had to rent a U-Haul to get them and the gear home, which ate up every last cent we had made on the run and more. All the risk, all the sacrifice, all the fear, all the doubt, all the work gone. Poof. Now, that's rock-n-roll. One minute you're up, and one minute you're down, almost like gambling. One minute, the show is on, and the next, it's off. With rock-n-roll, anything can happen at any time. No rhyme or reason either sometimes. It is what it is.

We left home in the midst of a pandemic to entertain a few crowds and try to scratch and claw our way into 2021 with something under our belts, and instead, we dug ourselves deep into a hole of debt.

When will we be able to play again? Tour again? Who knows? 2020 was the gift that just kept on giving. Or really the gift that just keeps taking. #Fuck2020!

A few days after we got home, Dave Sharpe got the sniffles, and we all sort of held our breath until he got a negative test result. His girlfriend had the sniffles when we got home, so we all think he caught it there and not at the shows. It's amazing how quickly a stuffed-up nose, a throat tickle, or a dry cough can change the whole complexity of your day right now.

This time of year, and during the change of seasons, my sinuses and allergies always go crazy. You know that feeling when your ears itches so badly, but you can't do anything about it? Have you ever tried to use your tongue to scratch it from the inside? Your eyes tear while sneezing? No? Well, I do. And it sucks. It's gotten so bad that I get monthly allergy shots. I also have the telltale heart beating like a drum always in one ear during the winter months. It was so bad at one point that I even had it checked out to make sure there wasn't anything else going on, and the doctor said I was fine—losing my hearing slowly, of course, but my ear was fine. It's just all due to sinus congestion and an uncomfortable postnasal drip from seasonal allergies. When the windows and doors close up in the cold months and the dry, forced heated air comes on, I get it bad.

The main symptom of covid that everyone is talking about is the loss of taste and smell. While I was out with Ellefson, I heard about a foolproof test to assure you that you can still smell.

Bumblefoot told me, "Take your finger and stick it up your own ass. If it smells like shit, you're in the clear."

You won't read about that quick and easy method on the CDC website, because it doesn't make anyone any money.

When you're broke and desperate, like musicians in 2020, you've gotta find a way to survive. Bumblefoot is a pro's pro. Thanks for the amazing advice, Bumble!

December 16, 2020, proved to be one of the weirder days of a bizarre year. I was hired to play drums on a few tracks by my old Gargantua Soul bandmate, Marc Amendola, for a new recording project. I was hired and paid by him per song to do a job and play drums in my own studio, which I wanted to sound test anyway. I didn't have to go anywhere and still made money, so it was a no-brainer. In the end, it actually came out decent, and I had fun catching up with Marc on a bunch of stuff, as well as reminiscing about our time working together. Everyone involved in Gargantua Soul can list the reasons the band didn't break through, and maybe in some ways, we're all correct. Maybe it wasn't one thing. Maybe it just wasn't meant to be. Or maybe it was; what do you think?

The last time we had gotten together was about a decade earlier when Gargantua Soul did a reunion show.

The reunion wasn't very good.

I won't say the reunion was bad because of any of the guys or of past friction, I just found it kind of boring going backward, to be honest. It was like going on a date with an ex after several years. Been there. Done that. I didn't feel any of the vibe or magic I'd had on stage with those guys years earlier. The chemistry had changed or diluted or…

I still have respect and love for what we did and for the guys as individuals, but I don't have much desire to try that again.

Look, the music business is a cold, difficult, dark sea to navigate.

As I recorded my drum parts today, Marc and I talked about this book.

He asked, "So, what are you going to say about me?"

I was noncommittal but told him I planned to dig into our pasts.

He persisted. "What will you say about our band?"

I simply said, "I'm going to tell the truth."

He seemed a bit concerned by that answer. He asked, "Do I have anything to worry about that might come out in your book?"

I shrugged. "Do you?" Then I laughed. I told him I was trying to just paint the picture from my point of view and that from what I remembered, my comments about him were mostly neutral. I wanted to tell the story about the band imploding for fans of the band to know what happened, for my son to know what I went through on my journey, and I guess I needed to get it out for myself. Maybe seeing it in writing would help me process it, all these years later.

The recording session was the first in my new band room. It sounded great. It felt great. He seemed happy. And the client was happy with what we did.

This is the part in the book where we discuss *The Karate Kid*, or maybe more accurately: this is where we discuss the time I flew to Atlanta in the midst of a pandemic to appear in an episode of *Cobra Kai*. Okay, well, it turns out I flew all the way to Atlanta in the midst of a pandemic only to find out I wasn't hired for a part in *Cobra Kai*, but instead, I played a burned-out drummer in a pilot for a new TV show. Still cool, but ... *Cobra Kai* is one of my favorite shows, ever. I don't know what details I can give on the show just yet, but if it gets picked up, I'll let you all know.

Amendment: The show didn't get picked up, but Nickelodeon aired the pilot of *California Dreaming* a few times in December of 2021, and the reviews weren't half bad.

When I first started this book in December of 2019, I had no clue what was coming. It's hard to even put myself back in that naive and narrow mindset anymore. I am a different person, with a new point of view. I want to be out there playing shows, winning over fans, and being proud in every project I get involved with going forward.

I recently broke down and got myself vaccinated. Am I happy about it? Well, here is an essay I recently posted with my thoughts on the whole thing:

> *I'm sure I'll get shit for this, and that's okay, because idgaf; plus, I'm allowed to feel how I feel ... So, I'll just come out & say it. I'm fully vaccinated as of last Thursday, and I'm still fully one hundred percent against it. I feel kind of duped and pressured into getting it, and I really hope it doesn't bite me or anyone else in the ass down the line. It's not even really about the science behind the vaccine that I'm against; I just can't stand all the contradictions and hypocrisy around it all even though I know of friends who have had both covid and the shots, and both have had issues. One person recently told me that one of the shots caused major issues with her health since May!?! Makes me hate it even more, like politics and religion. Honestly, you should all thank me now, because I did it for YOU! That's right. Ha-ha ... Just playing! All kidding aside, I mainly did it for the elderly and immunocompromised people in my family and selfishly to be able*

to tour and fly anywhere I want freely out of the country regardless so I'm able to play/work. I'm sure it'll soon end up being mandatory, if it's not already in certain countries. We will see what happens ... not now, maybe six months from now, one year, or five years? Not a lot of people know this, but let this sink in, and feel free to do your own research as well. What the news and media does not talk about are some weird facts that always seem missing, like that around fifty-one hundred people have died so far from these particular vaccines alone. But all you see is them pushing people to get it and not even mutter a word about this stuff, because it doesn't help promote their agenda. Well, why is it concerning you say? Because, obviously, we all know there's adverse reactions to all sorts of medicine, even aspirin, well, this is why. When the swine flu came out, there was only fifty-three deaths from that shot, and they shut the entire program down immediately. Fast forward to 2020, and now over five thousand have died from the shot, and no one seems to care? Is this really for the greater good of mankind? Well, why, then? Please do tell. Also, do you know the same amount, being around fifty-one hundred people, is about the same number of people who have died in total from ALL vaccinations combined together? Seems a bit odd to me, but hey, I'm not a doctor, scientist, or politician, so I shouldn't have an opinion and should fuck off, right? Maybe I should start some sort of "vaccinated people against the trial vaccination" group or something, because I'm sure there's plenty of people who feel like me out there too! I was just sitting next to one person who had her job threatened because of this, and she's pissed. Most of these people just stay silent to not upset anyone or be ridiculed. Call me dumb or whatever you want; I don't give a shit. We must always think outside the box, keep our eyes and ears open, and question everything or we have already lost. They're even threatening firing people at their jobs now, as well, unless they do it and giving weird huge initiatives to try to convince people to do so who aren't. That, to me, is also weird. It's your body no matter what, so you should be free to do what you want with it regardless of if it affects anyone else or not too, because it's still your body, and that's on you! I feel the same way about abortion to a certain extent and think assisted suicide should be legal as well. If you want to kill yourself, go right ahead. It should be your choice. I obviously hope nothing happens with the shot, and it's all good, but even if it's ten years down the line, we won't be able to prove it anyway, and they won't take any responsibility or accountability for anything by then either. You'll eventually see those cheesy legal commercials on TV, "Did you get the original COVID-19 shot and are now sick or suffering? We can fight for you and get you compensated." Etc., blah, blah, blah ... I figure I'm almost half dead anyway at this point, so what do I have to lose? But for my kid? No way! At least I did choose the best one, I think, after much research, being Pfizer that has the best effectiveness, ninety-seven percent, and less adverse side effects as well. I've just joined the dark side ...

FYI, I had almost zero reaction from it too.

I want to teach my son that he doesn't need to fear anything right now, that I got this. All he needs to do is work hard at school and leave the rest to me.

Orion, when you pick up this book to learn about your dad, I hope you can appreciate the humor, the sacrifice, the love, the anxiety, and the perseverance required to follow my passion for music and for connection and for you. I also hope you chase down your dreams with the same reckless abandon no matter what you do, though maybe avoid eating any weed at the Canadian border.

Well, since there's absolutely nothing on my radar as far as touring or recording, maybe this is the right spot to say goodnight.

CHAPTER FIFTEEN
The Poland Pickle and the Video Seen Around the World

Wait, what happened with Ellefson?

Okay, so I guess we can't just end a book without a little drama. The last few months have certainly been full of it: vaccine rollout, the Capitol was stormed, and Ellefson made the news in a major way. I will walk you through things from my POV and let you all decide how you feel.

Look, the eyes are out there, and they're always watching. You've got to be smart not only in public and on social media, but apparently you need to start making better choices in private as well. Because that's what this boils down to, right? Ellefson was having a private conversation. It wasn't illegal. The female was of age.

The only problem is this whole cancel culture is watching and waiting to pounce. People no longer want to put people on pedestals; they want to tear them down. They have realized they get way more attention if they can help ruin someone's life rather than make a positive impact on the world.

Here's an experiment to try: make a positive post on a good deed you saw someone do recently, and then make a negative post attacking something someone did that you don't like, and then see which post gets more reaction. It'll be the negative one, every time.

I don't think Ellefson was aware of how that technology worked. That's not an excuse. Again, I am just spit-balling from my POV. Ellefson is too trusting and perhaps a little naive, and those two facts got him into this situation more than anything else.

Yes, Ellefson should've known better. No, those videos shouldn't have gotten out.

Look, everyone jerks off. If they say they don't, they are liars.

In some people's eyes, what he did might be ethically and morally wrong, but all the guy did was what we all do. The only people he needs to answer to are his wife and the God he believes in.

All of a sudden, one of the nicest dudes in the music industry is a bad guy for jerking off to a younger woman, when a large percentage of people condemning him go on porn sites and do the very same thing.

And he deserved to lose his career in Megadeth over this? What ever happened to sex, drugs, and rock-n-roll?

The comments I've seen have overwhelmingly supported Ellefson, and it seems like the fans are pissed that he got thrown out.

Ellefson has pulled out of the spotlight completely for the time being. He has things he could say, but it seems like he is content to let his initial statement stand as the last word on all this nonsense. Out of respect for his family, Ellefson is keeping all the attention this situation created on himself, so they don't have to get thrust into the same shit spotlight.

Ellefson and I see this situation differently. Whereas he is humble and classy, I lean more to the Tommy Lee side of things. I would've capitalized on the whole situation. Instead of shying away from it, I would've gone full steam ahead. Once Megadeth kicked me out, I would book a solo tour the same night and city as every one of their shows. I'd start my set an hour or so after they got done playing, and I'd make sure me and my band sounded even better than them. I'd call it the MegaCock tour. The merch would all say, "Rock out with your cock out." We'd play all the best Megadeth stuff that fans want to hear that the band never plays and make it a huge spectacle.

Mustaine has a laundry list of fucked-up stories about him, so it feels a tiny bit hypocritical to throw Ellefson out after years of support and friendship. Yeah, I know there was the whole lawsuit thing years ago and whatever, but firing Ellefson is extreme. I could see Mustaine saying, "Hey, you embarrassed the band. We're going to do a tour without you, while you handle your business" or something. That seems reasonable. Their new album is basically done. David is on it. So, what? They rewrite and rerecord all of Ellefson's parts? Yup. They going to screw him out of publishing and credit? Yup. After all they've been through? Yup. Way to stay classy.

If you haven't seen the videos yet, I'll save you the trouble of finding them by saying I was impressed by the man's girth and stamina, especially for his age, though I cannot unsee it now that I peeked.

Is that enough detail? Can we move on?

Oh, and just to put my money where my mouth is, I'll admit I got caught jerking off once too. You want to talk about embarrassing? This was shortly after Jessica and I started dating, Orion was just about to be born so she was very prego, and it was Jessica's stepfather who caught me. Instead of hiding in shame and making myself look more guilty or making the situation more awkward, I turned it into a self-deprecating joke at the hospital in front of everybody there—family, friends, staff, and whoever was unlucky enough to be there. I owned what I did, and sure enough, the embarrassment passed eventually. I'm only human.

After the rough draft of this book was done, Ellefson and Thom split their partnership. It all happened quickly and mostly behind closed doors. There's still a lot I don't know, but as I'm trying to make sense of it all, I figured I'd share where I'm at with it as of today (June 30, 2021).

I know it was not an amicable split. I know there was animosity and accusations. It got ugly.

Obviously, there was more to the story when Ellefson had put me in charge of the money on tour, and then Thom had treated me like a second-class citizen, though I thought Thom and I had patched all that up on our last string of dates.

From what I heard, Thom didn't know about the split until he heard from sources that Ellefson was spreading the word to everyone and anyone who would listen that Thom was no longer his partner and when working with David, they should steer clear of him.

Thom put out a statement saying he is the victim and actually the martyr in this situation. Following his statement, many bands and musicians started to release their own stories about Thom's business dealings. You know everyone likes to fuel the fire and kick people while they're already down. They claimed he ripped them off, mismanaged them, lied, and many other claims that you can go read about yourselves.

I don't know the truth behind what they say. I only know my experiences in dealing with Thom. I knew going in what the situation was, so I never expected to see any money from our deals. I used him to open doors. Other bands might not have strictly wanted to deal with Thom to pivot to bigger and better things like I did, so I could see them feeling ripped off and betrayed. Maybe it's true, maybe it's not.

Did I ever see paperwork or sales statements that are a part of every label deal? Nope. Never. I assume none of the other bands did either, which is why it's easy to point fingers and ask, what is Thom hiding?

Did any band on the label ever see a penny? I don't know. All the money for physical merch and digital sales went through the label first. Were there unkept promises? Pay to play? Shady investment opportunities? Were bands encouraged to spend big on themselves to entice fantasy tour slots? I heard a lot, but I was too busy hustling to take part in any of that stuff.

Labels have costs, no doubt. There's just no record of what money was spent on behalf of each band or what money came in from sales. No shared spread sheets. The website that sold the merch is down. There was a warehouse full of merch/CDs/records/stickers for EMP bands that sat for years, unknown to the bands. That's now gone. How many tens of thousands of dollars of that came at the expense of Ellefson and the bands on his label who were under Thom's care? How much rent did Ellefson pay out of pocket for that storage?

I spoke with Douglas Esper from Chuck Mosley's band (the coauthor of this book). Chuck passed in 2017, so he was trying to help keep all things Chuck out in the world. The original idea to tour acoustically came as a cost-effective way to promote the CD/record that came out on EMP in 2016. Chuck only ever got two cases of vinyl (about fifty copies) and a couple hundred CDs to sell on the road. The rest will be thrown out in a dumpster. And I imagine the rest of the EMP bands will suffer the same sad fate.

After years of dealings with Ellefson and Thom, I decided to put my energy into reclaiming the rights to all the DBW material. I'm exploring options to rerelease them in digital and physical formats.

I mean, look, I don't know what the truth is, but it always seems to come out eventually. There is enough drama and accusations surrounding the label, the tours, and the general business dealings. I've reached a point that it might be better to not have business dealings with anyone in or from that camp, no matter what the bottom line is. Dead By Wednesday has a good reputation, solid track record and a great back catalogue, so having control of it is in our best interest right now.

As I was working on this epilogue, more stuff about Thom surfaced. Some even speculated that Thom set up David with the video leak, even though he immediately came to his defense after. Like a fire fighter starting a fire so that he can be the hero to put it out. But no one has any proof, at least that I know of. Thom responded with a long post announcing his retirement from the business. This came as a surprise, considering, on paper, he and I were still actively working on Chris Poland's new record. Are both Thom and Ellefson retired for good?

I love Ellefson and Thom and hope the best for them. Maybe we work together down the road, and maybe we don't, but we've shared some incredible experiences. I hope whatever they decide makes them happy.

Thom had finished some vocals for the project, which has me caught in the middle of the two (again). One of the songs has lyrics that sounded to me like a thinly veiled shot/threat at Ellefson. I spoke to Thom about it, but he claimed the words were more general than anything specific between the two. I felt uncomfortable. As this is the Poland album, I'm calling this the Poland Pickle. I have no idea how it plays out. I want to have the music we did together finished and out in the world, especially because it rules and sounds a bit like a better produced, old-school Megadeth. Dave Sharpe and I put in our time, energy, and money to see it happen, but we don't really have much say in any of it.

If Poland and the other guys want to keep going to finish the record, I am all for it. Right now, it's me, Dave Sharpe, Chris Poland, and Ricky Bonazza from Butcher Babies on bass for the recordings.

I am following the lead of Chris Poland. These are mostly his riffs and his band; whether it becomes just a studio thing, or we tour, I don't know. Thom did some positive things for me, so I'm not on some teardown-Thom campaign. The good things he's done for me have outweighed the bad, and I'm a guy that judges you by how you treat me. People can disagree, because they had a different experience with him, and I totally understand. I never made a penny dealing with Thom, but I played with John Bush, Ellefson, Poland, Bumblefoot, Bello, DMC, and so many others through that relationship. If the project moves forward, is Thom still the singer? I don't know; again, I don't have much say.

I'm staying as active with my bands as I can during all of this. Not just in writing, recording, and performing, but also, I'm getting back to booking and promoting as well. A week ago, I was in Florida with Dead By Wednesday to open dates for the return of Puya. I put that run together myself and can't wait to do it again. Esteban got a taste of the road with us and seemed to enjoy it, so that's a good sign. Dead By Wednesday might finally have the lineup we've needed for years to propel us forward as a unit.

January 10, 2022. One final update.

A few months back, Marc Rizzo called me up to help on a new project with his buddy, Tony Campos, who you know from bands like Static-X, Fear Factory, Prong, Ministry, and Soulfly. Was Tony also in Brujeria? Well, no one can give up that info without fearing death, so I'll let you decide.

Rizzo wanted to stay busy and have some fun, so he recruited me to play drums for this new three-piece. We started learning cover songs remotely, while coming up with a name and booking some dates. We started with obvious covers. Meaning, we dipped into the vast catalogue of ex-bands we had all been in. Even working online, Tony and I hit it off. Once we actually got together, I'd like to think we became fast friends. A while ago, Rizzo was in a similar style project called HAIL, another all-star-type band with Ellefson, Jason Bittner, and a few others. We couldn't reuse that name, but I liked it. We tried a few variations of it and finally settled on Hail the Horns, or HTH. It seems all the bands I end up in have some sort of shorter nickname or abbreviation: G-Soul, DBW, HTH, etc.

We hit the road for a string of dates. I felt a little under the weather but nothing bad. My drum tech, Talon, helped me by setting up and sound-checking for a few nights so I could get extra rest. When I got on stage, however, I didn't hold anything back. I sang and played for ninety minutes, like a beast. After the shows, I went straight to the hotel with some Nyquil to help me sleep. Those nights in a cheap motel, with the stale air recycling back at you, over and over, can be brutal, but I got through it.

I went to a pharmacist and talked through my symptoms, and they concurred with me; it seemed like more of a sinus infection than anything. I deal with sinus issues a lot, even when not traveling across areas with rapidly changing temperatures and pressures and air qualities, so this and the headache was nothing new.

I wasn't coughing. I only had a little congestion. I went about my day.

Until we went to a diner and everything, and I mean *everything*, smelled off. The whole place smelled rancid. I couldn't even stomach the smell of the coffee. And I love coffee! Then I got this weird metallic taste in my mouth mixed with chemicals, like when you've worked close with a lot of ammonia or bleach, and you feel like it's all around you.

The next day. No taste. No smell. Nothing.

Our run was done, so I went home for some rest. I developed this odd sensation where everything felt weird to the touch. The itching and burning got so bad I didn't want anything to touch my skin. Even wearing a shirt was uncomfortable. The only other time I had heard anyone talk about something similar was when they had taken too many pills and got this way. Along with the metallic/chemical taste in my mouth, it made the sickness feel manmade or manufactured.

My sister was pregnant, so before getting together for Thanksgiving, Jessica suggested I got tested for covid.

A couple days later, I got a call from the Connecticut covid people, and the women asked, "Is this Christian?"

I said, "Yeah."

She then said, "How you feeling? You better sit down."

My results came back positive.

I told the rest of the guys in HTH and crew, and they all got tested as well. I felt bad knowing I might've given it to them, as we had shared one van and room on the road.

Covid didn't hit me hard, but I took it seriously after almost two years on nonstop virus talk. I've had all sorts of illnesses and never experienced that itchy-touch sensation before or tasted such an unnatural metallic flavor, nor have I ever fought off a virus where my mucus remained completely clear the whole time. Right? Think about that. Typically, you start coughing up yellow, green and brown and all sorts of stuff your body is trying to get out. Not with covid. It was always clear. I am one hundred percent convinced this virus was manmade. There's still a lot of misinformation out there, but it's becoming generally accepted that we're all going to come in contact with covid at some point, and our immune systems will have to either fight it or lose to it. That sounds heartless and cold, but it's the reality. Those who are immunocompromised have a big challenge in front of them. Those who are old, sick, and haven't taken care of themselves might not make it. For some reason it seems to attack the people who are overweight and have diabetes more seriously too. It effects everyone differently. I look back at the people who said, right from the start, we should all just infect each other and get it over with, and I wonder if they were correct. Should we have tried for herd immunity right away?

Could we just say, "Hey, if you're not feeling well, wear a mask or stay home," without making everyone hysterical over it? I mean, people are canceling stuff last second, because they might've come in contact with someone who might've come in contact with someone who might've had covid. That doesn't work.

Meanwhile, someone's making a lot of money off all these plastic gloves, masks, and tests the government is forcing us to take.

I think that's the worst part about this whole thing. The government and big pharma now know they can scare us all so quickly to get us to obey, and every time they do it, it will mean billions more in their pockets. I can guarantee this pattern will continue from here on out. There's no way they give up this money-making scheme or power moving forward. Every couple years, we're going to have a new strain, a new bug, a new shot, a new booster. Delta and omicron and the flu will combine into a superbug and keep morphing and mutating.

Coauthor's note: At this point in our conversation, Christian was taking a walk, and he came upon a rabid fox. The fox came toward Christian, almost getting hit by a car in the process. The fox continued to head toward Christian, but his movements were erratic and illogical. I listened as Christian narrated what was happening. At one point, he said, "Oh, shit. This thing is coming toward me again, I'm gonna pick up a stick just in case—" and then the line cut off. I tried calling him back a few times before he was able to answer. The rabid fox eventually left him alone.

Okay, I won't end this book on a low note. Here's some good news.

My sister had her baby! So, I am uncle Opus yet again. I call him Jah; in Rastafarian, it means God. He's absolutely gorgeous. We can now add African American blood into our already super-mixed-race family, and I couldn't be happier! I'm glad she and I have reconnected after a few years of a rough patch. She was in a bad spot, but she's doing great, and we're all very proud of her. She's a great mom so far too.

Dead By Wednesday is almost done with our new album, *Capital Conspiracy*, showcasing our new singer Esteban, which I hope will be out later in 2022, maybe before or around when this book is released. My hope is we'll also be out on the road, but who knows? All I can do is control what I can control. We have a solid lineup of musicians all working together to create something brutal and honest. I am excited and refreshed.

Jessica and I have moved into our new house, and she has really made it a home. We are still doing Sunday dinners with family, and our son was able to stay at his school even after the move. He has really grown up in front of our eyes during this pandemic, and we're so proud of him. My Trivia nights are back, and I can't tell you how great it is to see familiar faces at Erick's bar on Tuesday nights.

I earned my red belt with a black tip in martial arts (ITF) recently with my former teacher, Mr. Cuddy in high school, so my next goal is black belt by 2023-24. My body feels great. My mind is clear. I have so much drive and energy, and I feel like I still have a ton to prove. There are so many milestones ahead, songs to write, things to learn, and people to entertain and meet. I need to stay focused and ready and aware to take hold of any opportunities that come my way and to make my own opportunities happen for when they don't.

I may not be famous, maybe just popular. I am not necessarily a universal household name … yet. I am not rich or notorious. I am not on MTV—well, even though, I guess, technically, I was on MTV for that *Wanna Be a VJ?* TV-show contest and for DBW's "Pawns" video being in rotation on MTV2's *Headbangers Ball* once upon a time—but that's okay. I am having a shitload of fun playing in bands with my friends and creating music, watching my son grow up, pushing and improving myself every single day, all while making an honest living. When you play drums, you provide a service. It's a job. It might be a fun job, but it's still a job. Like a plumber (My grandfather used to always say, "You could always be a plumber. They make good money.") I'm providing a service and should be getting paid for that service, like they do. They show up, fix a pipe or two and you pay them. No questions asked. Well, I show up, set my drums up, rock a house or two, so in theory it's the same. Of course, I would willingly accept fame and fortune, anyone in this business who says otherwise is full of crap. But then again, I would just be happy being respected, honored, and labeled as a genuine, talented, and legitimate musician after I'm gone …

You might not know who I am now, but write down my name, and say it out loud, then go research and Google my music. You either have the fire burning inside or you don't. There is no in between. The flame may have gone down a bit at times, but it has never fully gone out. If this is the career path you choose to do, remember it's like what Yoda says, "Do or do not, there is no try." Stopping is not an option for me … I'll break when I'm dead.

PS. For the last time, Lars was right!

www.ingramcontent.com/pod-product-compliance
Lightning Source LLC
Chambersburg PA
CBHW030033100526
44590CB00011B/177